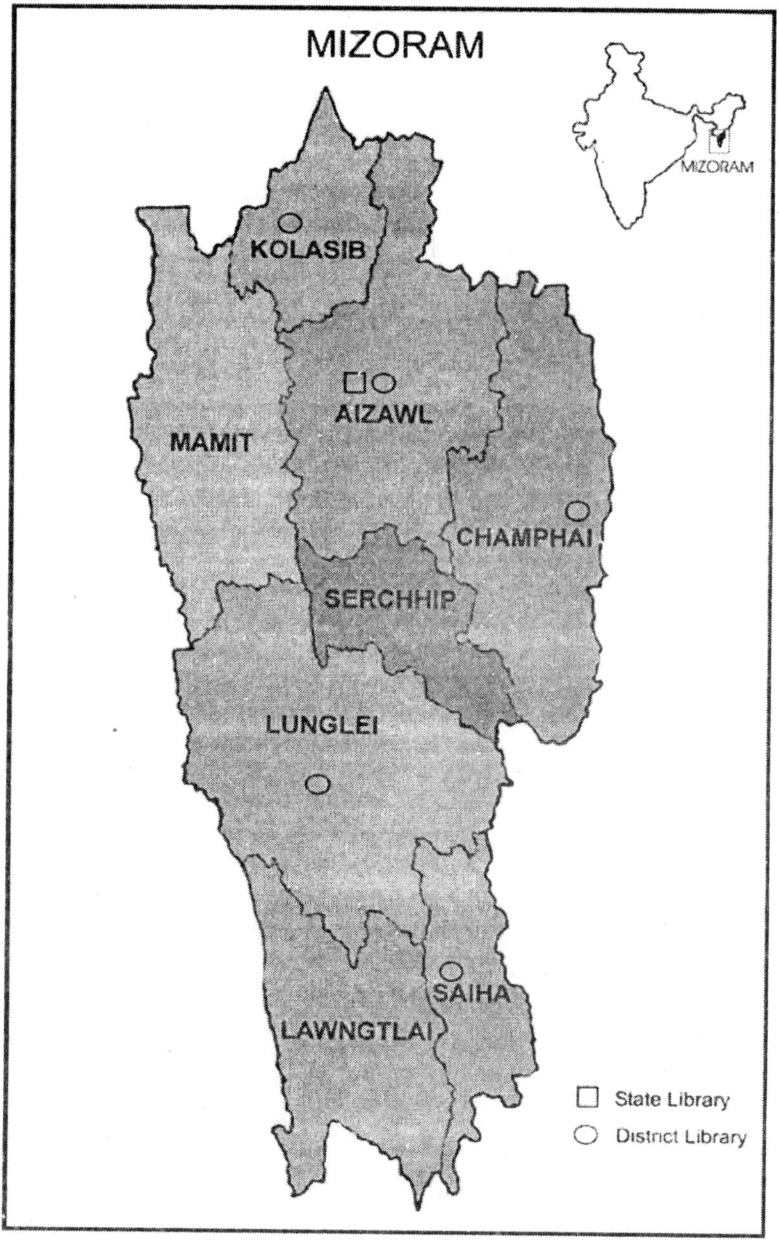
MIZORAM
MIZORAM
KOLASIB
AIZAWL
MAMIT
CHAMPHAI
SERCHHIP
LUNGLEI
SAIHA
LAWNGTLAI
State Library
District Library

PUBLIC LIBRARY IN INDIA

Impact on Socio-cultural and Educational Development of Mizoram

R K Ngurtinkhuma

Today & Tomorrow's Printers and Publishers
4436/7, Ansari Road, Daryaganj, New Delhi - 110 002
Ph : 23242621; 23241021; Fax 23242621;
E-mail: ttpp@vsnl.net

ISBN 81-7019-456-3 (India)
ISBN 1-55528-313-6 (USA)

Published by
Today and Tomorrow's Printers and Publishers
4436/7, Ansari Road, Daryaganj, New Delhi - 110 002 (India)
Ph : 23242621; 23241021; Fax 23242621; E-mail: ttpp@vsnl.net

MIZORAM UNIVERSITY

(A Central University)
Department of Library and Information Science
Tanhril, Aizawl, 796004
Phone- (0389)-Tel: 2331607/2331608

Dr Pravakar Rath
Professor and Head

Dated 12th August ,2010

Foreword

Public libraries as "People's University" play an important role in bringing all round developments of a society and nation. Government of India and state governments have been making all efforts to enact pubic library act which is otherwise known as library legislation to provide a legal framework with adequate financial support to run the public libraries smoothly and effectively. The basic objectives of developing a sound public library system in each state are to bring socio-economic, cultural and educational development of the state and people at large. Public libraries have great impact in promoting reading habits of the literates and neo literates, their thinking and attitude and make them most enlightened citizens of the country. Educated people get an opportunity of employment and thereby leading to economic development. Public libraries are considered as "Learning and Resource Centers" or "Community Information Centers" or "Knowledge Centers"

Understating the value, importance and impact of public libraries, Dr R.K Ngrutinkhuma has carried out an innovative research work entitled "Impact of State and District Libraries on socio-cultural and educational development of Mizoram". This research publication which is an outcome of a scientific study depicts that Mizoram being the second largest state in educational literacy along with other factors, public libraries have also contributed a lot in the socio-cultural and educational development of the state. The present publication in the form of book shall be an immense help to the students, teachers, researchers, planners and policy makers interested in the areas of public library system and services in designing, developing and implementing and effective and efficient public library system.

Prof. Pravakar Rath

PREFACE

Public library is one of the types of library dealing about the public in general and individuals of the society in particular. It is regarded as a gateway to knowledge for the community. It is a local center of information, making all kinds of knowledge and information readily available to its users.

The knowledge of public library in India is very old but its services and importance for the upliftment of the society is not much aware by the society. Most of the states in India have a public library serving the general public through various means of dissemination of information in order to help in their information needs. At the same time, more than ten states had legislated Public Library Bills to overcome the problems faced by the local people due to their ignorance, illiteracy or poverty.

The government of India has taken several steps to develop and support public library services in our country. There are various developmental plans through its agents but the state governments or other organizations are not much aware or responding in this regards. Public library is one of the most important agents to overcome poverty and illiteracy as well. The people of India need to contribute for the development of public library by understanding its impact and advocacy for the society.

This book is divided into nine chapters studying and evaluating various topics of public library elements in different approaches as below:

Chapter 1 is about the discussion of public in general, defining public library and its need to study about it in regards to its support and impact for the development of the society. It also includes about the problems that arises for this study with methodology.

Chapter two discuss about the public library scenario in India. It discuses each states of India in regards to public library services dividing into states with public library acts and states without library acts in India. National Knowledge Commission's recommendations in libraries and National Policy on library and Information science were also discussed.

Chapter three deals with the public library scenario of Mizoram discussing State and District Libraries in the state in regards to their services, staff, collection, finance, etc. with latest statistical data.

Chapter four study about the contributions of Raja Rammohun Roy Library Foundation, Adult Education and Young Mizo Association for the development of public libraries in Mizoram which is supported with statistical data.

Chapter five is about the contributions of library associations for the promotion of public libraries. The contributions of Mizoram Library Association in this regard are discussed in detail to encourage other associations for the development of the society through their activities.

Chapter six gives us about the dynamic socio-culture of Mizo that is very different from other societies of India. The impact of public library for the development of socio-cultural of Mizo society is presented in this chapter.

Chapter seven deals with the history of educational developments in Mizoram under the aegis of public library. Its impact on education in the state particularly in informal education of the state is discussed in detail.

Chapter eight deals about the analysis of data and findings which is drawn from data collected from various sources.

Chapter nine is about the conclusion and suggestions from

the study of the problem that arise on public library as gateway of information to the society.

This book is the first of its kind that depicts about the public library services and systems in Mizoram. I wish to open doors for young generations to come forward for the development of public library services in India.

R K Ngurtinkhuma

ACKNOWLEDGEMENT

I am very happy to complete this book for publication. I wish its readers to gain tremendous information through this book.

I would like to acknowledge my heartfelt thanks to the publisher, Today and Tomorrow Publishers, New Delhi for their tireless works and efforts to publish this book. It is due to their desire and ability that it has come out with modest quality of publications.

My heartfelt thank goes to Prof. Pravakar Rath of Mizoram University, Aizawl who has taken pains for the publication of this book in its shape. He encourages me and rendered his full support throughout my work of publication. It is my moral duty to acknowledge him for his generous efforts for this book.

It is earnest acknowledgement also goes to my colleague, Dr. R N Mishra, who help and encourage me in my work. I also thank to my colleagues and well-wishers, for their suggestions, supports and comments for its publications.

This publication is an outcome of the support of my wife, C Lalhmingthangi, and beloved son and daughter; they gave me moral and physical support from the beginning till end of my work. I convey special appreciation and gratitude for their patience and care. I earnestly acknowledge their invaluable encouragement and back-up

Above all, I am really obliged to the Almighty God for His gracious guidance and love. He is my guide, supervisor and mentor of my life. Praise be always with Him.

R K Ngurtinkhuma

ACKNOWLEDGEMENT

CONTENTS

Public Library in India : 1-19
R. K. Ngurtinkhuma
Today and Tomorrow's Printers & Publishers, New Delhi-110 002 (India)

Chapter 1

INTRODUCTION

Learning is a life long process. Every activity of human being, whether economic, education, health, business or developments are organized through learning. These organizations may be of different kinds, but are constantly changed in contributing learning and knowledge of which library is one of them. Library also serves also as a 'learning and resource center'. The change of human value system has prompted great demand of information in different areas of life. Latest development of information systems, such as computers, telecommunications and other technologies are being cope up with the library to meet the demand of library users and hence the notion of library as "storehouse for books" have been come up to the extent of "digital library" and "virtual library". The doors of the great library in ancient Thebes bore the words "The Healing Place of the Soul". (Holgate;2006;6).

A library may be small or big, but falls under the broad categories of library systems, such as, national, academic, public or special. With the passage of time and also with the production of different writing materials this knowledge-communication system became very much congenial and therefore, a library in whatever forms it exists be a center of communication between the originators and users of thoughts and ideas. But the Public Library System, as the name implies, is user-friendly system as anybody can make use of this system without disseminating caste, creed, sex, religion, age, community and status.

Public library, from time immemorial, has been considered as social institution based on the democratic principle "of the people, by the people and for the people". It is the living force of the world in different walks of life. Pierce Butler stated that, "The American library, especially, bears many traces of the peculiar social forces by which it was created. In the minds of its active creators there was always a clear and rationalized belief that this social institution is so necessary an agent for public enlightenment that its support, like that of schools, should be assumed by the state". (Butler;1933;1). This is the only institution, which caters all categories of users irrespective of age, race, sex, colour, creed and religion. Public Libraries serve as a catalyst for socio- cultural and educational development by providing access to information and knowledge. Therefore, the public libraries are considered as effective tools to mould the character of the citizens, which has wider impact on societal as well as national development. The IFLA/ UNESCO Public Library Manifesto 1994 elaborates the significance of public libraries as "the local gateway to knowledge, provides a basic condition for lifelong learning, independent decision-making and cultural development of the individual and social groups", and further stated impact of public libraries for education and society as "a living force for education, culture and information, and as an essential agent for fostering of peace and spiritual welfare through the minds of men and women". (IFLA/UNESCO; 1994). On defining a public library it may be acknowledge that, "an organization established, supported and funded by the community, either through local, regional or national government or through some other form of community organization. It provides access to knowledge, information and works of the imagination through a range of resources and services and is equally available to all members of the community regardless of race, nationality, age, gender, religion, language, disability, economic and employment status and educational attainment". (IFLA/UNESCO; 2001;2,3). Encyclopedia of Library and Information Science defines it as, "a public institution supported by taxation, one that opens its collections, facilities and services, without distinction, to all citizens". (Kent;1978;267). According to Dr. S R Ranganathan, the Father of Library movement in India, public library is, "one which is open to any member of the public and annually free of any charge paid as so much service". (Ranganathan;1960;21). IFLA/UNESCO Public Library Manifesto 1994 reads the following key missions that relate to information, literacy, education and culture should be at the core of public library services:

1. creating and strengthening reading habits in children from an early age;
2. supporting both individual and self conducted education as well as formal education at all levels;
3. providing opportunities for personal creative development;
4. stimulating the imagination and creativity of children and young people;
5. promoting awareness of cultural heritage, appreciation of the arts, scientific achievements and innovations;
6. providing access to cultural expressions of all performing arts;
7. fostering inter-cultural dialogue and favoring cultural

diversity;

8. supporting the oral tradition;
9. ensuring access for citizens to all sorts of community information;
10. providing adequate information services to local enterprises, associations and interest groups;
11. facilitating the development of information and computer literacy skills;
12. supporting and participating in literacy activities and programmes for all age groups, and initiating such activities if necessary. (IFLA/UNESCO;1994;2).

By considering different corners of the definitions of public library given above and the missions laid down by the IFLA/UNESCO Public Library Manifesto, it can be stated the purpose of public library as follows:

1. It is established, supported and funded by the community under the clear mandate of law.
2. It is a living force for education, culture and information, an essential agent for the fostering of peace and spiritual welfare through the minds of men and women.
3. It provides equal free resources and services to the society.
4. It provides knowledge, education, information and cultural development to all members of the community regardless of race, nationality, age, gender, religion and language or social status.
5. It is the responsibility of local or national authority.

1. Significance of the Present Study

Libraries are the fundamental sources of information to its clients by providing various categories of knowledge of the users. Everybody needs some sort of information to quench his or her thirst in one-way or the other. In this kind of act, public library presents various information needs to the society through its services to the community. Public libraries are of different in nature of functions and services, organization and structure. But, by and large public libraries are local center of information, established to serve the society in free of cost. Public libraries are considered basically significant in view that they generate everlasting efforts continuously to meet the changing situations and problems in the society. By taking public library in India, they can be various levels depending upon the organization and set up of the government. Nature and levels of public libraries may be different in various states of India. The nature of services provided is of the same by providing information to the community for the development in socio-cultural, education and other walks of life the society. Some of the levels of public libraries in India are:

- State Central Library;
- State Library;
- District Library;
- Sub-divisional Library;
- Tehsil Library;
- Taluka Library;
- Block Library; and
- Village Library.

In Mizoram, there are only two levels of public

libraries established and administered by the state government, viz., State Library and District Library. These two levels of library are serving the society since last forty years. Therefore, it is quite significant that the assessment of the role of these two levels of public libraries for socio-cultural and educational development in Mizoram are adequately helpful to the entire society and the country at various levels of libraries and information centers.

2. Statement of the Problem

State and District libraries of Mizoram while providing its services to the society rendered valuable activities to the community to generate and development the society at different ways of life. It is an imperative need to assess the services and activities of these public libraries in the interest of the society to fulfill the requirement of the community in its services to the nation. By taking into consideration of the IFLA/UNESCO Public Library Manifesto 1994, these public libraries have to achieve its mission in serving the society. The present study examines the public library systems with their service facilities, activities of various professional associations and organizations for the community developmental works. While catering such activities, the prime importance taken into consideration is the role of State and District Libraries and its impact on educational and socio-cultural development in the state of Mizoram. The present study further elaborates how far public library services and activities have been instrumental for all-round development of the state for the last forty years.

Mizoram has developed a sound public library system for over a period of forty years, and also being the 9th state in India enacting a Public Library Act(1993), but so far, no study has been undertaken to explore and assess the impact of public libraries on socio-cultural and educational development of the state. NGOs, particularly Young Mizo Association, are touching different corners of the state for the establishment of local/village library. Mizo has distinct social life from the rest of the world. The ethical code of Mizo social life, a kind of self-sacrifice, is very valuable moral life that all the community is associated and the core of social life among the Mizos. The educational development of Mizo is also very fast growing during the last century. These two changes or development during the past may have some impact within the society and it is high value to assess the activities and services of State and District libraries in Mizoram to the society.

3. Scope of the Study:

The scope of the present study is limited to State and District Libraries of Mizoram. However it provides an over-view of the public library scenario in India. Keeping in view of the Socio-Cultural and Educational Development of Mizoram, an investigation is made to trace out the impact of State and District Libraries in enhancing the growth and development of the state on socio-cultural and education as well. Among the four types of libraries, i.e. National, Public, Academic and Special, State and District Libraries fall under the category of public library system, and therefore, while taking up a research work on State and District Libraries, public library system was also included in the study.

The state government of Mizoram established one State Library at Aizawl and five District Libraries at the five district headquarters, viz., Aizawl, Lunglei, Saiha, Kolasib and Champhai, but three districts; namely, Serchhip, Mamit and Lawngtlai have no district library till today. By this date, there are 424 government recognized village libraries, which are generally run by voluntary organizations and other NGOs. These recognized libraries are not under the supervision and control of the government, but they are receiving some of the government grants and other special assistance particularly through State Library Committee. This study is confined the existing State Library and five District Libraries in the state and hence the number of libraries undertaken for study is 6(six).

4. Objectives of the Study:

It is widely acknowledged that Public Libraries are established on democratic principle and well versed to the community being an agent of information in the knowledge society. Any kind of public libraries, big or small, has to ascertain some guiding principles to serve the community and to provide best information services. State and District libraries in Mizoram, falling under the category of public library system, are also serving the society for almost forty years. By acknowledging this kind of services undertaken by public libraries, the present study has formulated the flowing objectives to:

- present the current library scenario in Mizoram with special reference to Public Libraries.
- examine the present structure, functioning and services provided by the State and District Libraries of Mizoram.
- examine the impact of State and District Libraries on socio-cultural and educational development of the state.
- explore any other agencies and organizations contributing for the development of public libraries

of the state.

- know the effectiveness of State and District Libraries in the state towards Socio-cultural and educational development.
- suggest and recommend measures for the improvement of State and District Libraries in the state.

5. Review of Literature:

To achieve objectives of any system fully, it needs to assess certain methods of studies to identify deficiencies that encompass within the scope of the subject. There has been many changes in the filed of public libraries due to the exponential growth of an information systems as a result of ICT developments. This explicit growth has also witnessed a developing information society in India. By taking account to the changes of information systems, different kinds of public libraries are also needed to strengthen and develop through latest technical devices that can be accounted in its services to serve the community.

Many states in India are moving in their own way to provide best information to its users through library and information services. State and District libraries are such public libraries that the local community through latest ICT. Mizoram is also one of the states in India that can serve its community by using different modes of communication to develop local community through State and District libraries.

A comprehensive review of literature is an essential part of any scientific investigation. It do not only gives an idea about the work done in the field and assists in the delineation of the study in hand, but also provides a basis for theoretical framework and an insight into the methods and procedures. It also provides significant methods for the basic interpretation and findings. The review of literature also eliminates gap within the area of subjects and that can direct scholar to fill up the gap for research work. Therefore, it is an essential work for the researcher to identify already available literatures to know the status quo of knowledge in the area of study.

The survey of literature done by the researcher is in the pursuit of the present research problem that can facilitate the research problems and its objectives. A large amount of literature review are available in the form of library and information science journal articles and completed research works are reported in the library literature are also scanned. Already carried out studies on public libraries and particularly on related state and district libraries, are favorably considered. Dissertations submitted as a practical requirement for the degree of Master of Library & Information Science and activities of state and district libraries of Mizoram or other related areas are also scanned.

A number of works have been carried out with regard to the role of public libraries at national and international level. However, there is hardly any documentary source on public libraries, particularly on State and District Libraries in Mizoram in the form of books, articles and reports. Public library is considered as, 'Peoples' University' where general public can meet their information on educational, recreational and socio-cultural needs. UNESCO has done significant work for the developments of public libraries especially in developing countries, which has also worked out as standards for public libraries.

The study of public library made by I.V.Ramanayya may be mentioned that, "Library is a center of social activity and a center of nigh schools for daily labourers. The role of public library is both in the creation and in the fostering of the learning in the adult for his own uplift through self-education and literacy. Library is the only institution which has equipment to the cause of spreading adult education and literacy". (Ramanayya:1967;174-177). This study reveals that public libraries, in general, have contributions to the local community as a social nigh schools for self-education and literacy.

Another study worth mentioning here is that, "Information is a basic resource for the development of the individual and the society. Contributions of INSDOC (now NISCAIR), UNISIST, and NISSAT are of immense help for information seekers and the public library can also serve as an information system of national importance as well. It is for a local public library to ensure universal accessibility to information". Here, B.P.Barua stressed public libraries as accessibility of information to the community. (Barua;1990;19-24).

Two scholars, M.Jatana and S.Khosla also stressed the status of public library as an essential civic amenity, providing services to all, irrespective of caste, creed and class. They regarded public library as a social institution, catalytic change agent in rural areas as a tool for dissemination of information, keeping alive the cultural heritage and writing amongst the general mass. Library develops the character and conduct of rural people. It is a heritage for cultural development as well as to eradicate superstitions, blind faiths and beliefs. Public library should be declared as the Fundamental Right as a follow up of compulsory education. (Jatana/Khosla; 2003;66-73).

Another study had been carried out some works on the contributions of public libraries, like State, Teshilla, Village libraries and stated, "If today the potential of these systems is to be tapped, it could be tied up with the Adult Education Programme especially till such time as the latter creates an infrastructure of its own". (Esparanza;1986;189-193). It is clear that public libraries are related to adult education programme.

P.B.Mangla also stated public library as a vital agency for continuous education and information to serve the community. He also stressed the needs of library legislation and need for suitable reading and other materials, need for professional manpower. He suggested that:

1) Formulation and implementation of a Nation Policy for Library and Information Service so as to establish a well planned network of public library service in the country.

2) Training of the required manpower.

3) Developing relevant programmes of cooperation and coordination amongst the developing countries and with the developed ones so as to gain from each others rich experiences; and

4) Allocation of 10-15% of the budget meant for the informal education for public library services. (Mangla;1984;1-15).

T.N.Rajan discusses some features of the modern libraries as a product of the social milieu by pointing out the need for social studies and research in the library and information filed in order to serve the community more effectively. In his article he narrated some roles that a library can play for the development of the country with a need of strengthening of National Information System. (Rajan;1980;19-22).

D.R.Kalia, S.C.Biswas, Krishan Kumar and B.P.Barua had formulated guidelines for the public library systems and services in India. They stress the objectives of public library to the community and proposed different levels of public libraries in the states with a systematic functioning. The primary roles of such categories of public libraries at different levels were also highlighted. The public library services for the community were also given as recreation, research, education and recreation center. They also proposed library structures and furniture as well as human resources with the application of latest ICT in such public libraries for the better development of local community through public library services. (Kalia;1991;31-84).

R.S.Shastry has elaborated the role of public library as an agency that brings about change in the society by alerting and educating the people. According to him public libraries established and organize on the initiative of the people played a singularly role in raising the awareness of people against injustices of the alien rule. He stated the new role of public library as a switching system to connect the user with other people, other places, other systems acting primarily as a filter and negotiator in the process. And he stresses the new role of public libraries as the comprehensive repository of the literary, historical and cultural heritage of the society. (Sastry;1994;3-7).

Another learned Prof. Alaka Buragohain contributes article on the public library scenario in India. She emphasized on the role of public library system in continuing education with the major drawbacks in the provision of the existing Library Acts in Indian states with the solution of a comprehensive multipurpose public library system for social and cultural renaissance in India. (Buragohain;1999;5-13).

K.Veeranjaneyulu and T.Sreenivasa Rao stated the importance of a public library as a chief instrument for accumulating and using man's intellectual heritage. According to them, libraries are the inheritors and repositories of the culture and civilization of the past without which we would have remained ignorant of the past and without a base to bud up our future. They stressed the importance of public library that it play a vital role in collecting and preserving the cultural heritage of the locality and make it readily available to the people to enrich their cultural awareness. It is an institution par excellence which provides all information demanded by all the people. (Veeranjaneyulu /Rao;1999;39-41).

Dr. V.Venkatappaiah stresses the need to formulate a policy covering various areas of services supporting education, preservation of cultural heritage, reading materials, human resources, private and aided libraries, comprehensive library legislation and restructuring the existing library acts in the states for public library services in view of the recent developments emerging in the field. He proposed a policy for literacy and education on the following priority basis:

- Illiterates and neo-literates, semi-literates and the participants of non-formal education;
- People pursuing self-education;
- People interested in self-employment schemes;
- Semi-skilled;
- Children and youth;
- Casual readers, housewives; and
- Higher education and research, etc.

Dr. Venkatappaiah also proposed a public library to

act as a principal center for promoting awareness about cultural heritage, appreciation of arts, etc. as below:

- Preserve cultural heritage;
- Provide access to all forms of cultural expression;
- Make efforts to foster inter-cultural dialogue;
- Favour cultural diversity; and
- Support oral tradition.

He also proposed the different areas of public library services as:

- Irrespective of age, sex, caste, religion or social status;
- More particularly, it should cater to the needs of human beings starting from illiterates, neo-literates, semi-literates, dropouts, etc.;
- To the people living in rural areas, backward and remote areas;
- To the physically handicapped, prisoners and patients in the hospitals; and
- To the people at all levels with certain limitations. (Vankatappaiah;1999;20-26).

The above literature dealt with some of the impact and role of public libraries as an agent for the development of the community as a whole. Some of them have suggested policy and other measures for the strengthening of its services to the public. These literatures do not study the role of State and District Libraries of Mizoram as an agent of Socio-cultural and Education Development of the state. Still then, there is no any study carried out on the role of

State and District Libraries of Mizoram in the socio-cultural and educational development of the state. Therefore, this study is taken up to assess the role of these two levels of libraries within the state.

6. Methodology:

Research method is the foundation of any research project carried out for a systematic study of the problem. It provides guidelines and channelises the available information of the given subject in a structured manner. It provides scientific thought to available resources and relevant data for the research problems. Research findings can be drawn on the basis of a systematic method of research. Thus it is very vital to follow certain methodology to carry out the research problem. The present research is carried out with the following methods through out the research work for the innovative conclusion of the research problem.

1) Questionnaire Method

Two types of questionnaires are designed to collect data and circulated to the selected respondents as:

1) to collect data and other necessary information relating to the research topic, a structured questionnaire was designed and circulated to the Librarian/in-charge of the State and District Libraries in Mizoram.

2) to collect data and other information relating to the research topic another questionnaire was designed and circulated to the selected renowned academicians, intellectuals, students, various library

users of different categories and reliable NGO officials within the state to explore the factors responsible to influence socio-cultural and educational developments.

2) Interview Method

To obtain the best result on the services, organization, administration and development of libraries in the state, Semi Structured Method of Interview was conducted to the selected library users, library personals, social workers, intellectuals and senior citizens of the state and State and District Library Authorities.

3) Observation Method

The researcher carried out observation method in order to assess the real situation of the functioning of the State and District Libraries. Photographs, pictures and illustrations to supplement the study.

In addition to the above methodologies, the researcher explored and made use of documentary/primary sources of information such as official records and communicating Government reports and statistics to know the initiatives taken by the Government for the development of State and District libraries vis-à-vis socio-cultural and educational development of the state.

Library is as old as human society and is available at very country serving the people in various field of knowledge. It is one of the best means of communication that all the community within a society can have free access to its services. It is one of the most recognized institutions of a society to acquire knowledge and understandings in various information needs without hesitation. The public library services have been a lifeline and help to the people of India since ancient times. There is tremendous growth in its infrastructure and its services to serve the people from village to cities by giving knowledge and information to various communities, irrespective of race, tribe, religion, sex or gender. The study of State and District Libraries in the Socio-cultural and Educational Development is also a part and parcel of public library system and services, and as such, it is quite essential to comprise the study of public library system and services to have authentic acquaintance of this research work.

REFERENCES

Barua, B.P. "Universal Accessibility to Information - Role of a Public Library in Indian Context". *Granthana.* 1(1), 1990; 19-24.

Buragohain, Alaka. Public Library Scenario in India: Problems and Prospects. *Herald of Library Science.* 38(1-2), Jan.-Apr., 1999; 5-13.

Butler, Pierce (1933). An Introduction to Library Science. Chicago: University of Chicago.

Esparanza, M. Role of Public Libraries in Socio-economic Development. *Herald of Library Science.* 25 (3-4), July-Oct. 1986;189-193.

Holgate, Steve. Americans Love Self-help Books. *Span.* Jan/Feb., 2006; 6.

IFLA/UNESCO Public Library Manifesto 1994. (http://www.ifla.org/VII/s8/unesco/eng.htm) Accessed on 2.3.2007

IFLA/UNESCO. The Public Library Service: IFLA/UNESCO Guidelines for Development (2001). Munchen: K G Saur.

Jatana, M and Khosla, S. Public Library - A Dynamic Community Centre for Socio-cultural uplift of Rural India. *Herald of Library Science.* 2 (1-2), Jan-Apr. 2003; 66-73.

Kalia, D.R. et.al. Guidelines for Public Library Systems and Services. *Granthana.* II (1), Jan., 1991; 31-84.

Kent, Allen, (et.al). *eds.* (1978). Encyclopedia of Library and Information Science, vol.24. Chicago: Mercell Derek.

Mangla, P.B. "Role of the Public Library in Developing Countries with particular Reference to Literacy". *Journal of Library and Information Science.* 9(1), June, 1984; 1-15.

Rajan, T.N. The Role of Libraries in a Changing Society. *ILA Bulletin.* XVI(1-2), Jan.-Jun.,1980; 19-22.

Ramanayya, I.V. "Role of Public Library in Adult Literacy Work". *ILA Bulletin.*.III (3&4), July-Dec.1967; 174-177.

Ranganathan, S R (1960). Library Manual. Bombay: Asia Publishing House.

Sastry, R.S. Public Libraries Modernization and Development. *ILA Bulletin.* XXX 1-2), Apr.-Jul., 1994; 3-7.

Veeranjaneyulu, K and Rao, T.Sreenivasa. Role of Public Library in Development of Culture and Civilization – An Overview. *Herald of Library Science.* 38(1-2), Jan.-Apr., 1999; 39-42.

Venkatappaiah, V. State Policy for Public Library and Information System and Services. *Herald of Library Science.* 38 (1-2), Jan.-Apr., 1999; 20-26.

Public Library in India : 21-81
R. K. Ngurtinkhuma
Today and Tomorrow's Printers & Publishers, New Delhi-110 002 (India)

Chapter 2

PUBLIC LIBRARY SCENARIO IN INDIA

India celebrated its 60 year of Independence in 2007 and taking stock of developments in various fields. It is also an important landmark in the history of public library services in India. Maharaja Sayaji Rao Gaekward has introduced free compulsory elementary education backed by libraries in 1883 in the district of Baroda and henceforth for the first time in India free public library services were introduced as a system in 1907 and extended to the entire state. It can, therefore, be traced out that 2007 was the centenary year of free public library services in India.

By 1856, most of India was under the control of the British East India Company. In 1857, a nationwide insurrection of rebelling military units and kingdoms, variously referred to as the First War of Indian Independence or Sepoy Mutiny, seriously challenged British rule but eventually failed. As a consequence, India came under the direct control of the British Crown as a colony of the British Empire. During the first half of the twentieth century, a nationwide struggle for independence was launched by the Indian National Congress and other political organisations. Millions of protesters engaged in mass campaigns of Civil Disobedience with a commitment to *ahimsa* or non-violence, led by Mahatma Gandhi. Finally, on 15 August 1947, India gained independence from British rule, but not before losing its Muslim-majority areas, which were carved out into the separate nation-state of Pakistan. Three years later, India became a republic, and a new constitution came into effect on 26 January 1950.

India is, according to 2001 Census report, administratively divided into 28 states, 7 Union Territories, with National Capital Territory of Delhi. There are as much as 593 Districts, 5463 Sub-Districts, 3799 Community Development Blocks, 4378 Urban Agglomeration/Towns, 384 Urban Agglomeration, 5161 Towns, 593731 Inhabited Villages and 44656 Uninhabited Villages. The population of the country is increasing every year. The totals population, according to 2001 census, is 1,028,610,328, which is the second largest population of a country next to China. Its literacy rate is 560,687,797 that is 64.8% of the total population. At the time of India's independence in 1947, its literacy rate was 12.2%. Since then, it has increased to 64.8% (53.7% for females and 75.3% for males). The state of Kerala has the highest literacy rate (91%); Bihar has the lowest (47%). The national gender ratio is 944 females per 1,000 males. India's median age is 24.9, and the population growth rate of 1.38% per annum; there are 22.01 births per 1,000 people per year.

1. Public Libraries in India

Public library is largely regarded as the People's University. It has tremendous developments in India from the early period to till date at various stages. Most of the Indian states now have free public library services to develop the people of India at different levels, which can be stated as below briefly:

1) Ancient Period (before 1200 AD)

The history of the development of the public library may be said to be as old as that of education in India. During Vedic times, the pupils stayed in the *guru-gruha* for several years for education. Since ancient times, India is being very much pertinent in search of knowledge and wisdom. Oral communication was the best means amongst the people of India and writing was not available. "The earliest written and recorded materials found in India are the inscriptions on stone pillars of King Asoka (300 BC); these inscriptions could be called the first outside open libraries". (Patel;2004;3). Later, *Ashrams* came into existence in India and students study under the supervision of well-known teachers. They kept many manuscripts for use of the teachers and students as well as for the visitors. Many students joined ashrams and such big ashrams were known as *vidyapeeth*, where numbers of teachers are engaged to teach the students. These educational institutions collected many different manuscripts and other materials which can help in their teaching and daily routine. They kept and preserved carefully. "The reading materials, of course, related to many subjects formed the source material for transmitting knowledge in different streams of education and culture. The collections might be likened to modern libraries since they were carefully maintained and extensively used by students and teachers alike". (Ekbote;1987; 3). Such *ashrams* or *vidyapeeths,* where manuscripts and other reading materials were reserved, may be regarded as a kind of library as they serve information and knowledge to the students and community in different ways. Pandey S K Sharma stated that: "In India, since the ancient times libraries have been functioning as light houses for those who wanted to read and to extend the boundaries of various disciplines. References are available to prove that Nalanda University (in Bihar) had its own multistoried library in 600

AD with massive collection of manuscripts. The collection of the library was housed in three buildings, each having nine floors and three hundred rooms. This library was opened by the then Emperor of India, King Davapal. The library was open for any body that was known scholar and took interest in reading, interpreting and even copying the documents kept in the library. Chinese traveler Whuen Sang is known to have consulted this library in the seventh century and to have taken from here hundreds of treatises to China and Japan. This library was completely destroyed by Bakhtiar Khilaji, who invaded India in 1205 A.D. and burnt the library. The library kept on burning for about six months". (Sharma;1987;97).

Libraries in ancient India also developed at other famous centers of learning, such as *Vikramshila* and *Odantapuri*. Universities of ancient India, like Taxila and Vikramshala also have valuable collection on *tantras* and manuscripts in their libraries.

2) Medieval Period (1200-1757 AD)

Muslims mostly rule the Medieval Period of India. Historically, it is also known as Mughal Period. There were great changes not only in social and political, but also on education and library system during this period. The Muslim rulers made great contributions to Indian culture and libraries played a significant role in the socio-cultural development of the nation. "The period of Mughal is considered as the golden period of Indian history for its educational, literary, and library activities". (Khursid;2004;6).

Babur, king of Kabul invaded India and annexed Delhi to his kingdom and established the first Mughal Imperial Library in 1526. (Patel;2004;6). Babur inherited manuscripts from his father and kept in his library and also collected books from different sources of his kingdom. Babur died in 1530 and was succeeded by his son Humayun. (Smith;1981;321). Humayun much lived in Agra and established library in his palace. He set up a library at Agra Fort, which was managed by Lal Beg. (Sharma;1987;98). In his library, he kept books, gilded pen cases, portfolios, picture books and beautiful works of calligraphy. After the death of Humayun, his son, Akbar, succeeded him in 1356. Akbar is regarded as one of the greatest Mughal king. Akbar improved the management of library with some technical works. He appointed Sheik Faizi to manage and control library services. Akbar was very interest in manuscripts and appointed calligraphers to copy good manuscripts. He established a separate library for women at Fatehpur Sikri and made great improvement to the library. At the time of his death in 1605, the Imperial Library has twenty-four thousand books. (Patel;2004;6). Jahangir, another rule of Mughal period, made a law that when a wealthy man died heirless, the property should be used for building and repairing schools, monasteries, libraries, and other institutions.

Some wealthy and scholars, like Abdul Rahim Khan-i-Khanan, Shaik Faizi, Gulbadan Begum and ruler of Mysore and Jaipur also have their private libraries. Some Hindu learning centers also have libraries. "The libraries of these centers contain huge collections of manuscripts on religion and philosophy as well as other subjects like medicine, science and history". (Datta;2004;172-173). Christian missionaries have also contributed for the libraries since the coming of Vasco da Gama in India.

During the Mughal period, library technical works, viz. Accessioning, Classification and Cataloguing were also carried out in some ways. The head librarian was known as *"Nizam"* and the assistant librarian *as "Muhatin"* or

"Darogha". Other staff of libraries during Mughal period is Scribes, Book Illustrators, Calligraphers, Copyists, Translators, Bookbinders and Gilders.

3) The British Period (1757-1947)

The Britishers came to India primarily to establish trade and commerce. Some of them were very interested for the upliftment of rich cultural heritage of India. A number of Academic institutions were established during the British period by the East India Company and by the Christian missionaries. The University of Calcutta was established in 1857 and its library was opened in 1873. Other Universities, University of Bombay and University of Madras were established in 1879 and 1907 respectively. There were only nineteen Universities in India before 1947. Universities were equipped with libraries in accordance with the Indian University Act of 1904. The Bengal Royal Asiatic Society set up library in 1784, Bombay Royal Asiatic Society in 1804 and Calcutta Public Library in 1835. Establishment of these libraries enlightened the community and may be regarded as the foundation of the concept of public libraries to the Indian people. Some of the important libraries set up in 19th. Century in India are Andrews Library, Surat in 1850, Gaya Public Library, Gaya in 1855, Long Library, Rajkot in 1856, Connemara Public Library, Madras in 1860, Government Library, Janagarh in 1867, Adyar Library, Adyar in 1886 and Dahi Laxmi Library, Nadiad in 1892. (Sharma;1987;99). Apart from these, other libraries, like Gujarat Vernacular Society along with a library, in Ahmedabad 1848 and Barton Library, Bhavnagar in 1882 were also established. Some of the Indian states also established public libraries. Such as Baroda established Baroda State Library in Baroda in 1877, Cochin established Public Library and Reading Room in Trichur in 1873, Dhar established Victoria General Library in Dhar in 1856, Indore established General Library in Indore in 1852, Jaipur established Maharajah's Public Library in Jaipur in 1899. Others states also established such kind of libraries, viz. Jammu and Kashmir in 1879, Kahtiawar, in 1886, Kolhapur in 1850, Nizam's Dominion in 1891 and Travancore in 1829. (Patel;2004;9). The first significant date in the development of public libraries in India is 1808 when the Bombay Government initiated a proposal to register libraries, which were to be given copies of books published from the 'Funds for the Encouragement of Literature'. (Bhattacharjee;2002;82).

The contributions of His Highness the Maharaja Sayajirao III, Gaekwar of Baroda towards library movement in India cannot be overlooked. He is remembered today as the Father of Library Movement in India. At the age of 18, in 1881, he was entrusted with full power of the government of Baroda in the Gujarat speaking region of the Bombay Presidency and the Peninsula of Kathiawar. Baroda's population was predominantly rural, the main occupation was agriculture. The people in general were economically poor and socially backward. According to him, education was the foundation to reconstruct a new social and economic life and education should be the right of the humblest villager. He introduced free and compulsory education in his princely states. Baroda became the first territory not only among the native states but also in British India to have compulsory free primary education. He opined that primary education was to be the very base and decided to preserve it by means of libraries, which were the only agencies for perpetual universal self-education. He decided to establish library as an experiment in one of the towns of a *taluka* and in order to implement his idea immediately; he issued orders to his ministers. "In conformity to his ruler's instructions, the Minister of Education prepared a detailed plan to open Circulating Libraries in the State, which was approved in March, 1907. Every public library instituted through the State's financial assistance was to be named as Circulating Library". (Nagar;1983;26). In 1906, he went to America as an observer, a student desirous of acquiring all the knowledge and experience that could enable him to make his own State a model one in India. He was very much impressed by the library services of America for the development of the people in their social, economic and educational life. He then invited an American, William Alanson Borden, a pupil-assistant of Charles A Cutter, who is working as Librarian of the Young Men's Institute, New Haven, Connecticut to come and established library services in India. In response to his invitation, Borden reached Baroda on November 6, 1910, and became the Director of State Libraries. It can be traced back that public library movement started since 1910 in India. Borden makes a survey of libraries in Baroda and concludes that there were over 241 libraries, holding a little over 100000 volumes. But he did not find any of those libraries adequately housed, nor did he find them shelved in such a manner as to make them most attractive to readers or convenient to those in charge. He then make proposal for the best services of libraries in the State as follows: (Nagar;1983;38).

1. Should Your Highness feel disposed to grant me the necessary authority, I propose to organize a Department of Public Libraries, to rank with the other Departments of Your State, with the necessary equipments of officers and clerks, etc. and to bring all the libraries above mentioned under its control and management;

2. To unify all the collections of books in Baroda City into one Central library;

3. To add to this Central library, general and technical books;
4. To erect a suitable library building of fireproof construction, with reading grooms, study rooms, Women's Library, Children's library, Lecture hall, Library school, and executive offices;
5. To make that library to be Free Public Library of Baroda City, and also the main storehouse for all the valuable historical documents and papers now in private hands in the State, but which the owners would probably be glad to have stored in a safe place;
6. To make it also the center from which traveling libraries should start and from which the books, new and old, could be distributed to the various branch libraries in the different towns, cities, and villages of the State.

The Maharaja apparently accepted Borden's proposals, and ordered that the whole scheme might be implemented in parts. The Library Department was created under Order No.9/19, January 30, 1911, for organizing libraries in Baroda. As the Director of state libraries, he planned a network of free public libraries consisting a state central library, four district or divisional libraries, forty-five town libraries, and more than a thousand village libraries-all integrated into one chain system. Borden played a leading role for the establishment, management and organization of public libraries in India. As a result of system, within two decades 85% of the Baroda urban and rural population had access to libraries. (Patel; 2004;10). Borden developed library classification scheme to suit Indian libraries. Another great contribution of Borden was the establishment of the first library school in India, in which he trained his own assistants and successors. Borden conducted the first formal library-training programme in India at Baroda in 1911. He was instrumental in the foundation of the Baroda Library Club and its journal, "Library Miscellany", published quarterly in three languages between 1912 and 1919.

University of Madras created the post of University Librarian in 1923 and Dr. S R Ranganathan joined the post on 4 January 1924. (Ranganathan;1957;19). Ranganathan published his Five Laws of Library Science in 1931, Colon Classification in 1933 and Classified Catalog Code in 1934. He also prepared Model Public Library Bill and drives to legislate library bill in Indian states. He made a tremendous contribution for the development of libraries in India.

Scholars, educationists and people of library bent of mind founded Calcutta Public Library in 1835 and the same was opened on 21 March 1836 for the public. In 1944, Calcutta Public Library was shifted to a new and spacious building, constructed in honor of the Governor-General of India, Lord Metcalf. Indian War of Independence broke out in 1857 resulted in to Europeans of Calcutta withdrew their support for the library management in 1899. Consequently, the management and establishment of the library were gradually waning and by the end of the century, the activities of the library came into standstill.

Lord Curzon, the then Viceroy and Governor-General of India visited Calcutta in 1899 and found a miserable condition of Calcutta Public Library. He bought the rights of the Library from the proprietors and later merged it with the Official imperial Library consisting of government departmental libraries of the East India Company. He then declared open of a new Imperial Library of India on 30 January 1903 in the Metcalf Hall. In 1948, one year after the independence of India, Imperial Library was transformed into National library of India and was housed to the Viceroy's Palace in Calcutta, namely, the Belvedere Palace.

4) Post-Independence Period (1947 onwards)

Public libraries in India made a tremendous growth after the independence of India in 1947. The central and the state governments took a number of steps forward for the development of the nation from the point of education and considered library as essential part of it. The programs executed by provincial and central governments since 1910 for the social and adult education of the populace paved the way for the enactment of library laws and rules for grants-in-aid in the country. Hence public library became part of the education budget. To enhance the level of literacy of 16% in 1941, the government undertook some programmes such as extension services, continuing education, social education, non-formal education and adult education. The government further initiated steps for the development of community and organized some projects in this regard. Libraries were considered to be an essential part of the Community Development Project that was launched during the first plan period. (Naidu;1990). In order to accelerate the pace of socio-economic development, the government considered public libraries to be an integral part of development projects. (Jambhekar;1995).

The Connemara Public Library in Madras became the State Central Library in 1950 under the provision of Madras Public Libraries Act 1948, and became one of the three depository libraries in 1955. Delhi Public Library was established in 1951 as the first UNESCO Public Library Pilot Project under the joint auspices of UNESCO and

Government of India to adopt "Modern Techniques to Indian Conditions" and to serve as a model public library for Asia. In 1954, the Delivery of Book Act was passed to include newspaper. The act obligated every publisher in India to deposit one copy each of its publications to the National Library in Calcutta, the Asiatic Society Library in Bombay, Connemara Public Library in Madras, and Delhi Public Library in New Delhi

The Advisory Committee for Libraries as constituted in 1957 by the Government of India, with K P Sinha as the Chairman. The Committee submitted its report in 1959 with a drafted Model Library Bill. The Planning Commission constituted a Working Group on Public Libraries in 1964 and the Commission submitted its report in 1965 with a Model Public Libraries Act. The model bill was sent to all the states/UTs, which do not have Public Libraries Act. In 1972, the Government of India, Planning Commission constituted Working Group on Development of Public Libraries to make recommendations for library development. Raja Rammohun Roy Library Foundation, an autonomous body under the Department of Culture, Ministry of Education, was established in 1972. The main objective of the Foundation was to assist state library services in developmental works.

In 1979, a library section was established in the Department of Culture under the Ministry of Education, which section was under the charge of an Under Secretary. The objective was to promote the development of public libraries in India. (Jambhekar;1995). A Working Group on Modernization of Library Services and Informatics was appointed by the Planning Commission in 1983 and submitted its report in 1984 with the formulation of National Policy on Library Services and Informatics. Delhi Public Library became a copyright library in 1982. National Literacy Mission was adopted in 1986, which emphasized education for women and also establishment of rural libraries. Library networks and systems were strengthened at the national level institutions in the development of literature in neo-literates. Fourteen states namely, Tamil Nadu, Andhra Pradesh, Karnataka, Maharashtra, West Bengal, Manipur, Kerala, Haryana, Mizoram, Goa, Orissa, Gujarat, Uttaranchal and Rajasthan have enacted Public Libraries Bills during 1948 to 2006.

The Government of India, Department of Culture, appointed a Committee on National Policy on Library and Information System in 1985. The National Policy on Education, 1986 states that a nationwide movement for improvement of existing libraries and the establishment of new ones will be taken up, provision will be made in all educational institutions for library facilities, and the status of librarianship improved. (Jhambekar;1995). The National Book Policy, 1986 also had an impact on libraries, as:

1) Provision of reading material for children by all the agencies involved;

2) That 10 percent of the annual education budget of the governments be used to purchase books for libraries.

These goals are to be achieved by using formal, non-formal, and open channels of learning. Rural libraries should become the focal point for post-literacy and continuing educational programs. Publishers, voluntary organizations, and school library programs undertaken as part of the "Operation Blackboard Scheme" of the National Education Policy on Education, 1986 were given assistance. The following five libraries were regarded as national importance and may be stated in a very brief manner:

a) **National Library, Kolkata** was established in 1836 in the name of Calcutta Public Library. It was not a

Government institution running on a proprietary basis. The then Governor General, Lord Metcalf transferred 4,675 volumes from the library of the College of Fort William to the Calcutta Public Library. This and donations of books from individuals formed the nucleus of the library. Prince Dwarkanath Tagore was the first proprietor of the Calcutta Public Library. Both the Indian and foreign books, especially from Britain, were purchased for the library. In the report of 1850 we find that the library started collecting books in Gujarati, Marathi, Pali, Ceylonese and Punjabi. The Government of Bengal and North Western Provinces regularly made by individuals as well as donations. The Calcutta Public Library had a unique position as the first public library in this part of the country. Such a well-organized and efficiently run library was rare even in Europe during the first half of the 19th century. Because of the efforts of the Calcutta Public Library, the National Library has developed rare books and journals in its collection.

The Imperial Library was formed in 1891 by combining a number of Secretariat libraries. Of these, the most important and interesting was the library of the Home Department, which contained many books formerly belonging to the library of East India College, Fort William and the library of the East India Board in London. But the use of the library was restricted to the superior officers of the Government. Lord Curzon, the then Governor General of India, was the person who conceived the idea of opening a library for the use of the public. He noticed both the libraries, Imperial Library and Calcutta Public Library, were under-utilized for the want of facilities or restrictions. So, he decided to amalgamate the rich collection of both of these libraries. He was successful in effecting the amalgamation of Calcutta Public Library with the then Imperial Library under certain terms.

The library, called Imperial Library, was formally opened to the public on 30th January 1903 at Metcalf Hall, Kolkata. The aims and objectives of the Imperial Library, well defined in a Notification in the 'Gazette of India' *as ' It is intended that it should be a library of reference, a working place for students and a repository of material for the future historians of India, in which, so far as possible, every work written about India, at any time, can be seen and read.*

John Macfarlane, the Asst. Librarian of the British Museum, London, was appointed as the first Librarian of the Imperial Library. After his death, the famous scholar and linguist Harinath De took over the charge of the library. After his death J. A. Chapman became the librarian. Mr. Chapman showed keen interest in the affairs of the library and worked hard to improve its status. After his retirement, Khan Bahadur M.A. Asadulla was appointed as the librarian and he continued as the librarian till July 1947. The policy of acquisition broadly adhered to by the Imperial Library was enunciated by Lord Curzon in his speech at the opening ceremony of the library, "The general idea of the whole Library is that it should contain all the books that have been written about India in popular tongues, with such additions as are required to make it a good all-round library of standard works of reference."

After the independence the Government of India changed the name of the Imperial Library as the National Library, with an enactment of the Imperial Library (change of name) Act 1948 and the collection was shifted from the Esplanade to the present Belvedere Estate. On 1st February 1953 the National Library was opened to the public, inaugurated by Maulana Abul Kalam Azad. Sri B.S. Kesavan was appointed as the first librarian of the National Library.

The reviewing Committee in its report of 1969

suggested that the following should be the basic features of the National Library; Acquisition and conservation of all significant printed materials produced in the country to the exclusion of ephemera:

- Collection of printed materials concerning the country wherever published and also acquisition of photographic record of such materials that are not available within the country;
- Acquisition and conservation of manuscripts having national importance;
- Planned acquisition of foreign materials required by the country;
- Rendering of bibliographical and documentation service of retrospective materials, both general and specialized;
- Acting as a referral centre purveying full and accurate knowledge of all sources of bibliographical activities;
- Provision of photocopying and reprographic services; and
- Acting as the centre for international book exchange and international loan.

b) Khuda Bakhsh Oriental Public Library, Patna was open for the public in October 1891 with 4000 Oriental manuscripts. Maulvi Khuda Bakhsh donated his entire collection to the nation by a deed of trust. Acknowledging the immense historical and intellectual value of its rich and valued collection, the Govt. of India declared the Library as Institution of National Importance by an act of Parliament in 1969. The Library is now fully funded by the Ministry of Culture (Govt. of India). This autonomous institution is being governed by a Board with the Governor of Bihar as its ex-officio Chairman and Director is carrying the responsibility of day-to-day management of Library affairs.

c) Rampur Raza Library, Rampur was founded by Nawab Faizullah Khan in 1774 AD. It was brought under the management of a Trust till the Government of India took over the library on 1 July 1975 under the Act of Parliament, which declared it as an institution of National importance. It contains very rare and valuable collection of manuscripts, historical documents, specimens of Islamic calligraphy, miniature paintings, astronomical instruments and rare illustrated works in Arabic and Persian languages besides 80,000 printed books. Nawab Faizullah Khan who ruled the state of Rampur, from 1774 to 1794, established the library with his personal modest collection kept in the Tosha Khana of his Palace. Now the Library occupies the position of an autonomous institution of national importance under Department of Culture, Government of India and is fully funded by Central Government. The Library has now attained an International status of higher studies.

d) Thanjavur Maharaja Serfoji's Sarasvati Mahal Library, Thanjavur is one among a few medieval libraries existing in the world. It contains very rare and valuable collections of manuscripts, books, maps and paintings on all aspects of Art, Culture and Literature. The Encyclopedia Britannica in its survey of the Libraries of the world mentions this as "the most remarkable Library in India". The Library houses a rich and rare collection of manuscripts on art, culture and literature. Conceived and christened as the Royal Palace Library by the Nayak Kings of Thanjavur (1535-1675 AD). And the Maratha rulers (1676-1855) nourished it for intellectual enrichment. In 1918 this Library was made as a public Library. A body constituted by the

Government and financed by the Central and State Governments now administers the library.

During the reign of Nayaks of Thanjavur (1535-1675 A.D.), "Sarasvati Bhandar"(Collection place of Manuscripts) was formed and developed. The Maratha rulers who captured Thanjavur in 1675 A.D. patronized the culture of Thanjavur and developed the Royal Palace Library till 1855 A.D. The Sarasvati Bhandar was situated within the Palace campus and the Manuscripts used for the purpose of reading by the Royal personages. Among the Maratha Kings, King Serfoji II (1798-1832), was an eminent scholar in many branches of learning and with great enthusiasm he took special steps for the enrichment of the Library. It is a fitting tribute to the great collector Serfoji that the Library is named after him. Till the survival of the last Maratha Queen, the Library was the Palace property. After that, the Library together with the Palace properties formed the subject of litigation in Civil Courts. The Royal Family members voluntarily came forward to delete this Library from the suit properties formed an Endowment and dedicated this Library to the public with one lakh rupees for its maintenance and upkeep. Accordingly, the Government of Madras in their G.O. Ms. No.1306 Home (Education) dated 5th October 1918, took possession of the Library under the Charitable Endowment Act and framed scheme for the Library management.

In 1983, the Library was declared as an Institution of National Importance. The Government of Tamil Nadu abolished the Five Member Committee of administration and made it as a Registered Society under G.O. 209 (EST) dated 1-2-83. The Society was constituted and got registration on 9-7-1986 under the Tamil Nadu Registered Societies Act of 1975. The Society consists of ex-officio members of Central and State Governments, nominated Scholars, Member from the Royal family and the Director of the Library. The

Hon'ble Education Minister of the Government of Tamil Nadu is the ex-officio Chairman of this society.

e) **Harekrushna Mahtab State Library, Bhubaneswar** was conceived during 1st Five Year Plan under the advice of Government of India and was completed in 1959, enshrined within a beautiful land of 3 acres in a prime location of Capital City of Bhubaneswar. In 1967, it was named as Gandhi Bhawan commemorating birth centenary of Mahatma Gandhi, the father of the nation. In 1987 it was renovated and entire space of the four storied building was utilized for the functioning of two Libraries i.e. State Library for the entire State of Orissa and another Public Library for Bhubaneswar City. In 1987, Government decided to rename the State Library and the Public Library as Harekrushna Mahtab State Library (in memory of Dr. Harekrushna Mahtab, the builder of modern Orissa) and the Bhubaneswar Public Library respectively. The former is a Reference Library and lending of books is not permitted whereas the latter is a Lending Library for the public of Bhubaneswar City. These two Libraries have managed to function over the limited space. Total readers seats available are about 350 against the present demands of 600-700 readers per day.

2. Library Legislation in India

Since the beginning, the public libraries served as the local information centers making the source of knowledge readily available to the public. The local community from the local fund or individual munificence could not achieve the services of a public library. Public leaders, scholars and learned societies have realized that the only way to establish and develop a public library system is through legislation. The UNESCO Public Library Manifesto, 1972 stated that,

"The public library should be established under the clear mandate of law", which is substantiated by the IFLA/ UNESCO Public Library Manifesto 1994 as;

"The public library shall in principle be free of charge. The public library is the responsibility of local and national authorities. It must be supported by specific legislation and financed by national and local government. It has to be an essential component of any long-term strategy for culture, information provision, literacy and education".

Libraries are recorded under the Article 246 of Indian Constitution, Seventh Schedule List II of State List No.12 and the Indian Constitution (Seventh Amendment) Act, 1956, Section 27 reads, "Libraries, museums and other similar institutions controlled or financed by the State; ancient and historical monuments and records other than those to be of national importance". Provision of public library service is the responsibility of the State Government as the subject matter of libraries is relatable to entry 12 of the State List in the Seventh Schedule to the Constitution of India (Trehan;1986;7).

Dr. S R Ranganathan regarded as the pioneer of library legislation in India. The concept of legislation for libraries is a contribution of S R Ranganathan to Indian public libraries. He made library legislation obligatory for the implementation of the second law of library science, "Every reader his/her book". According to Ranganathan the second law can be properly carried out only by legislation. (Ranganathan;1957;160).

Public libraries also considered as community information centers providing access at local level to a wide range of knowledge and information for the benefit of the individual and society as a whole. To ensure sustained development and information network services public libraries should be based on legislation. "Public library legislation may be in various forms depending upon the government structure. It can be simple, allowing the establishment of public libraries but leaving standards of service to the level of government directly responsible for the library, or more complex, with specific detail on what services should be provided and to what standard". (IFLA/ UNESCO;2001;15). But no British Government passed library Act for creation of public library system in Indian states. (Buragohain;1999;8). There have been different efforts to work out library legislation models in India. In the pre-independent and post-independent of India, there have been five models of public library bills suggested by experts and national level professional associations and organizations.

1) Model Public Libraries Act of Dr. S R Ranganathan

The first Model Public Libraries Acts was prepared by Dr. S R Ranganathan in 1930 and revised in 1957 and 1972. It was discussed at the First All Asia Educational Conference held at Banaras during 26-30 December 1930. It was introduced in West Bengal Legislature in 1931 and in Madras Legislature in 1933. The Bill could not be passed due to financial clauses on library grant, library cess etc. Salient features of final version are:

- establishment of public libraries in city, rural and other areas;
- constitution of State Library Authority i.e. Minister of Education;
- constitution of State Library Committee as an advisory body of the State Library Authority;
- Constitution of Local Library Authority for each city

and one for each district;

- State Library Authority, Government and Local Library Authority may determine library rate in such a manner and may determine collection of library cess from time to time.

2) Model Public Libraries Bill of Ministry of Education

The Government of India, Ministry of Education appointed an Advisory Committee for Libraries in 1957, under the Chairmanship of Shri K P Sinha, former Director of Public Instruction, Bihar. This committee recommended the need for library legislation for each state. As a follow-up action of the Advisory Committee, the Ministry of Education, Government of India appointed a committee under the Chairmanship of Dr. M D Sen. The Committee drafted Model Public Libraries Bill in the year 1963. The salient components of this Bill are:

- Constitution of State Library Authority as an apex body to advise the Government in the matter of library developments;
- Constitution of State Library Directorate for direction and controlling of library services;
- Constitution of District Library Committee in each district;
- Treatment of employees as government servant;
- Collection of library cess at the rate of 6 paise per rupee on house tax and property tax.

3) Model Public Libraries Bill of the Planning Commission

The Planning Commission, Government of India, constituted a 'Working Group on Libraries' in 1964 to plan and advice on the development of Libraries during the Fourth Five Year Plan. The Working Group recommended a Library Development Scheme to be implemented during the Fourth Plan period with a financial commitment of Rs.309 million, which was appended by Model Public Libraries Bill and submitted its report in 1965. Bill was not considered even by a single state. The Bill included the following features:

- Establish, maintain, develop and integrated adequate public library service in the state;
- Constitution of Committee of Experts to prescribe the standards of service;
- Constitution of State Library Council to advise the government for the promotion and development of library service;
- Establishment of State Library Directorate to control, direct and supervise library system in the state;
- Establishment of State Central Library, State Regional Libraries and District Libraries;
- Treatment of employees in the system of State Government Servants
- Government shall be the financial source and shall maintain the public library system in the state.

4) Model Public Libraries Bill of Indian Library Association

The Indian Library Association (ILA) formed in 1933, has keen interest in library legislation. The ILA discussed library legislation at its various seminars organized in 1964, 1978 and 1981. Consequently, ILA Council at its meeting held on 23 June 1989, keeping in view of the developments and experiences gain from the existing Acts, resolved to prepare a Model Library Bill. Accordingly, as asked by ILA, Dr. Velaga Venkatappaiah, Chairman, Central Sectional Committee on Public Libraries of the ILA prepared a Model Public Library Bill. ILA accepted the draft Bill with minor changes at its National Seminar on Public Library Legislation in 1990 at the final product of the Model Public Libraries Bill was published in 1991. The Bill was circulated to all the states and union territories but few states reacted favorably to the Bill. This Model Bill was again discussed in a National Seminar on Library Legislation and revised as the Model State Public Library and Information Service Act in 1995. In view of emergence of Information Technology at all levels, the model act was again revised in 2000. The important components of this Bill are:

- State Library and Information Service, based on a State Policy;
- Constitution of State Library Authority at the apex level with Minister of Libraries as Chairman as policy making and executive body;
- Establishment of Directorate of Public Libraries for directing, controlling and supervising;
- Constitution of City, District Library Authority for rendering service from district to village level;
- Provision for network of Public Library and Information Services from state to village level;
- Constitution of State Library and Information Service;
- Collection of Library cess on house tax and property tax, entertainment tax, professional tax, vehicle tax,

etc.;

- Constitution of State Boards for education, book production, co-ordination, etc.;
- Accountability of public expenditure and services.

5) Model Union Library Act

The Government of India appointed a committee to explore the possibilities to establish a National Central Library at New Delhi in 1948. Dr. S R Ranganathan, a member of the committee drafted a Library Development plan in 1950 with a 30-year programme and a draft Library Bill for the states and Union Public Library Act. This was revised in 1959 and again in 1972. However, libraries falls under the state list of the constitution and it may not be possible to pass Bill as a Union Act, unless and until the constitution is suitably amended for this purpose. The main features of this model Act are:

- Constitution of a National Library Authority;
- Establishment of national central libraries;
- Constitution of National Library Committee as an advisory body to the National library Authority;
- Constitution of National library fund;
- Amendment to the delivery of Books and Newspaper Act, 1954.

The IFLA/UNESCO Public Library Manifesto 1994 reads that, "The public library is the local center of information, making all kinds of knowledge and information readily available to its users". (IFLA/UNESCO;1994) Public libraries, to become an enthusiastic source of information and knowledge for the local community, needs certain forms of developments in terms of infrastructure, collection and the trinity of library as well. It cannot survive by the local contributions and dedication alone, but through the support of government. “The pubic library, as a democratic institution operated by the people for the people, should be established and maintained under the clear authority of law; supported wholly or mainly from public funds; open for free use on equal terms to all members of the community regardless of occupation, creed, class or race”. (Ekbote;1987;34). Efforts have been going on well under the initiatives of professional associations and learned societies in this context. “In India, the post independence era was favorable to the establishment of public libraries based on legal basis”. (Viswanathan;2005;46).

a) States with Library Legislation

During the last six decades, 14 (fourteen) Public Library Bills were enacted in different states of India, such as:

1) The Tamil Nadu (Madras) Public Libraries Act 1948;

2) The Andhra Pradesh Public Libraries Act 1960

   (previously known as The Hyderabad Public Libraries Act 1955, but renamed as a result of State Reorganization);

3) The Karnataka (Mysore) Public Libraries Act 1965;

4) The Maharastra Public Libraries Act 1967

   (The Kolhapur Public Libraries Act was passed in 1945. Consequent upon the state reorganization, the state of Kolhapur was merged with Maharashtra state. Then Maharashtra Public Libraries Act came into being in 1967);

5) The West Bengal Public Libraries Act 1979;

6) The Manipur Public Libraries Act 1988;

7) The Kerala Public Libraries Act 1989;

8) The Haryana Public Libraries Act 1989;

9) The Mizoram Public Libraries Act 1993;

10) The Goa Public Libraries Act 1993;

11) Orissa Public Libraries Act, 2001;

12) Gujarat Public Libraries Act, 2001;

13) Uttaranchal Public Libraries Act, 2005.

14) Rajasthan Public Libraries Act, 2006

1) Tamil Nadu

Tamil Nadu is the first state that enacted Public Libraries Act in independent India. It came into force with effect from 1 April 1950. The objectives of the Act are contained in its Preamble as, 'An act to provide for the establishment of public libraries in the province of (Madras) Tamil Nadu and the organization of comprehensive rural and urban Library Service therein". It has 19 sections. The salient features of this Act are given below:

1) This Act facilitates establishment of Public Libraries in the State.

2) Constitution of State Library Committee for the purpose of advising the government on such matters relating to libraries.

3) Provision for appointment of Director of Public

Libraries to control, direct and supervise public libraries.

4) Constitution of Local Library Authorities, one for the City of Madras and one for each district.

5) Every Local Library Authority shall levy in the area a library cess in the form of a surcharge on property tax or house tax at the rate of six paise per rupee.

6) The Government shall contribute Library Fund to each of the Local Library Authority, except the City of Madras, to the amount of library cess collected.

7) The Act amended Sec.9 of the Press and Registration of Books Act, 1867, Central Act XXV of 1867 to the effect that every printer shall deliver five copies of each book to the State Government out of which four will be deposited in the State Central Library, Madras.

Tamil Nadu was very rich in public libraries. The Connemara Public Library was opened for the public in 1896 and became the State Central Library from 1 April 1950. There is a tremendous growth and development of public libraries since an enactment of Tamil Nadu Public Libraries Act 1948 being the first state in India with Library Legislation. The state has public library service units, as – 1 State Central Library, 29 District Central Libraries, 1548 Branch Libraries, 506 Village Libraries, 649 Part-time Libraries, and 8 Mobile Libraries. The Department of Public Libraries has been offering extension services, like – Mobile Library Service, Home Delivery Service, Library Service for Children, Library Service for Police Personnel, Library Service for state workers and remote settlers in the hills, Hospital Library Service, Rural Library Service, Part-time Library Service, Library Service for Students, Library Service for research scholars and Library Service for competitions for various civil services.

2) Andhra Pradesh

The state of Andhra Pradesh was formed in 1956, comprising Andhra areas of composite Madras state and Telengana area of Hyderabad area, whereas Madras Public Libraries Act in force in Andhra area. To solve administrative problems on two acts in operational in one state; both the acts were amalgamated, modified and up-to-date as Andhra Pradesh Public Libraries Act 1960. It received the Governor assent on 18th. February 1960. Andhra Pradesh is the second state that has enacted Public Libraries Act in independent India. Its Preamble reads that, "An Act to consolidate and amend the laws relating to the establishment and maintenance of Public Libraries in the State of Andhra Pradesh and matters connected therewith". It has seven chapters. Important features of this Act are as below:

1) Constitution of 'The Andhra Pradesh Granthalaya Parishad', as a corporate body, having perpetual succession and power to the provisions of this Act.

2) Constitution of Directorate of Public Libraries to direct, supervise and control Public Library System.

3) Constitution of Zilla Granthalaya Samastha, one for the City of Hyderabad, one for the district of Hyderabad and one for each districts.

4) Provision to collect library cess by every Zilla Granthalaya Samstha in its area as surcharge on property tax or house tax up to eight paise per rupee.

5) The accounts of Zilla Granthalaya Samstha shall be open to inspection.

6) Provision of Government Grant-in-aid to private libraries.

7) Provision for constitution of a Library Service for the Ziila Granthalaya Samstha for the appointment of Librarians.

Andhra Pradesh is one of the leading states in India for the promotion of library services in India. It is the second in India with Public Libraries Act in 1960. The structure of public library services can be classified into three categories consisting of: (Patel;2004;156).

- **Government Libraries**

  1 State Central Library, 6 Regional Libraries, and Mobile Library,

- **Zila Grandhalaya Samstha Libraries**

  23 District/City Central Libraries, 1448 Branch Libraries, 355 Village Libraries, Mobile Libraries, and Book Deposit Centers,

- **Aided Libraries**

  Gram Panchayat Libraries, Cooperative Society Libraries, and Private Libraries.

3) Karnataka

Karnataka is the third state in an independent India that have enacted Public Libraries Act. The objective of this Act can be seen in its Preamble that reads, 'An Act to provide for the establishment and maintenance of Public Libraries and the organization of a comprehensive rural and urban library service in the State of Karnataka (Mysore)'. Important features of this Act are given below:

1) Constitution of State Library Authority to meet twice

in a year, Minister of Public Libraries as its Chairman and State Librarian as ex-officio Secretary.

2) Provision for creation of an independent Department of Public Libraries with a profession as its head, to supervise, direct and control library services.

3) Provision for the establishment of State Library as apex of public library system in the state.

4) Constitution of Local Library Authority, City Library Authority and District Library Authority.

5) Provision for setting up of Advisory Library Committee for Branch and Village Library Services.

6) Collection of library cess on tax on lands and buildings.

7) Additional sections in State Central Library

   i) State Bureau of Copyright Collection

   ii) State Library for the Blind

   iii) State Bureau of Inter Library Loan

   iv) State Bibliographical Bureau

   v) State Bureau of Technical Service.

Karnataka is the third state in India that enacted Public Library Bill in 1965. The Belgaum Native General Library, established in 1848 by M.J.D.Invararity, was regarded as the first library started in Karnataka state. There were other seven libraries or reading rooms in Belgaum, namely, Library at Chikkodi established in 1886, Nippani Library in 1875, Gokak Library in 1865, Athani Library in 1865, Sampagaon Library in 1866, Khanapur

Library in 1868, and Saundatti Library in 1870. The existing public libraries in Karnataka are - 1 State Central Library, 1 Indira Priyadarshini Chidren's Library, 1 Public Technical Library, 27 District Central Library, 19 City Central Library, 14 Mobile Libraries (District & City), 490 Branch Libraries (District & City), 107 Service Stations (District & City), Reading Rooms, Gram Panchayat Libraries, Aided Libraries (District & City), Slum Libraries and Reading Rooms in Slum Areas.

4) Maharashtra

Consequent upon the constitution of Maharashtra state, The Maharashtra Public Libraries Act, 1967 succeed Kolhapur Public Libraries Act 1945. The fourth state in an independent India that has enacted Public Libraries Act is Maharashtra state. Preamble of the Act read that, "To provide for the establishment, maintenance, organization and development of public libraries in the state of Maharashtra". Important features of this Act are:

1) Constitution of State Library Council. Minister for Education shall be the ex-officio President of the Council. The Council will advise the State Government on all matters connected with the administration of this Act.

2) Constitution of a separate department of Libraries and the appointment of a professional Director;

3) Establishment of Maharashtra State Library Service;

4) Establishment of State Central library and a Divisional Library for each Division;

5) Constitution of District Library Committee in each of the district. Chairman of the Education Committee

of a Zilla Parishad in the district shall be ex-officio President of the Committee.

6) Constitution of Library Fund by the State Government for carrying out the purpose of this Act. The State Government will contribute not less than a sum of twenty-five lakhs to the Library Fund every year.

The Birtishers started public libraries in Maharashtra after defeating Marathas in 1818 but no Indians were allowed membership of these libraries till 1830. Pioneer libraries established by Indian in Maharashtra were at Ahmednagar in 1838, Bombay in 1845, and Poona in 1848. In 1939, the government constituted a Library Development Committee to prepare a plan for public library development in the state of Bombay. The report was implemented from 1955 to 1967. After an enactment of Maharashtra Public Libraries Act 1967, public library system was developed through voluntary organizations with grants from the government. As on 1998, Maharashtra has different categories of public libraries as – 1 State Central Library, 6 Divisional Libraries, 31 District Libraries, 63 Taluka Grade A Libraries, 144 Taluka Grade B Libraries, 58 Taluka Grade C Libraries, and 3842 Recognized Libraries.

5) West Bengal

The West Bengal Legislature passed this Act and assent of the President was first published in the Calcutta Gazette, Extraordinary on the 7th January 1980. West Bengal enacted the Public Libraries Act in 1979 to become the fifth state of India with library legislation. Its preamble stated that, *"An Act to provide for the establishment of Public libraries in the State of West Bengal and to regulate, guide, central, supervise and to grant recognition to the existing libraries in the State as also to provide for a comprehensive rural and urban library service in the State of west Bengal".* Some of the important salient features of this Act are:

1) Constitution of State Library Council for the purpose of advising the Government on the matters of public library services. Minister-in-Charge of Library Services shall be the Chairman of the Council;

2) Constitution of the Department of Libraries to supervise and direct the maintenance of Public Libraries;

3) Constitution of Local Library Authority for each district. The District Magistrate shall be the Chairman of the Local Library Authority. Provision for constitution of Executive Committee for Local Library Authority;

4) The Government is empowered to appoint District Library Officers and District Librarians in districts. The Government, in consultation with the Local Library Authority may place a person in charge of a District Library to be called as District Librarian;

5) Financial management of local libraries rests upon the Local Library Authority. Means of augmenting funds are:

a) Contributions, gifts and income from endowments;

b) Grants from the government

c) Collection of Local Library Authority under the Act.

In 1780, Mr. John Andrews run a commercial library in Fort William and the first public library; Calcutta Public Library was established during the British period in 1836, which is now known as National Library. By 1900, there were 50 public libraries in Bengal. The state government took up a seven tier library development scheme, which envisaged setting up of public libraries at different levels-State Central Library; District Library; Sub-Division/Area Library; Rural Library; Village Library; and Delivery Stations/Book Deposit Centers. (Patel;2004;114) By 1996, West Bengal has one State Central Library, 22 District Libraries, 120 Sub-Divisional/Town Libraries, and 2276 Rural/Area/Primary Unit Libraries. There are also around 3000 non-governmental/non-sponsored public libraries. West Bengal is the fifth state in India with Library Legislation in 1979.

6) Manipur

Manipur is the sixth state in an independent India that has enacted Public Libraries Act in 1988. The preamble stated the objectives of this Acts as, "An Act to provide the establishment and maintenance of Public Libraries in the State of Manipur and matters connected therewith". Salient features of this Act are given hereunder:

1) Constitution of a State Library Committee, to advise the State Government on all matters arising under this Act and to exercise and perform such other powers and duties as may be prescribed.

2) Constitution of a separate Department of Public Libraries under the Director, as its head.

3) Constitution of District Library Authority for each district to supervise library services in the area of its jurisdiction.

4) Provision to constitute Executive Committee and Sub-Committees of District Library Authority to

inquire into and report or advice on any matters, which it may refer to them.

5) Constitution of Library fund formed mainly with the contribution of the State Government.

Manipur is the sixth state in India with Public Library Acts in 1988. Manipur Club established in 1927 was changed over into Manipur Book Club/Manipur Club Library and again changed into Jubabati Memorial Library in 1933. Imphal Public Library, also known as Khwai Public Library was established in 1938 but was functioning till 1960 and later it was demolished in 1994. District Library and Children's Library-cum-Museum were merged on 26 August 1970 and came to be known as State Central library. There are 9 District Libraries, 1 State Central Library, and 215 Libraries organized by Voluntary Organizations.

7) Kerala

Kerala Public Libraries Act, 1989 is also known as Kerala Granthasala Sanghom, 1989. Kerala enacted its pubic Libraries Act in 1989 to become the seventh state in India with library legislation. Preamble of this Act stated its objectives as, *"An Act to consolidate and unify the library laws in the State and to provide for the recognition in the entire library system in the State of Kerala with a view to the development and maintenance of comprehensive rural and urban library service and for matters connected therewith or incidental hereto"*. Important features of the Act are:

1) Constitution of Kerala State Library Council with Executive Committee to advise the government on all matters connected with this Act and to supervise and direct all matters relating to library service in

2) Secretary of the State Library Council shall be the Chief Executive Authority of the State Library Council;

3) Constitution of District Library Council to supervise, co-ordinate and control the Library service under its jurisdiction and to promote co-operation between libraries and cultural and educational institutions in the country;

4) Constitution of Taluk Library Union, with the power to supervise, co-ordinate and control the library services in the Taluk and to give directions and advise to affiliated libraries in regard to their day to day function and management;

5) The Government may make every year a grant to the State library council with a maximum of one percent of the education budget of the State.

6) The State Library Council shall maintain a fund called State Library fund. Library cess collected and grants of State and Central Government will be credited to the State Library fund.

7) Transfer of Kerala Granthaala Sangham with its staff, assets, and liabilities to the State Library Council.

8) Collection of Library Cess in the form of a surcharge on the building tax or the property tax at the rate of 5 paise for the whole rupee.

Christian missionaries started libraries in Kerala during the 19th century. The history of public library movement in Kerala started in 1829 with the establishment of Trivandrum Public Library. There are more than 5000 public libraries in Kerala now, one in every 8 square kilometers. Public libraries can be grouped into four categories, as – Libraries directly run by the Government, Libraries run by the local bodies, Grant-in-Aid libraries affiliated to the Kerala Grandhasala Sangham, and Libraries run by the Local Library Authorities. The Kerala Grandhasala Sangham was established in 1947 and was registered under Section 9 of the Travancore Company Act, 1939 and in 1948 the Government approved it as the Central Agency of the Libraries. It plays an incredible role for the promotion, development and encouraging the people of the state through library services. Kerala enacted Public Library Bill in 1989 to become the seventh state in India with Library Legislation.

8) Haryana

Haryana is the eighth state in India with library legislation. The preamble stated its objectives as, *"An Act to provide for the establishment, maintenance and development of Public Libraries in the State of Haryana and for matters ancillary thereto"*. Some of the important features of this Act are:

1) Constitution of State Library Authority to advise the Government on all matters for the promotion of library services in the State. Minister-in-charge of libraries will be the Chairman;

2) Establishment of State Library Directorate to execute the programmes approved by the State Library Authority;

3) Establishment of State Central library;

4) Constitution of District Library in each district and Municipal/City/Town library; Block library; Village library; and Smaller book deposit centers;

5) Provision for three types of library funds, such as State Library Fund, District Library Fund, and City/Town/Block/Village Library Fund;

6) Levy of Library cess in the form of surcharge on property tax and house tax as decided by the government from time to time;

7) Provision to recognize state library associations, and co-operative institutions by the State Library Authority.

Before the creation of this separate state, some public libraries were already established, Guru Gobind Singh Municipal Library (formerly Fyson Library) in 1926, Shri Parmeshwari Yuvak Librray in 1927, and Sri Bal Amar Samiti Library in 1932. A State Central Library (Jagnayak;1999;67) was started in 1967 by th4 Government of Haryana. Besides it has started 12 District Libraries, 11 Sub-Divisional Libraries and 11 Municipal Libraries. Many philanthropic trusts and local bodies/organizations had also established public libraries, which took active role in the promotion of reading habits and library services in the state. The Haryana Library Association was founded in 1967. The Haryana Public Libraries Bill was passed in 1989 and independent Directorate of Libraries was established in January 1993. Mobile library services to reach the interior of the remote villages with reading facilities were started and the people are very much encouraged for the development of libraries at villages and panchayat levels as a social education center and community information center as well.

9) Mizoram

Mizoram is the ninth state of India to have library legislation. Preamble of this Act stated its objective as, *"An*

Act to provide for the establishment, maintenance and development of comprehensive public libraries system in the State of Mizoram". Important features of this Act are:

1) Constitution of State Library Council to advise the Government on all matters relating to libraries and also in regard to promotion and development of libraries in the State;

2) Constitution of the Department of Public Libraries to control and supervise the public library system in the State;

3) Constitution of State Library, District Library, Sub-Divisional Library and Village Libraries;

4) Provision of grant-in-aid to recognized libraries;

5) No library cess. All expenses shall be made from the Government funds.

10) Goa

Goa is the tenth state to have library legislation in India. Preamble of this Act stated that, *"An Act to provide for the establishment, maintenance and development of Public Libraries in the State of Goa and for the matters ancillary hereto".* Important salient features of this Act are:

1) Constitution of State Library Council with the Minister-in-charge a the Chairman to advise the Government on all matters arising under the Act;

2) Constitution of State Library Directorate for controlling and directing the public library system in the State;

3) Organization of State Library, District Library, Taluk Library, and Village library;

4) Creation of Public Library employees similar to the employees of State Government;

5) Recognition of one State Library Association as co-operating institution;

6) State library fund from different sources, viz. Government contribution, Government Grants, and any other contribution from the public;

7) Levy of Library Cess in the form of a surcharge on Indian Made Foreign Liquor at the rate of 50 paise per bulk litre of beer.

Under the order of the Viceroy, *Dom Manuel de Portugal e Castro*, a public library, *Publica Livraria* was opened and attached to *Academia Militar* in 1832 and it was named as *Bibliotheca Nacional de Goa* in 1959 and came under the administration of Education and Health Services department. The Government of Goa constituted a State Level Expert Committee in 1978 and State Library Advisory Board in 1983 for the development of library services in the state. The public libraries of Goa can be categorized into five levels, as State Library, Taluka Libraries, Village Libraries, Government Aided Libraries, and Municipal Libraries. Goa is the tenth state in India with Public Library Act in 1993.

11) Orissa

The establishment of Diamond Jubilee Library at Kendrapara in 1897 and at Baripada in 1898 started the development of public library and followed by establishment of other libraries in the state. Three Government functionaries, Department of Information and Public Relations, Department of Sports and Culture, and Department of Housing and Urban Development operated public libraries in the state for some times. In 1975, the Department of Cultural Affairs, Government of Orissa took complete charge of Public Libraries from the Department of Education. There is one State Library, 13 District Libraries, 4 Sub-Divisional libraries, 6 Ex. District Board Libraries, and 4 Memorial Hall Libraries.

12) Gujarat

Objective of Gujarat Public Libraries Act provided in its preamble is to provide for the promotion and development of public libraries in the State of Gujarat and for that purpose to constitute State Library development Council and for the matters connected therewith or incidental thereto. Important features of this act are:

1) Constitution of State Library Council with Minister –in-charge of Libraries as its Chairman;
2) Establishment of Public Library Department with Director as its head of office;
3) Establishment of District and Taluka Libraries at the headquarters of taluka;
4) Constitution of District and Taluka Library Advisory Committee;
5) Formation of State Library Development Fund;
6) Recognition of libraries run by voluntary organizations.

The first considered public library in Gujarat was called, "Himabhai Institute of Library" established in 1849 in Ahmedabad Other pioneer public libraries are Andrews Library established in 1850, Lang Library in 1857, Lakhajirao Pusthakalaya in 1868, Bhagavatsihji Library in 1884, State

Library in 1865, Barton Library in 1882, Takhsinhi Library in 1877, and Victoria Jubilee Library in 1891. There are 2 State Central libraries, 18 District Libraries in all the districts, 45 Taluka Libraries, 129 Mahila Libraries run by voluntary organizations, more than 300 Book Service Centers and Mobile Library service.

13) Uttaranchal

Uttaranchal is the 27th state of Indian Union, separated from Uttar Pradesh and coming into existence on 9.11.2000. The state comprises ten districts, namely Uttarkashi, Dehradun, Tehri Garhwal, Chamoli, Pithoragarh, Nainital, Uddam Singh Nagar, Pauri Garhwal and Hardwar. Public Libraries within these districts were automatically came under the Uttaranchal administration. The state literacy rate is 72.28%. The state government is very interested to serve the people through public libraries and the Uttaranchal Public Libraries Bill was enacted in 2005 to become the thirteenth state in India with Library legislation. Some of the well established libraries by the state government of Uttar Pradesh were taken over while coming up into existence.

14) Rajasthan

Libraries were established in Rajasthan as early as 14th. Century and maintained in the form of *Pothi-Khanas* consisting rich collections of manuscripts on different disciplines. Rana Kumbha's Saraswati Bhandar Library was established in 1448. Raja Man Singh established library, *Pothi-Khana* in 1592 by keeping rare and important manuscripts. Pioneer Public Libraries were established in Bharatpur in 1907, Sikar in 1908, Kota in 1910, Fatehpur in 1910, and Jodhpur in 1915. There are 5 Divisional libraries, 24 District Libraries, and 8 Tehsil Libraries with 600 Book Deposit Centers on 15 August 1956. Mobile van was also provided to Division Libraries to supervise library services in the state.

b) States/UTs without Library Legislation.

Public library systems and services of Indian states and Union Territories are highlighted hereunder:

1) Arunachal Pradesh

Arunachal Pradesh, formerly known as North East Frontier Agency, introduced library service since 1950s. During the Seventh Five Year Plan period, the state government took up the scheme of developing libraries in the state and set up a number of libraries at block and circle levels. Mobile library system was introduced in the state capital. The state has six categories of library, such as – 1 State Library, 2 Branch Libraries, 13 District Libraries, 2 Sub-Divisional Libraries, 20 Block Libraries, and 45 Circle Libraries.

2) Assam

In 1865, George Williamson, a tea-planter of Golaghat bequeathed 10,000 pounds for the purpose of educational and set up of libraries in Assam and the government taken up as an experiment measure to established public libraries at the initiatives of British government in 1902-1903 at Dhubri, Guwahati, Nagaon, Jorhat, Tezpur, Shillong, Sibsagar, Goalpara, Dibrugarh, Hailakandi, etc. and then handed over to the Local Boards.

The people were awakened and established rural libraries in some areas. The Assam Library Association came into existence in 1938 and extended all possible help to established public libraries in different areas. The Central Library, established in 1954 at Shillong and the Assam Government Public Library established in 1903 was amalgamated in 1956 and renamed as the State Central Library. In 1955, seven District Libraries were set up at Guwahati, Nagaon, Jorhat, Dibrugarh, Tezpur, Dhubri and Silchar. Book Mobile Service along with 70 Deposit Centers for Circulation of Books was organized to villages in 1959. Assam is running 1 State Library, 1 Branch Library, 22 District Libraries, 14 Sub-Divisional Libraries, and 1 Children Library.

3) Bihar

The ancient Educational and Cultural Centers like Nalanda, Vikramshala, Pataliputra and Taxila had magnificent libraries and Bihar Library Association was founded on 15 October 1936. The Association popularized importance of libraries and in 1937 prepared a Draft Scheme for the development of libraries in Bihar. There is one State Central Library at Patna, having seven wings, viz., State Reference Library, State Lending Library, State Library for Blind, State Bureau of Inter-Library Loan, State Bibliographical Bureau, State Bureau of Technical Service, and State Institute of Library Training and Research. (Thakur;2006). At present, there is 1 State Central Library, 6 Divisional Libraries, 7 Special Libraries, 17 District Central Libraries, 2 State Libraries, 11 Sub-Divisional Libraries, 328 Block Libraries, and about 4400 Village Libraries in Bihar. The Library service is at the government level is under the control and supervision of the Commissioner of Education. In the state of Jharkhand area, there are 5 District Libraries,

4 Sub-Divisional Libraries and other Village Libraries are under the public library sector. The state of Jharkhand came into existence on 15 November 2000 by separating some areas of Bihar state.

4) Himachal Pradesh

Under the scheme of Integrated Library Service formulated by the Union Ministry of Education, a small library system was introduced in 1952. A State Central Library was established in Solan in 1959, and within two years sic District Libraries were opened. It has 1 State Central Library, 11 District Libraries, 15 Community Central Public Libraries, and 101 Senior Secondary School (Public) Libraries in the state. The School Libraries are also used as public libraries after the school hours. (Jagnayak; 1999;66) Two Mobile units are set up in 1961 to cater the needs of the community particularly in the rural areas of the state.

5) Jharkhand

The state of Jharkhand, separated from Bihar, is having 18(eighteen) public libraries established by the state government. These public libraries may be classified into four groups as below:

i) Three State Public Libraries, one each at Ranchi, Chaibasa, Dhanbad and Dumka.

ii) One Divisional Library at Hazaribagh;

iii) Five District Libraries, one each at Gumla, Lohardaga, Daltonganj and Godda; and

iv) Eight Sub-Divisional Libraries, one each at Garhwa,

Lahetar, Pakur, Simdega, Chatra, Sahebganj, Saraikela, and Khunti.

The library building are, generally, not functional to cater more readers at a time. Furniture is inadequate and water supply system is poor. No electricity connection was available to some of them due to non-payment of bills. Collection and subscription of periodicals/newspapers are not adequate to serve the library users as well.

6) Jammu & Kashmir

The state is divided into 14 districts. The Christian missionaries started education. Until 1947, the state has only two public libraries, namely, Sri Pratap Singh Library in 1893 in the city of Srinagar and Sri Ranbir Singh Library in Jammu. The state government establishes the department of public Libraries in 1961 for the establishment and promotion of public library services in the state. The state has 2 Central Libraries, 14 District Libraries, 51 Tehsil Libraries, and 18 Block Libraries.

7) Madhya Pradesh and Chhattisgarh

The state of Madhya Pradesh including Chhattisgarh lies in the heart of the country came into existence on 1 November 1956. Madhya Pradesh was divided into two states, viz., Madhya Pradesh and Chhatisgarh on 1 November 2000; hence the state of Chhattisgarh came into existence. It has 5 Regional, 42 District Libraries, 6 Information Centers, Private Public Libraries, and Gram Panchayat Libraries. The Madhya Pradesh Library Association was formed in 1957.

8) Meghalaya

Meghalaya has taken up the State Library of Assam established in Shillong in 1903 as its State Central Library. It has one State Central Library, four District Libraries, and Libraries run by voluntary organizations in different localities. The Meghalaya Library Association was established in 1994.

9) Nagaland

Nagaland has established a State Central Library at Kohima in 1981 functioning under the Directorate of Art and Culture. It offers computer facilities and reprographic services to its readers. There are eight District Libraries and four of them have completed computerization. 330 Rural libraries are registered under the department of Art and Culture.

10) Punjab

The first public library in Punjab, known as Punjab Public Library was established at Lahore (now in Pakistan) in 1884. Other pioneer libraries are Dyal Singh Public Library was established at Lahore in 1896 through a trust created in the name of Dyal Singh, Sir Ganga Commercial Public Library established in 1923, and Dwarka Das Public Library at Lahore in 1921. Pioneer Municipality Libraries in the state were established in Ludhiana in 1878, Lahore in 1884, Patiala in 1897, Amritsar in 1900, Kapurthala in 1904, and Sangrur in 1912. There are 2 State Central Libraries, 14 District Libraries, and 97 Municipal Libraries. Dr. A.C.Wooner founded the Punjab Library Association in 1915 at Lahore.

11) Sikkim

Sikkim public libraries came into existence under the influence of academic libraries in the state. After 1975 the Government of Sikkim realized the importance of public libraries and has started a few libraries but public libraries have not made much progress in a systematic way. All the four districts have a separate District Library at the district headquarters. These libraries were controlled, supervise and administered by the Cultural Department of the Government of Sikkim.

12) Tripura

From the nucleus of "Ujjayanta Palace Library", the then Maharaja Birchandra Manikya established a library in the Royal Palace in the year 1896 in Agartala was called as "Birchandra Library" and declared open to the public. This library was taken over by the government in 1953 and named as Birchandra Public Library and from 1977; it was designated as a State Central Library and renamed as Birchandra State Central Library. Libraries are look after by the Government of Higher and Technical Education and at present the position of public library in Tripura is – 1 State Central Library, 3 District Libraries, 7 Sub-Divisional Libraries, 10 Block Level Public Libraries, 2 Rural Libraries, and 1 Children Library. The departments of Social Education and Panchayat Raj also run some public libraries in the state.

13) Uttar Pradesh

Uttaranchal state came into existence on 9 November 2000 separating some areas from the state of Uttar Pradesh. Some libraries were established in the early days, such as, Raza Library, Rampur in 1750, Allahabad

Public Library (Azad Park Library), Allahabad in 1763, Maulana Azad Library, Aligarh in 1877, Bharati Bhawan Library, Allahabad in 1889 and Lyall Library, Aligarh in 1899. The state has a State Central Library at Allhabad, 69 District level libraries, about 62 other prominent public libraries run by voluntary organizations.

14) Andaman and Nicobar Island

Andaman and Nicobar Island, one of the Union Territories of India, have never experienced the services of libraries until a small library was set up in the cellular jail in the early 1930s. In 1957 an Information Centre was set up at Port Blair. In 1964, this Information Centre was converted into District Library and later on considering the public interest the District Library was enlarged and reorganized into the State Library in 1977. Library service is under the Department of Education and financed by the Andaman & Nicobar Administration and the department came forward with an idea of spreading education through the libraries. At present, there is 1 State Central library, 1 State Library, 2 District Libraries, 12 Zonal Libraries, and 3 Public Libraries.

15) Dadra and Nagar Haveli

In the Union Territory of Dadra and Nagar Haveli, there is a State Central Library at the capital city Silvasa and Public Library, known as Central Library at Naroli, Kanvel, Randha, Kilvani, Dapido, Amoli, Dushni and Mandoni. The Central Library at Silvasa and Naroli were established in 1954 and 1965 respectively. Central Libraries at Silvasa, Dadra and Kanvel are functioning in their own buildings whereas the remaining libraries were in a rented building and primary schools. There are no public libraries run by voluntary organizations in this Union Territory. The library services were under the control and supervision of the Director of Education.

16) Daman and Diu

The Assistant Director of Education under the control of the Department of Education supervises library services in the Union Territory of Daman and Diu. There are 3 Municipal Libraries at Moti Daman, Nani Daman, and Diu. Establishment of a Central library, 2 District libraries, and Mobile Library is under consideration.

17) Lakshadweep

There was no library service in this Union Territory before independence. The first public library was established at Karavati in 1951. However, the island has the apex library of this Union Territory established in 1958 as Freedom Fighters Central Library, which was subsequently named as Lakshadweep Central Library. It has well organized public library system in which Lakshadweep Central Library serves as the State Central Library. These libraries were earlier known as Reading Room-cum-Library. Library services are looked after by a Library Development Officer who performs the supervision function under the overall control of the Director of Social Welfare and Culture. To develop and sustain library movement, the administration has constituted a state level committee known as 'Lakshadweep State Library Committee' in 1994 comprising 10 members including Library Development.

18) Pondicherry

The history of Library in Pondicherry began with the establishment of a '*Bibliotheque Publique*' (Public Library) in 1827 with a modest stock of books collected from several Government establishments functioning in this region. The British Indian Government also donated some books to this library from time to time. It was renamed as *'Romain Rolland Library'* in 1967 after the French scholar Romain Rolland. The General Assembly, in 1892, authorized the opening of the library at Karaikal and constituted a Commission to advise the administration on measures to be taken for the development of the Library. The Library was originally named as *'Bibliotheque Coloniale'*. This library was renamed as *'Bibliotheque Publique'* in 1952 and subsequently categorized as Regional Library and called as Government Public Library. The first library was actually started by the 'Association of Old Students' in 1918 at Mahe. The Old Boys Association donated all the books and furniture of Mahe Public Library. In 1964, the Union Territory Administration has evolved a policy of opening Branch Libraries at rural areas of the territory and the number of Branch Libraries opened in four regions are, 46 in Pondicherry region, 14 in Karaikal region, 3 in Mahe region, and 2 in Yanam region. The Director of Education from 1954 to 1991 controlled the library services. Since 1991, Director of Art and Culture is the head of the Library services.

19) National Capital Territory of New Delhi

Before the independence, Delhi was very poor in library services, particularly in public libraries, due to political structures, lack of educational facilities, and attitude of the authorities. Harding Library was established in 1862 and housed in a portion of the Town Hall. In 1942, Delhi Municipal Committee changed the name of the library to the Harding Municipal Public Library, which was further rechristened in 1970 as the Hardayal Municipal Public

Library after the famous freedom fighter and intellectual Lala Hardayal. The British Council Library and American Information resource Centre are also being developed for the public and function with the latest technology which enrich public library services in Delhi. Marwari Seth Kedar Nath Goenka in the Chandi Chawk area of Delhi set up the Marwari Library, the first of any type founded through community awareness in Modern India, in 1915.

Under the UNESCO's Pilot Project, the Ministry of Education, Government of India, founded Delhi Public Library in 1951. It was very much developed and became one of the depository libraries in India. The Delhi Public Library consists of the Central Library, Zonal Libraries, Branch Libraries, and Sub-Branch Libraries in addition to the Community libraries, Resettlement Colonies libraries, Sports libraries, and an adequately good network of Mobile Library Services to link up the remote urban and rural areas spread over the Union Territory of Delhi.

3. National Policy on Library and Information System (NAPLIS)

John Martin said, "Policy is a statement of a specific goal or goals which are to be achieved, or to be pursued; a statement of the means by which realization of the goals will be brought about; an assignment of the responsibilities for implementation of the means, and a set of rules or guidelines regulating the activity". (Hill;1989;20) According to P.B.Mangla, National Policy on Library and Information Science is to "provide a framework for properly planned and co-coordinated development of library and information structure in a country, resulting thereby in an enhanced and user-oriented information services to its user population". (Mangla; 2001).

The need for the formulation of National Policy on Library and Information Systems (NAPLIS) was brought to the notice of the Government of India by Indian library profession since 1950s by Dr. S.R.Ranganathan and in the recommendations of the Library Advisory Committee Report, 1958. Afterwards, professional organizations, like RRRLF, NISSAT and National Library urged upon the Government the necessity of enunciating such policy. The matter was discussed in the annual conference of IASLIC in 1979 at Roorkee and ILA in 1984 at Jaipur. Consequently, Indian Library Association submitted a draft policy statement to the Government in 1985. The Planning Commission Working Group in its report *Modernization of Library Services and Informatics for the 7th Five-Year Plan (1985-1990)* emphasized the need of such policy. The Raja Rammohun Roy Foundation, after nine years of its inception, took up the task in 1981 and after careful deliberations submitted a Draft National policy on Library and Information Systems to the government in July 1984.

On the basis of the draft policy submitted by the Raja Rammohun Roy Library Foundation and Indian Library Association, the Government of India, Ministry of Human resources Development, Department of Culture, set up a Committee in October 1985 under the Chairmanship of Professor D.P.Chattopadhyaya for the formulation of a National Policy on Library and Information Systems and the final report was submitted in May 1986 which includes:

- The Public Library system;
- The Academic Library System;
- Special Libraries and Information Systems;
- The National Library System and the Bibliographical Services;

- Manpower Development and Professional Status; and
- Modernization of Library and Information Systems.

Though the government has not adopted the recommendations as the official policy, but it serves as suggestive model for the development of libraries as a whole. The recommendations under the Public Library System are as follows: (India;1986).

- The most important task before the government is to establish, maintain and strengthen the free public libraries in the country and enable them to work as a system.
- The main thrust in this area should go to the rural public library. A village or a village cluster with an adequate population should have a community library, which will also serve as an information center. Resources of different agencies engaged in the work of public health, adult education, local self-government and such others may be pooled to build up this composite center.
- An important link should be established between the community library of the village and the village primary school. If the school does not have a library of its own, the community library should provide the children with an adequate book-corner.
- The community library should also importantly cater for adult education and make adequate audio-visual aids available to attract the illiterate villagers.
- The district library should serve as an apex library for each district with public libraries at city, town and village levels constituting important components in the district library system. In addition to the usual

services to be rendered by it, it should also provide for learning facilities and recreation for the handicapped. Wherever possible, district libraries and comparable city public libraries should provide literature in Braille. The district library and branch libraries should also arrange mobile and circulating library services within its area wherever it is necessary and feasible. Special services should be rendered to hospitals, prisons, and the infirm in their homes.

- Libraries for special groups should be built in areas of tribal concentration or minority communities to develop their distinctive cultures. The government will provide all encouragement for such communities to develop their own libraries through voluntary effort.
- Each public library should have a section for children and, in addition, separate libraries for children with attractive books and audio-visual supporting materials should be established wherever possible.
- The district library will take the leadership in establishing linkages between all other public libraries of the district and work towards resource sharing within the area.
- The key role of public libraries as chief sustaining agencies of distance education should be recognized and they should be adequately equipped with the relevant resources for this purpose.
- All the libraries within a state should form part of a network extending from the community library of the village through intermediary levels to the district and to the State Central Library. This State network should eventually connect with the national level.

- The role of the State Central Library is crucial in networking and the establishment of uniform library procedures within the States. The State Central Library/Directorate of Public Libraries has to perform as the coordinating agency for public libraries in the State.
- To bring about the development of the public libraries in a State it is vital that each State enact its own library legislation. The Central Government should revise the Model Public Library Bill, which it has already prepared, in the light of experience gained in recent years and urge upon the States the importance of enacting such legislation. Finances for library development should be found by each State either from its general revenues or from local taxation.
- The Central Government should assist the State in the development of public libraries in a larger way than it has done so far. The Raja Rammohun Roy Library Foundation as the national agency for co-coordinating and assisting the development of public libraries be suitably strengthened enabling it to discharge its responsibilities effectively.

4. National Knowledge Commission

National Knowledge Commission, the world's first body of its kind, was set up under the chairmanship of Mr. Sam Pitroda by the Prime Minister of India, Manmohan Singh to prepare a blueprint to tap into the enormous reservoir of our knowledge base so that our people can confidently face challenges of the 21st. Century. The Commission has a designated time frame of three years from 2nd. October 2005 to 2nd. October 2008.

The Commission argued Libraries as Gateways to knowledge and continued that a "Library is not a building stacked with books - it is a repository and source of information and ideas, a place for learning and enquiry, and for the generation of thought and the creation of new knowledge. Public libraries in particular have the potential to bridge the gap between the 'information poor' and the 'information rich' by ensuing that people from all sectors and settings of society and the community across India have easy access to knowledge seek".

The Commission clearly incorporated roadmap for the execution of its recommendations on libraries under different points of consideration. It gave a Library Charter that is incorporated below; Recognizing that the library's objectives are to:

- Disseminate knowledge as widely as possible;
- Serve as a major vehicle to facilitate creation of new knowledge;
- Facilitate optimal use of knowledge by all sectors, such a government, industry, rural sector and civil society;
- Ensure that people from all sectors and all parts of the country have easy access to knowledge relevant to their needs, in their own language.

The library undertakes to:

- Serve as local center of information and a gateway to national and global knowledge providing fair access to knowledge and information to as many as users as possible;
- Offer an inviting and attractive physical space with

clean drinking water and toilet facilities;

- Offer proactive services to its user communities;
- Ensure that users are treated with courtesy and respect by library staff;
- Pay attention to the needs of children, women, senior citizens and the physically challenged;
- Optimize its potential to provide access to information and knowledge to all;
- Help users developed information skills to make optimum use of resources;
- Improve its collections and services on continuing basis in consultation with users;
- To work more effectively and efficiently by undertaking every activity in a professional manner;
- To bridge the gap between the information poor and the information rich.

India now has become one of the most developing countries in the world. It spreads in various fields of knowledge and disseminates its resources to the world.

It is also one of theItIt has also establishedII It has also established public libraries and community information centers to give and help local community to acquire information from various agencies. Public library services have been expanded to serve the local people, but after 60 years of independence India, public libraries could not be administered and managed with the clear mandate of law in many states of India. As such, the development of the nation through library services is neglected in some states, and its services are beyond the reach of the rural poor. The next chapter describes about the public library scenario in Mizoram that is an important study to take up this research work.

REFERENCES

Bhattacharjee, R. (2002). Public Library Services in India; Systems, Modernization, Networking and Deficiencies. National Round Table on the Modernization & Networking of Libraries in India edited by H. K. Kaul. New Delhi: DELNET.

Buragohain, Alka. Public Library Scenario in India: Problems and Prospects. *Herald of Library Science*. 38 (1-2), Jan-Apr., 1999.

Datta, B K. (2004). Libraries and Librarianship. Quoted by Jashu Patel and Krishan Kumar *In*. Libraries and Librarianship in India. Westport: Greenwood.

Ekbote, Gopalrao (1987). Public Libraries System. Hyderabad: Ekbote Brothers.

Hill, Michael M. (1989). National Information Policy. Quoted by P.B.Mangla, National Policy on Libraries, Information Systems and Services; An Overview in 50 Years- Library and Information Services in India edited by M.K.Jain *et.al.* Delhi: Shipra.

IFLA/UNESCO (2001). The Public Library Service; IFLA/UNESCO Guideline for Development. Munchen: K G Saur.

India. (1986). Ministry of Human Resources Development (Department of Culture). National Policy on Library and Information System – a presentation. New Delhi.

Jagnayak, S. S. (1999). Public Library Development in India: An Historical Perspective since 1947. 50 Years of Indian Librarianship edited by G Devarajan. New Delhi; Ess Ess,. p.13.

Khursid, Anis (1972). Growth of Libraries in India. Quoted by Jashu Patel and Krishan Kumar. *In*. Libraries and Librarianship in India. Westport: Greenwood, 2004, p.6.

Mangla, P.B. (2001). National Policy on Library and Information Systems and Services; An overview in 50 Years- Library and Information Services in India. Edited by M.K.Jain, *et.al.* p.3.

Nagar, Murari Lal (1983). Foundation of Library Movement in India.

Ludhiana, Indian Library Institute and Bibliographical Centre.

Patel, Jashu and Krishan Kumar (2004). Libraries and Librarianship in India. Westport: Greenwood, 2004.

Ranganathan, S.R. (1957). The Five Laws of Library Science. Bangalore; Sarada Ranganathan Endowment for Library Science.

Sharma, Pandey S K (1987). Libraries and Society. New Delhi: Ess Ess.

Sharma, Pandey S.K. (1996). Public Libraries in India; Trends and Status. *In*. Public Libraries in developing Countries: Status and Trends edited by P K Mahapatra and V K Thomas. New Delhi: Vikas.

Thakur, U.M. Public Libraries in Bihar; An Overview. *Herald of Library Science* v.45 (1-2) Jan-Apr. 2006.

Smith, Vincent A. (1981). Oxford history of India. 4th. Ed. Delhi: OUP.

Mangla, P.B. *et.al* (eds). Library and Information Services in India: States and Union Territories . New Delhi: Shipra; 2001.

Trehan, G.L. (1986). Main Problems of Library Legislation in India. *In*. Library Legislation in India edited by R K Rout. New Delhi: Reliance.

Viswanathan, C.G. (2005). Public Library Organization. 4th. Ed. New Delhi: Ess Ess Publications

Public Library in India : 83-112
R. K. Ngurtinkhuma
Today and Tomorrow's Printers & Publishers, New Delhi-110 002 (India)

Chapter 3

STATE AND DISTRICT LIBRARIES IN MIZORAM

Mizoram completed its fortieth year of public library service in 2008. During these years, the state government established one State Library and five District Libraries and the government. The ethical code of the people of the state has distinct nature of livelihood to help and work for the others on voluntary basis and, most of the villages established village libraries run on voluntarily. The state government has recognized 242 Village Libraries at different areas of the state till date. The Mizoram Public Libraries Bill was enacted in 1993 by the State Legislative Assembly to become the ninth state with public library act in India. The public library system of the state is interesting for it has been serving to develop the society in various field of knowledge. It is not only the state government taking steps to develop library services within the state, but also NGO/CBO are also very active in organizing local/village libraries on voluntary basis.

1. Historiography of Mizoram

Mizoram, the 23rd. state of Indian union, is one of the seven sister states of the North Eastern Region. Situated between 21'58^{0}N to 24'35^{0}N latitude and 92'15^0 E to 93'29^{0}E longitude, covers an overall area of 21,087 sq.km. The length of the state, stretches from north to south is 277 km. and its width, from east to west, is 121 km. It is bounded to the north by the states of Assam and Manipur, to the east and south by Myanmar and to the west by Bangladesh and the state of Tripura. The total length of Mizoram's international boarder with Myanmar and Bangladesh adds up to 722 kms.

The origin of the Mizos, like those of many other tribes in North-Eastern India, is shrouded in mystery. Previously to outsiders, the Mizos were known by various names such as "Kuki", "Chin" and "Lushai". (Sangkima;1992;6). It is believed that Mizos are under the group of Indo-Tibetan Mongoloid race. (Liangkhaia;2002;13). The Burma Census Report of 1891 says that the Kukis of Manipur and the Lushais of Bengal and Assam, and the Chins originally lived in Tibet are of the racial stock. It can be learnt from the folksongs of the Mizos that there was a settlement in the Kabaw valley extending up to Khamti area in the north and south as Kale in Burma, now called Myanmar, and was ruled by three Mizo chiefs in different areas. (Hluna; 1992;7). The settlement at this area is estimated during 15th and 16th centuries.

Before the British conquest and subsequent rule, there was no demarcated boundary and hence no common name for the territory. Every village was a sovereign independent state under its chief. (Hminga;1987;6). Almost the whole of the territory was under the rule of Sailo chiefs. Mizos were then isolated from the others that resulted their social structure, political institutions, customs and traditions remain unaltered till they were under the British rule. The political contact of the British with the Mizos began following their occupation of Bengal after the Battle of Plassey. (Sangkima;1992;70). Mizo chiefs were in the habit of raiding the plains of Cachar and Chittagong tracts of Bengal, which were under the British Administration and hence resulted the involvement of the British Government. Almost every winter when the Mizos were free from *jhuming*, they committed daring raids upon the Kuki settlers in Cachar and Manipur killing many and carrying off many more as captives.

Mizos were constant source of trouble to the British due to their continuous raids to the Cachar settlers killing many persons. On January 23, 1971, Mizos killed James Winchester, a planter at Alexandrapore and his 6 year old daughter Mary Winchester was taken as captive. On July 11, 1871, the Governor-General-in-Council decided to send a military expedition against the Lushais. The force was to consist of two columns, one starting from Chittagong, the other from Cachar; a contingent force was also to be supplied by the Rajah of Manipur. (Woodthorpe;1978;37). The objective of the expedition was to retaliate the murder of Winchester and to deprive of his daughter Mary Winchester. The columns had returned to Calcutta in 1872 after recovering Mary Winchester and punishing the offenders by burning their villages and granaries and carrying away their cattle. (Hluna;1992;71). To avenge the killings, the Government of India decided on the 11th. September 1889 that operations should take place. This expedition was known as the, "Chin-Lushai Expedition of 1889-90". It was on a bigger scale than that of 1888-89 expedition because Bengal, Burma and Assam took part. (Reid; 1942;10-14).

By examining these three expeditions, it can be understood that there was no active consideration on the part of the Government to annex the area to the British territory. The future administration of the hills was, however, the subject of active discussion among the authorities even while the expedition of 1889-1890 was in progress.

(Sangkima;1992;74). The Government of Assam strongly advocated permanent occupation of the Lushai Hills by the British and suggested that the tracts should be divided into two halves for administrative purpose, as it was too big for one Officer alone to administer. The Government of India accepted the proposal, and subsequently it was divided into two administrative units, viz. The Northern Lushai Hills and the Southern Lushai Hills. The northern part was placed under the administrative jurisdiction of Assam with Captain H.R.Browne as Political Officer. He assumed office in May 1890 with Aizawl as his headquarters. Henceforth, Aizawl, chief Thanruma's village, came to be known as "Fort Aijal". The Southern part was made over to Bengal with C.S.Murray of Bengal police as Officer-in-Charge with its headquarters at Lunglei. In 1891, this tract was made a district with Captain Shakespeare as Superintendent. (Hluna;1992;32). Shakespeare took over charge from Murray on the 16th April 1891. (Lalrimawia;1995;52).

With the independence of India in 1947, the Deputy Commissioner replaced the Superintendent and the Lushai Hills continued to be one of the districts of Assam. The result of the partition was that the gateway of the district via Chittagong was sealed, while the Mizos found themselves abruptly separated from their kinsmen in the Chin Hills of Myanmar. In 1954, the Lushai Hills District was renamed "Mizo District" by an act of Parliament and given a new District Council of its own which was established as provided in the 'Sixth Schedule' of the Constitution of India. With the implementation of the North-Eastern Reorganisation Act, 1971, the Mizo District was upgraded into Union Territory on 21 January 1972 and renamed as "Mizoram". Consequent upon the 53rd. Constitutional Amendment, Mizoram was, by an Act of Parliament, elevated to the status of an independent state on 20th. February 1987 and continued to remain "Mizoram". Aizawl is the State capital of

Mizoram.

2. Growth and Development of Public Libraries

The development of Mizoram started with the mechanism and contributions of the Christian Missionaries of England. Education was started by the two Christian Missionaries, Rev. James Herbert Lorrain (Pu Buanga) and Dr. Frederick W.Savidge (Sap Upa) who traveled from London and arrived in Mizoram on 11 January 1894 under the Arthington Aborigines Mission. Their first important contribution for the people of Mizoram was preparation of Alphabets. They started a small school to provide primary education to those who could attend. (Lloyd; n.d.; 34). Due to their tremendous contributions and works, the Assam Government handed over school administration and inspection in Mizoram to the Christian Missionaries from 1904 to 1952. (Lianzawna;1996;15). It was followed by the development of college education and the first college in Mizoram was established under the initiatives of the Missionaries in 1958 at Aizawl under the name of Aijal College (now, known as Pachhunga University College) and Mr. Lalmakthanga was appointed as Librarian-cum-College Clerk in 1961, which was the first professional appointment in the field of Library in Mizoram. (Ngurtinkhuma;2006;19). Afterwards, the first public library, known as Aijal District Library, was established in 1969 at Aizawl (Lianzama;1993).

The then Mizo District (Mizoram) was getting steady growth and development in different aspects. The growth and developments resulted drastic change of social life, cultures and education to the people as a whole. The government took lot of initiatives for the promotion of the people in one or the other areas. Public Libraries are under the direction, supervision and control of Education department till the department was trifurcated in 1988.

Following the trifurcation of Education Department into School Education, Higher & Technical Education and Art & Culture departments, public libraries were fallen under the department of Art & Culture; academic libraries were under the Higher & Technical Education and school libraries under the School Education department.

Public library in Mizoram can be categorized into four groups, such as:

- Government libraries;
- Government recognized libraries;
- Libraries run by voluntary organizations; and
- Private libraries.

The so-called State and District Libraries falls under the category of Government library. At present, there is one State Library at Aizawl, the State Capital, and five District Libraries, one each at the district headquarters of Aizawl, Lunglei, Saiha, Kolasib and Champhai districts. The facilities, infrastructure, collection, administration, etc. are borne by the state government. Library staffs are also government employees and recruited by the state government authority as per rules. The second categories are those libraries run by NGO or other organizations to cater the local information need. The State Library Planning Committee recognizes these libraries. They are receiving some grants or assistance from the government and RRRLF schemes. There are 424 libraries under this category mostly in villages. The third categories are those libraries run by different NGOs or voluntary organizations. The local people establish them voluntarily to meet the local information needs. Management and financial contributions are borne by the local people on voluntary basis. The fourth categories are some private libraries established by some academicians or social workers. They were mostly housed in their private buildings and managed from their own resources. These libraries have good collections of cultural heritage. Many of their collections are mostly out of print materials.

a) STATE LIBRARY

The State Library of Mizoram, an apex public library of the state, was established in 1974 at the state capital, Aizawl to cater information needs of the community. It was housed in a rented building since its inception till today. The functions, services, and other activities undertaken by State Library are as given below:

1) Staff

Library staff is one of the trinity of library. There are 14(fourteen) staffs in the State Library. Out of fourteen staff, only two staff has professional degree in library science. The State Librarian acted as Controlling Officer of State Library and District Libraries as well. The staff position of State Library is one State Librarian, one Assistant Librarian, one Library Assistant, one Counter Attendant, five Clerical Staff and five IV Grade Staff.

2) Library Hours

State Library is open five days in a week, i.e. Monday to Friday. Library hours are predetermined by the office timings of the state government. In summer, it opens from 9:00 a.m. to 5:00 p.m. and in winter, from 9:30 a.m. to 4:00 p.m.

3) Membership

Membership is divided into two categories, namely Adults and Children. Anybody, who is interested, can become a member of the State Library by filling up of

Membership Card and depositing a membership Fee of Rs.10.00 in the case of Adults and Rs.5.00 for Children. Till date, there are 3539 adult and 3192 children members of the State Library. The average daily library user is between 40-50.

4) Sections

The State Library functions comprising various sections in which some staff manages every section. The functions of different sections are mentioned as below;

i) Acquisition Section

The acquisition section takes care of book selection, procurement of books, placing orders, physical checking of books, stamping, accessioning of books, verification of Bills and processing the same for payment.

ii) Technical Section

Technical works, such as Classification and Cataloguing of Books, Identifications of Subject Headings and transcribing are the main works done in this section. Books are classified according to the nineteenth edition of Dewey Decimal Classification (DDC-19ed) and follows Anglo-American Cataloguing Rules II (AACR-II) and Sears' List of Subject Heading (SLSH) to assign subject of documents. Among the different Book Numbering schemes, it follows the "first three letters of the author' surname' as book number.

iii) Circulation Section

Registration of membership, collection of membership fees, deposits, charging and discharging, reservation of books, recall of books, stack verification, display of new collections, collection of overdue charges are the main functions of this section.

iv) Periodical Section

As its name indicates, all related works on periodicals are taken care here. Selection and ordering of periodicals, receiving and registering of periodicals, payment of bills, display, reminders are the major functions of this section.

v) Reference Section

This section looks after all the reference books. Staff helps the users to locate their information needs and shelve used Reference Books on the respective racks. Temporary permission is given to the users to take the Reference Books for reprography/photocopying.

vi) Children Section

It takes care of the users, as most of them are children. Care of books; maintain discipline in the library and other related instructions are given to the children. Separate registration as well as Issue and return of children's' books are done here.

5) Collection

The total collection has grown up to 60009. Most of the collections are English and Mizo. The library has been subscribing eight local, six regional and two foreign journals. Three national and eleven local newspapers are also being subscribed. The library also has collected as much as 100 back volumes on different subject. The annual collection of book for the last seven years is illustrated with Table 3.1 as follows:

Table 3.1 : Year wise collections of books by State Library

Sl.No	*Year*	*RRRLF*	*State Govt.*	*Total*
1	2000	1,198	101	1,299
2	2001	960	1,070	2,030
3	2002	1,758	139	1,897
4	2003	407	122	529
5	2004	1,898	57	1,955
6	2005	1,936	126	2,062
7	2006	1619	3	1,622
Total	9,776	1618	11,394	

6) Services

The Mizoram State Library was established to cater information needs of the community in their day-to-day activities and develop the people in their social, economic, cultural and educational aspects. The library provides the following services not only to the readers but also to the general public as well.

i) Circulation Service

The Library is following Browne Issue System for the charging and discharging. Library member can be issued one book at a time for seven days. A fine is imposed as per rules after due date per day. The registered member can borrow one book for a period of seven days. Average issue of books per day is 18. An average of 50 users per day make use of this system.

ii) Audio-Visual Service

State Library is organizing some Audio-Visual programmes on special occasions. This programme is particularly meant for the children to provide good moral inculcate reading habits and make use of their leisure time in a productive way. Children's films and special films on animals, nature, festivals etc. are shown to the children.

iii) Book Exhibition

In collaboration with some publishers and the Government, the library organizes Book Exhibitions occasionally. Book Exhibitions were held in Aizawl and Lunglei on different occasions.

iv) Reprography

Reprographic service is being provided since two years back only. This is mainly for the library users. Re.1.00 is charged per page. Library users are very much beneficial by this service as they can get their desired materials on the spot by paying a nominal rate.

v) Library Awareness

The State Library in its extension services organized Library Awareness Programs at various district capitals during 2007 as below:

- Serchhip on 16 March 2007
- Kolasib on 20 April 2007
- Champhai on 27 July 2007

- Lunglei on 24 August 2007, and
- Aizawl on 15 November 2007

These programs are organized to give awareness about the library services for the local community to help them in their understanding bout the activities and best practices in utilizing the various information provided by the libraries and to encourage the community to make use of library services. The programme was attended by different section of the local community like students, social workers, service personals, pensioners, etc.

vi) Current Awareness Service

Current Awareness Service is being provided to serve latest information to the users. Documentation Bulletin, Content-by-Journal and Newspaper Clipping are the services rendered under CAS.

7) Building

Mizoram State Library, since its inception, is running in a rented building. Now it was housed in a three floor rented building with a separate hired building for Reading Room. The total floor area is 772.72 sq.m. The construction work of State Library Building is under progress at the New Capital Complex, Khatla, Aizawl with the financial assistance from Raja Rammohun Roy Library Foundation.

8) Budget/Finance

The source of finance for the establishment, management and development of State Library can be summarized as below:

- Membership registration fee
- Late fine
- Sale of waste papers
- Reprographic charges
- Assistance form Raja Rammohun Roy Library Foundation under Matching and Non-Matching Schemes.

Budget allocation of State Library for the last four years is present with Table 3.2 as follows:

Table 3.2: State Library Budget Allocations 2004-08

			Rupees in lakhs	
Head	*2004-05*	*2005-06*	*2006-07*	*2007-08*
Plan	17.23	18.87	12.89	27.45
Non-Plan	13.60	17.90	17.90	19.30
Total	30.83	36.77	30.79	46.75

9) Library Automation

The State Library is in the initial stage of Library Automation and important equipments are collected to start very soon. The library has already procured 6(six) Computers to carry out the work. Internet access, which is now used for E-mail and Web Browsing facilities, is provided to the users.

b) DISTRICT LIBRARIES

The growth and development of Mizoram in different aspects gave birth to the establishment of public libraries within the state. The Government of Mizoram established two District Libraries, one each in Lunglei and Saiha and three Sub-Divisional Libraries, one each in Aizawl, Kolasib and Champhai before 1985. But, after the formation of five more districts in Mizoram, the existing Sub-Divisional libraries were upgraded to the status of District Library and henceforth, there are five District libraries in Mizoram since 2001. Therefore, at present, there existed eight District Libraries in Mizoram, one each in Aizawl, Kolasib, Champhai, Lunglei and Saiha automatically. Mamit District having an area of 3025 Sq.Km with 62785 populations, Serchhip District having a population of 1421Sq.Km. with 53861 populations and Lawngtlai District having 2557Sq.Km. area with 73620 populations are not having District Library at present. State Librarian is the Controlling Officer of the district libraries. Each of these libraries may be discussed as below in brief.

1) Aizawl District Library

Aizawl District has an area of 3756 Sq.Km. with 325676 populations in 2001 census. Aizawl District Library is the first public library established in Mizoram. It came into existence on 12 February 1968 at Aijal, now Aizawl, under the control and supervision of Director of Public Instruction for Hills, Government of Assam. It was temporarily attached to the office of the Inspector of Schools, Aijal. By that time, District Library was already established in Silchar and consequently it was changed into Sub-Divisional Library on 1 August 1969 and housed in a rented building till today. Later, Mizoram being one of the states of India and consequent upon the formation of Districts in Mizoram and Aizawl as one of them, Aizawl Sub. Divisional Library was upgraded to the status of District Library in 2001.

i) Staff

The State Government of Assam appointed some of the staff for Aijal District Library to function under the Education department. The first appointed library staffs for the Aijal District Library is one librarian, one LDC, one Library Attendant and one Peon/Chowkider. The present staff position is one District Librarian, one Counter Attendant, one Clerical Staff and three IV Grade Staff.

ii) Membership

Membership is divided into two categories, namely Adults and Children. Any body, who are interested, can become a member of the Library by filling up of Membership Card and depositing a membership Fee of Rs.10.00 in the case of Adults and Rs.5.00 for Children. Till date, there are 3117 adult and 595 children members at the Aizawl District Library.

iii) Collection

The library is steadily growing in terms of collection. Now, it has 29655 collections of books. The average yearly collection of books can be calculated as much as 780. Eleven Indian Journals are being subscribed and three national and twelve local newspapers are also being subscribed. The library has no back volumes and foreign journals or newspapers. Growth of collection during the last six years in illustrated with Table 3.3 below:

Table 3.3: Growth of collection at District Library, Aizawl

Sl.No	*Year*	*Collection*	*Variance*
1	2001	558	-
2	2002	650	(+) 92
3	2003	879	(+) 229
4	2004	413	(-) 466
5	2005	1,252	(+) 839
6	2006	1,151	(-) 101

iv) Technical Work

To classify the documents, library is following 19th edition of Dewey Decimal Classification Scheme (DDC 19ed.) and Anglo-American Cataloguing Rules-II (AACR-II) for cataloguing of books and Sears' List of Subject Heading (SLSH) to assign subject of documents. Among the different Book Numbering schemes, it follows the "first three letters of the author' surname' as book number.

v) Services

The library has a Circulation Section, Reference Section, Periodical section and Children's' Section. One book can be issued to the library members for a period of seven days at a time. Overdue charge of Re.1.00 per day per book is imposed if not return on due date.

vi) Building

Aizawl District Library, the pioneer public library in Mizoram is not yet having its own building and housed in a rented building. Rented buildings are not functional for a library and as such the staff as well as the users faced difficulties in many ways. However, existing rented library building is of two floors having a total area of approximately 850sq.ft.

2) Lunglei District Library

Mizoram was given the status of Union Territory in 1972 and was divided into three administrative districts, namely, Aizawl, Lunglei and Saiha. Lunglei District (Mizoram Statistical Handbook 2006) has an area of 4536 Sq,Km. with 137223 population in 2001 census and now became the largest districts of Mizoram in area. Lunglei is the district capital.

Lunglei District Library was established on 22nd May 1975 by the education department right after the establishment of State Library at Aizawl. It was housed in a rented building for more than twenty years, but now settled in Saikuti Hall, maintained by the State Government of a storied building at the heart of the town.

i) Staff

From the very beginning, it is under staffed to function as an information center to the community. Three Librarians are being appointed to this library, they are- Mr. Hranghrima (1975-1998), Ms. Lallaisangzuali (1998-2005), and Mr. Rotluanga (2005 to present time). Out of the six posts created to this library, only four staff performed their daily duty. The present library staffs of Lunglei District Library is one District Librarian, one Counter Attendant and two IV Grade Staff.

ii) Membership

Before 1999, there was no proper registration for the membership. Any one who was interested to borrow books from the library can borrow the library books by depositing the prize value. But, since 2000, it follows the registration system of State Library that any person who is interested can apply and register as a member of the library by filling up the Membership Card and depositing a membership Fee of Rs.10.00 in the case of Adults and Rs.5.00 for Children. By this date, there are 445 adult and 78 children members at the Lunglei District Library.

iii) Collection

The library is steadily growing in terms of collection. Due to lack of finance in the budget for procurement of books, the library is very slow in collection development. Till date the library has 18561 collections of books, which is 516 books per year. Library also gets certain amount of books from the RRRLF against the matching fund. The library has been subscribing eleven Indian Journals and three national and seventeen local newspapers. The library has no back volumes or foreign journals. The growth of collection during the last five years is illustrated with Table 3.4 as below:

Table 3.4: Growth of collection at District Library, Lunglei

Sl.No	*Year*	*No. of Collection*	*Variance*
1	2001	1551	-
2	2002	809	(-) 747
3	2003	1375	(+) 566
4	2004	1008	(-) 367
5	2005	535	(-) 473
6	2006	695	(+) 160

iv) Technical Work

Due to non-availability of professional staff, the organization of the library was very inappropriate to serve its clients. Accessioning of books was started in 1983, after eight years of its inception. 19th edition of Dewey Decimal Classification Scheme (DDC 19ed.) and Anglo-American Cataloguing Rules-II (AACR-II) are used to assign classification number and cataloguing respectively. Sears' List of Subject Heading (SLSH) is followed to assign subject headings of documents. The *"first three letters of the author's surname'* is considered to assign book number.

v) Services

The service rendered by this library is very nominal. The library have Circulation Section, Reference Section, Periodical section and Children's' Section. Circulation and periodical section are the main service rendered by this library having an average of 12 daily issues per day and an average of 30 library users per day respectively. One book can be issued to the library members for a period of seven days at a time. Overdue charges is collected if kept beyond due date at the rate of Re.1.00 per day.

vi) Building

Lunglei District Library is in a rented building for more than twenty years. Now it is housed in the third floor of Saikuti Hall situated at the heart of the town. The floor area of the library is 1500sq.ft. The building is quite good and functional to serve the purpose, but being in the third floor, it is not very convenient for such public center being not easily accessible to the users.

3) Saiha District Library

Saiha District (Mizoram Statistical Handbook 2006) has an area of 1399 Sq,km. with 61056 population in 2001 census. Saiha is the district capital of Saiha District. It is within the area of Mara Autonomous District Council. Saiha district is in the southern most part of the state and the people of this area are poor and mostly live in villages. To serve the people of the area through library services, a District Library was established in Saiha on 1st. May 1975 and was known as Saiha District Library.

i) Staff

One of the trinity of a library is staff. The library staff should be well trained, professional and large enough to serve the users by providing best information in a systematic manner. Saiha District Library is not well equipped with adequate professional staff but perform their duty to serve the best to its clients. The staff position of Saiha District Library is one District Librarian, one Counter Attendant and two IV Grade Staff.

ii) Membership

Any persons who are inserted to become a member of this library can enroll themselves by paying a registration of Rs.20.00. There is no separate membership fee for adults or children. The library does not have proper record of library members. The average daily users of the library are 55.

iii) Collection

The library is steadily growing in terms of collection. Collection is carried out from the library budgets and the library also received some books though State Library

Committee under the RRRLF Matching Scheme. The present collection has gone up to 13575. The average yearly collection of books can is 411. The library has been subscribing two Indian Journals, one national and nine local newspapers. The library has no back volumes of periodicals and foreign journals or newspapers subscribed.

iv) Technical Work

Due to non-availability of professional staff, the library cannot perform technical processing work systematically. At the same time, accessioning was done nicely and books were classified according to 19th edition of Dewey Decimal Classification Scheme (DDC 19ed.) and were assign 'first three letters of the author' surname' as book number. Documents were not catalogued and assignment of subject heading was out of question.

v) Services

The library has Circulation section, Reference section and Periodical sections. One book can be issued to the library members for a period of seven days at a time. Daily average issue of books is 31. Overdue charges is collected if kept beyond due date at the rate of Re.1.00 per day. The services rendered by this library are very informative to the local community being they are in a remote area.

vi) Building

Saiha District Library has its own building at the heart of the town. The floor area of the library building is 640sq.m. It has stack area and reading room area separately, but they are not sufficient and functional to accommodate the library users comfortably for a long time.

4) Kolasib District Library

Kolasib District has an area of 1382 Sq.km. with 65960 populations in 2001 census. Kolasib District Library was established in 1980 as a Sub-divisional Library but consequent upon the formation of Kolasib District in 1998, and it was elevated to the status of a District Library in 2001.

i) Staff

The present library staffs of Kolasib District Library are five in number. It has only one professional staff and other supporting staffs are limited in the field of library services. The staff position of this library is one District Librarian, one Counter Attendant and two IV Grade Staff.

ii) Membership

Any persons who are interested can enroll themselves for the member of the library. Membership is divided into two, namely Adults and Children. Membership registration fee is for Rs. 5.00 only. At present, there are 1055 adult and 243 children members at the Kolasib District Library. Number of library visitors for the last seven years is present in Table 3.5 as below:

Table 3.5: No. of visitors at District Library, Kolasib

Sl.No	*Year*	*No. of visitors*	*Variance*
1	2000	3,987	-
2	2001	3,943	(-) 44

3	2002	3,727	(-) 216
4	2003	2,452	(-) 1,275
5	2004	2,111	(-) 341
6	2005	4,168	(+) 2,057
7	2006	5,304	(+) 1,136

iii) Collection

The library is steadily growing in terms of collection. Besides the procurement of books from the allocated fund of the state government, it receives some books from RRRLF Matching Schemes through the State Library Committee. Till date, the collection of books, as per accession register, is 15768. The average collection of books can be calculated as much as 985 per year. Two national and seven local newspapers are being subscribed but no journals are subscribed at present. The library has no back volumes of periodicals and no foreign journals or newspapers are on subscription list. Collection development for the last seven years is illustrated with Table 3.6 in the following:

Table 3.6: Growth of Collection at District Library, Kolasib

Sl.No	*Year*	*No. of collection*	*Variance*
1	2000	421	-
2	2001	171	(-) 250
3	2002	637	(+) 466
4	2003	1,203	(+) 566
5	2004	500	(-) 703
6	2005	472	(-) 72
7	2006	962	(+) 490

iv) Technical Work

Books are accessioned in the Accession Register systematically and some books are also classified according to 19th edition of Dewey Decimal Classification Scheme (DDC 19ed), but are not catalogued. The "first three letters of the authors' surname' is taken for the assignment of book number. No other technical works are carried out, but is going to start very soon under the initiatives of the newly recruited Librarian.

v) Services

The library have Circulation Section, Reference Section, Periodical section and Children's' Section. One book can be issued to the library members for a period of seven days at a time. Overdue charges is collected if kept beyond due date at the rate of Re.1.00 per day. The average daily issue of books is 20 and the average daily visitor is 20.

vi) Building

Kolasib District Library is in a rented building since its inception. Under the initiatives of the state government, a new building is constructed at the heart of the town and is in the final stage of its construction. The present rented library building has a floor area of 96sq.m. Being in a rented building, it was not functional to provide systematic services to the users.

5) Champhai District library

Champhai District has an area of 3185 Sq,Km. with 108392 population in 2001 census. Champhai District was being formed in 1998 separating from the Aizawl district. Champhai is the district capital and occupies the eastern part of the State bordering Myanmar on the east and

Manipur on the north. The library was established in 1982 under the name of Sub-divisional Library but consequent upon the formation of Champhai District, it was upgraded to the status of District Library in 2001.

i) Staff

Champhai District Library has only one professional staff supported by other tree staffs having less knowledge in the field of library services and systems. The present library staff of Champhai District Library is one District Librarian, one Countyer Attendant and two IV Grade Staff.

ii) Membership

Membership is open to those who like to register as a member of the library. Membership fee is fixed at Rs.10.00 only per head with a refundable deposit of Rs.100.00 and Rs.50.00 for adults and children respectively. There are two categories of members, namely, adults and children. The registered member of adults has gone up to 1056 and 47 in the case of children till date. Library visitor during the last six years is illustrated with Table 3.7 as below:

Table 3.7: No. of visitors at District Library, Champhai

Year	*No. of Visitors*	*Variance*
2001	2,911	-
2002	3,327	(+) 416
2003	3,372	(+) 45
2004	3,416	(+) 44
2005	3,489	(+) 73
2006	3,543	(+) 54

iii) Collection

Due to the inadequate resources of finance, the library cannot fast in collection development. At present, the collection has gone up to 14831. The average yearly collection of books is 1060. The library, besides its own collection, receives some informative and useful documents from RRRLF Matching Schemes through the State Library Committee. It has been subscribing six Indian Journals, three national and eleven local newspapers. The library has no back volumes of periodicals. During the last four years, 4,115 documents were added to this library. The collection development of Champhai District Library during the last six years is present with Table 3.8 as below:

Table 3.8: Growth of collection at District Library, Champhai

Sl.No	**Year**	*No. of Collection*	*Variance*
1	2001	523	-
2	2002	316	(-) 207
3	2003	1,222	(+) 906
4	2004	487	(-) 735
5	2005	407	(-) 80
6	2006	1,160	(+) 753

iv) Technical Work

Champhai District Library follows 21st edition of Dewey Decimal Classification Scheme (DDC 21ed) to assign class numbers and Anglo-American Cataloguing Rules-II (AACR-II) for cataloguing of books and Sears' List of Subject Heading (SLSH) to assign subject heading of documents. Among the different Book Numbering schemes, it follows the "first three letters of the author' surname' to assign book number.

v) Services

The library have Circulation Section, Reference Section, Periodical section and Children's' Section. Average daily issue of books is 25 and the average daily visitor is 20. One book can be issued to the library members for a period of seven days at a time. Overdue charges is collected if kept beyond due date at the rate of Re.1.00 per day. The library stack is divided into two; one is open access and the other is closed access. General books are on open access whereas reference books are kept in a closed access. The library organized user orientation programme to aware the services rendered by the library and to give better information to the community as a whole. Its reference service is much used by the locality and the students in particular.

vi) Building

Champhai District Library function in a rented building since its inception till date. It was housed in a first floor cement concrete building at Champhai Vengthlang area The floor area of the rented building was 180.8sq.m. The building is well ventilated and has good lighting system with natural light for the readers.

c) Library Hours

Five district libraries of Mizoram are under the control, supervise and direction of the Department of Art & Culture, Government of Mizoram. And as such, they do not have a separate library hours for their respective libraries, but are predetermined by the state government timing for its employees. Therefore, five-district libraries are open five days in a week, i.e. Monday to Friday, but closed on Saturday, Sunday and on public holidays. In summer, it was open from 9:00 a.m. to 5:00 p.m. and in winter, from 9:30 a.m. to 4:00 p.m.

d) Library Finance

The main source of finance to the five district libraries is State Government. The libraries are not allocated separate annual budget from the State Government but share the budget allocated for the district libraries. Table 3.9 as below illustrate the total annual budget allocation for the last four years in respect of five district libraries:

Table 3.9: District Library Budget

Rupees in lakhs

Head	*2004-05*	*2005-06*	*2006-07*	*2007-08*
Plan	6.79	7.36	7.66	7.40
Non-Plan	22.19	25.50	26.20	28.80
Total	28.99	32.86	33.86	36.20

The 11th Finance Commission had given grants to the tune of Rs. 2.6 crore which was fully utilized for up gradation of public libraries. Rs.209.90 lakhs was used for creating Corpus Fund and the interest accrued out of the fund are being utilized for purchase of books, periodicals, furniture, etc. for the development of public libraries in Mizoram every year. The 12th. Finance Commission has also allotted grants to the tune of Rs. 50.00 lakhs to be utilized annually @ Rs. 10.00 lakhs for development of public libraries. (Boichhingpuii; 2007;208). The functions, services and management of the above five district libraries are to the mark of the library standards and norms provided for the public libraries. They have common hindrances and come forward with their problems as below:

- Lack of professional manpower as well as other supporting staff.
- Inadequate finance
- Lack of physical facilities
- Inadequate equipment
- Non functional library building

REFERENCES

Boichhingpuii (2007). Status Report of Public Library Services in Mizoram. Proceedings of National conference on Public Libraries as Community Information Centers, Bangalore, 6-8 June 2007 edited by P.Y.Rajendrakumar and V.G.Talwar. Bangalore: Department of Public Libraries.

Hluna, J.V. (1992). Education and Missionaries in Mizoram. Guwahati: Spectrum.

Hminga, C.L. (1987). The Life and Witness of the Churches in Mizoram. Serkawn: Literature Committee, Baptist Church of Mizoram.

Lalrimawia (1995). Mizoram; History and Cultural Identity. Guwahati: Spectrum

Liangkhaia (2002). Mizo Chanchin. 5th.ed. Aizawl: LTL Publication

Lianzama, C. Status Report of Public Library Development in Mizoram. *Granthana,* IV(1&2); Jan.-Jul, 1993.

Lianzawna, C. (1996). Mizoram Education Chanchin. Aizawl: H. Rokhumi

Lloyd, J. Meirion (n.d.). On Every High Hill. Liverpool: Foreign Mission Office.

Ngurtinkhuma, R.K. (2006). College Library Scenario in Mizoram. 4th. Convention of Planner 2006 Souvenir. Aizawl: Department of Library & Information Science, Mizoram University.

Reid, Sir Robert (1942). The Lushai Hills. Calcutta: Firma KLM.

Sangkima (1992). Mizos; Society and Social Change. Guwahati: Spectrum.

Woodthorpe, R.G. (1978). The Lushai Expedition, 1871-72. Calcutta: Firma KLM

Public Library in India : 113-142
R. K. Ngurtinkhuma
Today and Tomorrow's Printers & Publishers, New Delhi-110 002 (India)

Chapter 4

PUBLIC LIBRARYASSISTANCE IN MIZORAM

Mizoram lies in the northeastern corner of India surrounded by two international boarders of Myanmar and Bangladesh. The main occupation of the people is shifting cultivation. The tribulation of *Mautam Famine* left a deep scar in the heart of some Mizos and was interlinked with a secessionist movement that was to follow. In 1961, one of the voluntary organizations, the *'Mizo National Famine Front'* purposefully deleted the word *'Famine'* from its name, with and avowed aim of attaining independence and sovereignty for the Mizo hills. Steadily, the movement gained strength and eventually took up arms on February 28, 1966 in a bid to achieve its goal. The Mizo Hills was immediately declared *a disturbed area* and security forces were inducted to maintain law and order. The state of disturbance was to last two decades during which the land of Mizos had to weather many storms and apart from lagging behind in the field of development. At long last, the two-decade old disturbance came to a welcome end on 30 June 1986 with the signing of an epoch-making *Memorandum of Settlement* by the Government of India and Mizo National Front.

The two decade-old insurgency resulted that the Indian Army grouped many villages together at the nearby central places to make easy administration from the point of security measures. As a consequence, the Mizos remained backward economically, politically and intellectually for a long time. Their long isolation from the rest of India made them shy, sensitive and suspicious of outsiders; and they could hardly identify themselves as Indians. (Thanhlira;1990;np). But, Mizos were hardworking and enthusiastic people to earn their livelihood and fight for their survival even at the crucial time of insurgency.

Village/rural libraries have been established and maintained in several states through some agencies, such as, Gram Panchayats, Cooperative Societies, Religious Endowments, Youth Organizations, and Voluntary Organizations. The Union Ministry of Rural Development had chalked out an ambitious plan of establishing 1000 community centers in every panchayat during the Eight Five Year Plan. This plan has been provided assistance from the departments of Social Welfare, National Literacy Mission, Education for All, etc. who have common welfare programmes. Mizoram being a remote state and most people live in villages are very keen in literacy and even the poorest of the poor have eagerness to take their children to attend school. Under the guidelines of Raja Rammohun Roy Library Foundation (RRRLF) on "Books for the Millions at their Doorstep," the State Government constituted a committee in 1981 known as "State Library Planning Committee" to facilitate better library services in public sector of the state (Ngurtinkhuma;2007;70).

In Mizoram (Census of India 2001), there are 22 Towns, 707 inhabited villages and 110 inhabited villages. The State Library Committee of Mizoram, since 1982 to till date, has recognized as much as 424 village/local libraries run by NGO's and other societies/organizations within the state. Out of the 729 towns/villages in Mizoram, only 424 libraries were recognized whereas 305 villages do not have recognized libraries. Many villagers are in a line for the recognition of their libraries waiting their turn. The recognized libraries, on the basis of State Government's contribution under matching scheme, received certain amount of assistance through State Library Planning Committee, which is equally shared in kind. The following Table 4.1 reflects figures on district wise statistics of Recognized Libraries in Mizoram for better clarity of information.

Table 4.1: District-wise Recognized Libraries in Mizoram

Sl.No	*Districts*	*Towns*	*Inhabited Villages*	*Uninha-bited Villages*	*No. of Towns and Inhabited Villages*	*Recog-nised Libraries*
1	Aizawl	4	96	7	100	164
2	Champhai	3	88	3	91	88
3	Kolasib	4	39	10	43	27
4	Lawngtlai	-	139	7	139	6
5	Lunglei	3	160	31	163	56
6	Mamit	3	82	41	85	32
7	Saiha	1	68	7	69	8
8	Serchhip	4	35	4	39	43
Total	8	22	707	110	729	424

The rural library is a good component of Public Library system. Which is termed as "People's University" and "Arsenals of Democracy". (Sharma;2007;25). Almost 80 Percent of the total population of our country lives in villages. Government sponsored libraries cannot reach each of the villages. Voluntary efforts therefore were made for the establishment of libraries by the youths; most of them are students with the help of book lovers of the locality. These libraries are managed and run by young students and other service holders of the village. The houses are built in public places with people's donations. The books, furniture needed for the purpose are collected locally. The libraries of such kind are opened for some hours of a day or on some holidays in each week to cater to the needs of the villagers to some extent. Thus these libraries help both literates and illiterates. Most of the rural people cannot think of purchasing the costly books, say, classics and other scriptures, which are borrowed from such libraries. Some one reads these books aloud which helped the illiterates for sharing the benefits of reading. Thus it indirectly serves the Adult Education Programme in a limited way. A village library has an important role to play in the national programmes of social reconstruction and nation building. It can contribute in sustaining the quality of life of the rural people in all aspects such as educational, economic, industrial, scientific and cultural etc. and they can promote the concept of a democratic society. Adult education centers can be established in the rural libraries for imparting education to the adults. The most appropriate place for serving to the peoples of different ages of the community is the public library. It is for that reason Melvil Dewey stated public library as 'Peoples University'. It means a place where people of all ages can freely acquire knowledge.

The Village Libraries can contribute tremendously for the development of rural community in different ways, i.e. socio-economic, socio-cultural, socio-educational and other related areas. Different types of activities of rural masses are centered round the village libraries. Therefore, it is the right time to launch comprehensive and integrated efforts for the improvement of Rural Libraries are the gateway of information & knowledge for the rural community.

1. Contributions of Raja Rammohun Roy Library Foundation

1972 was a significant year in the history of library movement in India. The country was celebrating the silver jubilee of its independence from the British Administration in 1972. Coincidentally it was an International Book Year with the slogan of 'Books For All' emphasizing promotion of reading habits among the masses. Not only that, it was the auspicious occasion of the bicentennial birth anniversary of an Indian social reformer, who stressed the need of modern education for the development of the nation. In this august year, Raja Rammohun Roy Library (RRRLF) came into being in May 1972 (RRRLF;1997;1). It is the nodal agency of Government of India to support public library services and systems and promote public library movement in the country. Raja Rammohun Roy Library Foundation is an autonomous organization, established and sponsored by the Department of Culture, Government of India. It is registered under the West Bengal Societies Registration Act, 1961. Its headquarters is located at Kolkata. In view of the expanding activities, the Foundation has opened zonal offices under the Assistant Field Officers for monitoring the impact and implementation of the assistance rendered by the Foundation such as-Eastern Zonal Office at Calcutta; Northern Zonal Office at New Delhi; Southern Zonal Office at Chennai and Western Zonal Office at Mumbai.

a) Objectives

Raja Rammohun Roy Library Foundation is a national agency for the promotion of library services in general and public library services in particular (Jayaswal; 1997;223). The main objective of the Foundation is to promote and support public library movement in the country by providing adequate library services and by developing reading habits all over the country with the active co-operation of State Government and Union Territories and of Voluntary Organizations operating in the filed of library services, cultural activities, adult education and the like. Objectives of the Foundation may be listed as below(RRRLF;1997;1):

- To promote library movement in the country;
- To enunciate a national library policy and to help build up a national library system;
- To provide financial and technical assistance to libraries;
- To provide financial assistance to organizations, regional or national engaged in the promotion of library development;
- To publish appropriate literature and to act as a clearing house of ideas and information on library development in India and abroad;
- To promote research in problems of library development;
- To advise the government on all matters pertaining to the library development in the country; and
- To propagate the adoption of library legislation in the country.

b) Assistance Programme

The Foundation promotes public library services rendering book and financial assistance to the public libraries under different schemes of assistance. The scheme of assistance is of two types, viz., Matching and Non-Matching schemes.

1) Matching Schemes

Assistance under Matching Scheme is given from the resources shared on matching basis with the States/Union Territory Administrations on the basis of developed states 50;50; developing and lagging states 60:40 and North-Eastern States 90:10. This revised matching scheme is effective from 2005. The Matching assistance can be given to achieve its main objectives for:

- Assistance towards building up of adequate stock of books and reading materials.
- Assistance towards development of rural book deposit centers and mobile library services.
- Assistance towards organization of seminars, workshops, training courses (orientation/refresher) and book exhibition.
- Assistance towards storage and display of books including reading room furniture.
- Assistance to public libraries below district level for increasing accommodation.
- Assistance to public libraries below State Central Libraries to acquire TV-cum-VCP sets for educational purposes/Computer for library application (networking of Public Libraries below State Central Libraries).
- Assistance towards Networking of Public Libraries.

2) Non-Matching Schemes

The Foundation fully gives assistance under this scheme from his own resources to implement its objectives for:

- Assistance towards building up of adequate stock of books through central selection.
- Assistance to voluntary organizations (NGOs) providing public library services
- Assistance to children libraries or children's section of general public libraries including women section and senior citizen section.
- Assistance to public libraries toward celebration of 50 years, 100 years and 125 years.
- Assistance towards collection and compilation of library statistics through official and non-official agencies.
- Assistance to centrally sponsored libraries.
- Assistance towards organization of seminars/ conferences by national level library organizations.
- Assistance towards establishment of children's corner.

c) Promotion of District Youth Resource Centres (DYRCs)

The development of DYRCs is being made commensurate with the decision of the inter Ministerial Steering Committee constitutes for the purpose with the representative from Ministry of Sports & Youth Affairs, Ministry of Culture, Raja Rammohun Roy Library foundation and Nehru Yuvak Kendra Sanghatana. The DYRCs are assisted for the following purpose:

- Towards building up adequate stock of books.
- Towards acquiring storage materials and library furniture.
- Towards construction of library building.
- Towards acquisition of computers with accessories.

d) Promotional Activities

RRRLF has undertaken a number of promotional activities for qualitative improvement of library services. It is associated and interacts with different national and international library professional associations like IFLA, ILA, IASLIC and different state level library associations. Some of the promotional activities taken up by the Foundation for the qualitative improvement of library services may be given as below:

- It organizes seminars and conferences on the topics related to the development of public libraries in India.
- It plays a major role in the preparation of National Policy on Library & Information Systems and also issued guidelines on public library systems and services.
- It instituted 'RRRLF Fellowship' to eminent men and women in the field of library services who have contributed significantly to the library movement particularly, public library movement in the country through active involvement in the movement, organizational initiative, intellectual leadership or are dedicated to the propagation of the reading habit among the mass. Fellowship carries a cash award of Rs.25, 000/- besides a plaque and a citation detailing the services rendered by the Fellow in the

country.

- 'RRRLF Best Library Award' for the Best State Central Library in India. The Award carries a Citation and a cash incentive of Rs. 1 lakh.
- 'RRRLF Best District Library Award' in each of the six regions. The Award carries a Citation and cash incentive of Rs.50, 000/-.
- The Foundation instituted 'RRRLF Best Rural Library Awards' one for each state since 2005.
- 'Raja Rammohun Roy Award' was introduced annually to the best contributor of an article covering the area of development of Public Library Systems and Services or suggesting measures for the promotion of reading habits.

e) Research Cell and Special Library

A research cell along with a special library on Library & Information Science and statistics unit supported by a computer unit are providing necessary input to its various activities. About 5000 important books and journals on Library & Information Science and allied fields have been acquired in the library. Besides carrying on Research Projects on public library or allied subject, the Research Cell renders advisory and consultancy services whenever required. It has prepared and published a report on loss of books in libraries for the Government of India.

f) Publications

The Foundation has brought out many useful publications for the promotion and development of public library services in the country. Some of its significant publications are;

- Indian Libraries; Trends and Perspectives
- Raja Rammohun Roy and the New Learning
- Directory of Indian Public Libraries
- RRRLF Newsletter (quarterly)
- Granthana- Indian Journal of Library Studies (Bi-annual)
- Annual Report
- Books for the Millions at their Doorsteps (Information Manual).

g) Modernization Programme

The Foundation is taking steps to meet the new technologies of information for the promotion of library services. It has a Computer Section for building-up data bank of Public Libraries for the country. This section is planned to give information storage, retrieval and data processing support for all the application areas. It has keen interest with enthusiasm to computerized state libraries in India. It gave computers to the state and district libraries to carry out Foundations' zeal to computerize such libraries. The work is going on to computerized shortly.

h) Achievement

The Foundation has taken pains in promoting and developing library services in the country since its inception. Central Government's grant allotment is increasing over the last years and state contributions for matching scheme is also increasing as well. This increased shows that the works carried out by the Foundation is growing and the State Government gives emphasis for the promotion of public libraries through the Foundation. During the VIII Five Year Plan period (1992-1997) the total plan grant from the Government of India was Rs.1175.50 lakhs with an average annual plan grant of Rs.235.10 lakhs and contribution of States under matching scheme reaches Rs.645.97 lakhs. The Government of India allotted an amount of Rs.3233 lakhs as plan grant during IX Five Year Plan period (1997-2002). The annual average plan grant was Rs.646.60 lakhs and the state contribution reaches Rs.1977 lakhs. During the last three years of the X Five Year Plan period (2002-2005), the plan grant stepped up to Rs.1150.21 lakhs including a special grant of Rs.150.21 lakhs for North-Eastern States and contributions received from various state governments also reaches Rs.769.59 lakhs. Plan grants and State contribution of matching scheme may be given in Table 4.2 as below:

Table 4.2: Plan grant and state contributions

Rupees in lakhs.

Five Year Plan	*Plan Grant*	*Average Annual Plan Grant*	*State Contribution*
VIII (1992-1997)	1175.70	235.10	645.97
IX (1997-2002)	3233.00	646.60	1977.00
X (2002-2005)	1150.21	383.40	769.59

Over the last thirty-two years, the Foundation has covered about a little thirty-one thousand libraries at different levels for assistance. The RRRLF assistance to libraries/kendras is illustrated in Table 4.3 as below:

Table 4.3: Assistance to libraries cover by RRRLF.

Category of Libraries/Kendras, etc.	*No of Libraries covered*
State Central Libraries	28
Divisional and District Libraries	451
Sub-divisional/Taluka/Tehsil Libraries	501
Towns and Rural Libraries	30134
Nehru Yuvak Kendras	272
Jawahar Bal Bhavans	49
Others	128
Total	31563

i) State Library Committee

The Foundation (RRRLF; 1997;10-11) renders matching as well as non-matching assistance to support and promote public library services in the States and Union Territories in accordance with rules and procedures. Every State/Union Territory Administration are advised to set up State Library Committee (SLC) consisting of the following members and will meet at least twice a year:

- Secretary/Director or person nominated by the Department controlling library services - Chairman
- Director or Officer-in-Charge of the Department, if he is not the Chairman
- Director of the Foundation or his representative
- Nominee of the Chairman of the Foundation;
- President or Secretary of the State Library Association;

- A representative of the Education Department, if library service is controlled by a separate department;
- An educationist or an author or a person representing the state level organization connected with book production to be nominated by the State Government; and
- Librarian of the State Central Library or any other public library nominated by the State Government shall be the Convener of the State Library Committee. Where this is not feasible, the State Government will nominate a suitable official looking after library service as the Convener.

The functions of the State Library Committee shall be:

- to prepare perspective and annual plan of library services in the State with particular reference to the assistance programmes of the Foundation;
- to ensure payment of State Government/UT Administration contribution and availing of the matching grant from the Foundation;
- to select books according to the felt need of the community and in conformity with the guidelines prescribed by the Foundation;
- to scrutinize and recommend proposals for other schemes of assistance to the Foundation;
- to ensure proper utilization of assistance by the Foundation; and
- to perform any other activity conducive to the development of library in the State or Union Territory.

Foundation's assistance is available for all categories of public libraries, viz., State Central Library, Regional/ Divisional Libraries, District Central Libraries, Sub-divisional Libraries, Tehsil Libraries, Taluka Libraries, Block Libraries, Branch Libraries, Municipal Libraries, Town Libraries, Rural Libraries, Panchayat Libraries, Village Libraries, etc. directly maintained or aided or recognized by the State Government. State Library Committee will decide number and categories of libraries for assistance under different schemes and consolidated list of books for different categories of libraries. However, Textbooks, costly books and foreign publications should not ordinarily be selected. The maxim "the best reading for the largest number at the least cost' should be the guiding principle for selection of books. The Foundation buys books at a graded rate of discount as mentioned below; (RRRLF;1997;16):

1	to	10 copies	-	10% discount
11	to	25 copies	-	15% discount
26	to	100 copies	-	20% discount
101	to	200 copies	-	25% discount
201	to	500 copies	-	30% discount
501	and above		-	35% discount

The Foundation also gives assistance to Public Libraries to acquire new computer or upgrade as the case may be for either of the following items, with accessories for educational purposes once in 10(ten) years:

I One TV-cum-VCP sets with accessories together with five educational videocassettes

II Computer System

A One Server

B Three (3) clients, nine (9) clients for State Central Library

C UPS in capacity rage of 0.5KVA to 3 KVA

D One Laser Printer and one Dot Matrix Printer; one Laser Printer,

one Inkjet Printer and two Dot Matrix Printer for State Central Library.

E Library Software

F Network Equipments

G Others;

1) One Web Camera

2) Two Barcode Reader

3) Two Speaker

4) One CD-Writer

5) One Scanner

H Cost of power cabling and installation of LAN

I Cost of Retro Conversion of total holdings (books).

Assistance is also given to both Government and Non-government libraries for construction of a new building or extension of the existing building. Maximum amount given to District Level Library is Rs. 10 lakh and Rs. 8 lakh for Sub. Division/Town Level Library once in ten years. For other libraries Rs. 4 lakh can be given for construction of library building.

RRRLF established by the Central Government as an agency for the promotion and development of public library survives in the country has been the lifeline of public library services in Mizoram. Raja Rammohun Roy Library Foundation is a national agency for the promotion of library services in general and public library services in particular (Jayaswal;1997;223). Like other states of India, the matching and non-matching schemes of RRRLF help library services and activities in different ways. The extensions of assistance in cash and in kind are of great value to the promotion of library services in Mizoram.

1) Matching Scheme

RRRLF Matching Scheme strengthened, developed and promotes public libraries in the State, particularly to the village libraries. The State can availed the valuable services of RRRLF after ten years of its inception. The contributions of the State Government to the RRRLF Matching Scheme since 1982-83 is present with Table 4.4 as below:

Table 4.4: Mizoram Government's contribution to RRRLF

Sl.No	*Year*	*Recognized Libraries*	*Mizoram Govt. Contribution (Rs)*	*Variance (Rs) (+)/(-)*
1	1982-83	25	20,000	0
2	1983-84	30	20,000	0
3	1984-85	39	30,000	(+) 10,000
4	1985-86	45	40,000	(+) 10,000
5	1986-87	55	60,000	(+) 20,000
6	1987-88	70	50,000	(-) 10,000

7	1988-89	77	1,00,000	(+) 50,000
8	1989-90	77	1,00,000	0
9	1990-91	77	2,00,000	(+) 1,00,000
10	1991-92	112	2,00,000	0
11	1992-93	150	2,00,000	0
12	1993-94	178	3,00,000	(+) 1,00,000
13	1994-95	188	3,00,000	0
14	1995-96	208	4,60,000	(+) 1,60,000
15	1996-97	300	15,00,000	(+)10,40,000
16	1997-98	327	15,00,000	0
17	1998-99	343	12,00,000	(-) 3,00,000
18	1999-2000	364	15,00,000	(+) 3,00,000
19	2000-01	390	12,00,000	(-) 3,00,000
20	2001-02	399	12,00,000	0
21	2002-03	411	12,00,000	0
22	2003-04	415	12,00,000	0
23	2004-05	418	12,00,000	0
24	2005-06	418	10,00,000	(-) 2,00,000
25	2006-07	424	5,00,000	(-) 5,00,000
26	2007-08	424	5,00,000	0

Since 2005, RRRLF revised Matching Fund share to 90:10 for NE States and State Government reduced its contributions accordingly. State Library Committee utilizes the share of RRRLF under matching scheme to give best result for the promotion and development of libraries in the State. All the recognized libraries have equal share and received assistance by kind from RRRLF. The total number of books received from RRRLF through Matching Scheme from the first time 1987-88 to 2006-07 is illustrated by Table 4.5 as follows:

Table 4.5:Year-wise procurement of books from RRRLF Matching Scheme

Sl. No	Year	No. of Books	Variance
1	1987-88	16,871	-
2	1988-89	6,293	(-) 10,578
3	1989-90	9,735	(+) 3,442
4	1990-91	13,316	(+) 3,581
5	1991-92	14,455	(+) 1,139
6	1992-93	17,029	(+) 2,574
7	1993-94	26,080	(+) 9,051
8	1994-95	19,760	(-) 6,320
9	1995-96	46,000	(+) 26,240
10	1996-97	21,420	(-) 24,580
11	1997-98	52,471	(+) 31,051
12	1998-99	51,891	(-) 580
13	1999-2000	39,338	(-) 12,553
14	2000-01	37,224	(-) 2,114
15	2001-02	44,420	(+) 7,196
16	2002-03	63,350	(+) 18,930
17	2003-04	32,316	(-) 31,034
18	2004-05	39,735	(+) 7,419
19	2005-06	38,745	(-) 990
20	2006-07	63,701	(+) 24,956

2) Non-matching Scheme

The state also received certain amount of assistance

through RRRLF non-matching schemes. This scheme is not receive annually, but on the basis of the foundation's resources. Most of the assistance received through this scheme includes books, bookracks, furniture, and assistance towards seminar. Two of the recognized libraries, namely, Lengpui YMA Library and Vaivakawn YMA Library received building grants under this scheme.

2. Adult Education Programme

The Education department of Mizoram serves the people of the state through its Adult Education Wing. The Social Education Wing came into existence in 1963 and it was substituted with "Adult Education" since 2nd October 1978. The primary function of the Adult Education Wing in Mizoram is to draw up and implement schemes for removal of adult illiteracy. As a part of elementary education, the main objectives are to impart functional literacy, which composed:

1) Literacy;
2) Functionality; and
3) Awareness.

The target group as envisaged by the National Literacy Mission comprises of illiterate adults of the age group of 15-35, which is extendable beyond 60 years subject to the willingness, and interest of the learners. The programme consists of the followings:

1) Conducting of survey of illiterates adults;
2) Formation of Village Adult Education Committee in all villages;
3) Running of Adult Education Centers for imparting

functional literacy;

4) Running of Circle Education Centers-cum-Rural Libraries for post literacy and continuing education for neo-literates;

5) Running of Vocational School for neo-literates for promotion of their vocational capability;

6) Publication of Primer, Guidebooks, and other literatures for the benefit of adult learners and neo-literates;

7) Conducting of mass campaign for total literacy to bring favorable atmosphere conducive to learning for illiterate adults;

8) Searching for people's participation in the implementation of adult education programme;

9) Publication of monthly departmental magazine from the state headquarters; and

10) Audio-visual Education.

Among the various schemes undertaken by the Adult Education Wing, Post literacy and Continuing Education programmes worth mentioning in connection with this studies. Literacy provides an entry point to the world of letters as a communication and information process. This is the basic step of Adult Education as a process of lifelong learning. The neo-literates are willing to continue their learning otherwise they may be relapse into illiteracy. It is, therefore, felt imperative to develop systematic post literacy programmes to give further education to the neo-literates and school dropout for the retention of their literacy skills to improve their living conditions. Hence, Continuing Education Centers were established in various villages. The main objectives of Post-literacy and Continuing Education as follows:

1) Provision of facilities for retention of literacy skills and continuing education to enable the learners to continue beyond basic literacy;
2) Creating scope for application an functional literacy of improvement of living condition and quality of life;
3) Creation of awareness about national concerns such as national integration, conservation and improvement and environment, women equality, observance of small family norms and sharing of common problems of the community;
4) Organization of short duration training orientation course and seminar;
5) Provision of facilities for libraries and reading rooms; and
6) Organization of cultural and recreational activities with effective community participation.

In order to facilitate Post-Literacy and Continuing Education of neo-literates and school dropouts, the Adult Education Centres established since 1979 were re-designated as Nodal Continuing Education Centres and Continuing Education Centres in 1998. Now, there are 40 Nodal Continuing Education Centres and 360 Continuing Education Centres running in the state. Rural libraries were attached to each of the centers. The centers have also been utilized by the local youths of the public for recreational and information centers. These centers were looking after by Preraks or *Assistant Preraks,* getting their honorarium as per Government of India financial patterns. Apart from other grants, they received books annually for their center libraries. Numbers of books distributed to these rural libraries is as follows Table 4.6:

Table 4.6 : Distribution of books to rural libraries of CEC

Sl.No	*Year*	*No. of Books Distributed*	*Variance*
1	1982-84	2,870	-
2	1984-85	3,212	(+) 343
3	1985-86	4,682	(+) 2,940
4	1986-87	3,080	(-) 1,602
5	1987-88	5,980	(+) 2,900
6	1988-89	5,033	(-) 947
7	1989-90	3,785	(-) 1,248
8	1990-91	14,796	(+) 11,011
9	1991-92	12,582	(-) 2,214
10	1992-93	9,592	(-) 2,990
11	1993-94	12,150	(+) 2,558
12	1994-95	8,475	(-) 3,675
13	1995-96	11,250	(+) 2,775
14	1996-97	3,230	(-) 8,020
15	1997-98	21,200	(+) 17,970
16	1998-99	20,400	(-) 800
17	1999-2000	No sanctioned	-
18	2000-01	No record found	-
19	2001-02	No record found	-
20	2002-03	No record found	-
21	2003-04	13,760	(-) 6,640
22	2004-05	16,160	(+) 2,400
23	2005-06	13,120	(-) 3,040
24	2006-07	18,200	(+) 5,080

Meanwhile, higher institutions have their own institutional libraries collecting their needs depending the course structures. The state government and UGC nicely funded college libraries with computer and its related facilities. And University library is also well organized to meet the information needs of the user with latest library technologies, like Internet and electronic resources. But, on the other hand, only educational books do not give self sufficiency to acquire information needs to the students, therefore, they rather need to access some sources from the public libraries. Public libraries, as its name indicate, collect all kind of materials that may be required by different information seekers and are of very helpful to all sorts of children, youth and adults.

3. YMA contributions for Public Library Development

Young Mizo Association (YMA), the largest voluntary organization in the state was the outcome of the works and contributions of the English Missionaries. The missionaries started evangelism, education and social development in Mizoram and have tremendous contribution in these regards. In continuation of their efforts for the upliftment of the people, they also started social activities and established institutions elsewhere.

On the night of 3 June 1935, some missionaries, church leaders, and well-known persons, Rev. David Edwards (Zorema Pa), Upa D.Thianga, Rev. L. Evans (Pu Niara), Upa Chawngzika, Miss K. Hughes (Pi Zaii), Pu Muka, Rev. Chhuahkhama, Pu Vankhuma, Pu L. Kailuia B.A., Pu L.H.Liana and Upa Ch. Pasena have had a meeting at Pi Zaii Bunglow at Aijal (now Aizawl), and discussed about the need for establishment of an association/ organization among the youths to guide and educate them in their future developments as a whole. (Vanlallawma;

1998;8) On this night, they concluded to establish Young Lushai Association so that all Lushais, Christians or non-Christians can join the association. They earmarked 15 June 1935 for the inauguration of the association formally and framed its objectives as follows: (Lalropuia;1985;1).

- To make best use of leisure time.
- To work for the development of Mizoram as a whole.
- To promote good teachings of Christianity.

As decided, the formal inauguration of the Young Lushai Association was held on the night of 15 June 1935 (Saturday) at the Nepali School at Aizawl. However, due to some political influences, the Committee changed the name of *Young Lushai Association* into **Young Mizo Association** on 7 October 1947. (Vanlallawma; 1998;33) .

1) Organizations

The activities influences different areas of the state and by now, most of the villages in Mizoram and Mizo inhabited areas of the country had established YMA. In the latest report, there is 1 Sub-headquarter, 49 Groups and 756 Branches. The apex body of the association is Central YMA. Central YMA is functioning at its own building at Aizawl with some full-time employees. The Central YMA has one each of President, Vice President, General Secretary, Assistant Secretary, Treasurer, Finance Secretary and 50 Executive Committee Members. Under the CYMA, there are 15 Sub-committees (YMA Chanchinbu) to pursue for the developmental works in different directions of the objectives; such committees are, Culture; Disaster Management; Finance; Land, Building and Property; Legal; Literature; Press; Project; Recreation; Research & Documentation; Resources; Kumpuan; Science &

Environment; Sports; and Youth Center.

2) Conferences

Group and Sub-headquarter YMA organize conferences in their area to have common activities for the development of the society in particular. These conferences are being annually. A General Conference is annually organized by the CYMA to discuss the action plan for the development and implementation of its objectives. Some of the topics of the YMA General Conferences includes – Our Duty; YLA and Social Life; Duty of Mizo Youth in the present day; Youth and Leisure; Self-sufficiency; Christianity and its Environment; Youth – Future of the Nation; Respect to Old-aged; Conservation of Wild Animals; Respect of Christian Teachings; Development of Social life; Education as Development; etc.

3) Activities

YMA has extended its helping hand to different quarters of its operations at different levels voluntarily. However, the activities concerning for the promotion of education and public library development may be mentioned herewith as: (Lalropuia;1985;4).

- The first approved guidelines for the implementation of its objectives included that YMA members should posses reading materials at their home.
- In the early days, they teach in the schools where there are no teachers.
- It publishes good books and started publication monthly bulletin of YMA in 1956.

- 20 Social Education Center, established by the Adult Education Wing of Education Department were under the management of YMA and 15269 persons became literate during 1973-1980 from these centers. 60 Libraries at the Social education Sub-Centers were taken care by YMA at different villages.
- In recognition of Children's Year, YMA established 4 Recreational center-cum-Library in 1979.

4) YMA Library

Since its inception, YMA is working very well for the educational development of the Mizo society through social education and the likes. Many branches established library at their locality to provide reading materials to the society as a whole. By understanding the importance of a library for the general community, the 42nd General Conference held at Khawzawl in 1987 resolved that **'All Branch YMAs should establish Library in their localities'.** In comply with this resolution, many of them started establishing a library and which have became as a living force for the community, particularly for the young persons. Out of the 424 Recognized Libraries in the State, 379 are established, managed and run by YMA at different localities.

Library is under the committee of the Recreation Sub-committee of the center. The committee organizes training programs for the local librarians and also pays a visit to local YMA Libraries to have ground reality and spot verification in connection to the library management. This Committee organized selection of 10 Best YMA Libraries in Aizawl City in 2006. The selected libraries with their marks in each of the criteria were given at Table 4.7:

Table 4.7: Aizawl City YMA Library to ten positions

Name of Library	Library Building	Book Accession	Book Classification	Arrangement of Books	Repairing of Books	Book Collection Devel.	Library Member	Library Sub-Committee	Library Hours	Budget	Addl. Point	Total
	10	10	10	10	10	10	10	10	10	5	5	100
Bethlehem vengthlang YMA Library	10	10	10	10	10	10	10	10	7	-	3	90
Chanmari YMA Library	10	10	10	10	10	7	10	10	5	5	-	87
Ramhlun North YMA Library	10	10	10	10	7	10	7	10	7	-	2	83
Bethlehem YMA Library	10	10	10	10	10	7	7	10	7	-	-	81
Zotlang YMA Library	10	10	10	7	10	7	-	10	10	5	-	79
Chaltlang YMA Library	10	10	10	7	7	-	10	10	5	5	-	74
Bungkawn YMA Library	10	10	10	7	7	-	7	10	5	5	-	71
Khatla YMA Library	10	10	2	5	7	10	-	10	10	5	-	69
Saikhama-kawn YMA Library	10	10	7	10	10	-	-	10	10	-	-	67
Dinthar YMA Library	10	7	7	10	10	5	-	10	5	-	1	65

Being a voluntary organization, the management and functioning of YMA Libraries are carried out through voluntary basis. In this regards, we may note the following points:

i) Most of the Branch YMA has Library Sub-committee to manage and organize library services;

ii) Library buildings are constructed voluntarily or housed in a private building voluntarily;

iii) Collection of Documents are mainly on donations and supplied by State Library Committee from RRRLF against State Matching Fund;

iv) Librarians are appointed from the locality on voluntary basis for a period of one year;

v) Library hours vary from libraries to libraries depending upon the convenience of the librarian or the local situation.

YMA Libraries plays a vital role for the local community as a center of social education, local information, cultural heritage, creativity, performing arts, local enterprise, literary and skill development. It is a crucial center of information in the knowledge society to educate the community through such kind of information in the form of paper and electronic documents and acted as a channel against the anti-social activities. YMA libraries are, mostly managed by local YMA Library Committee, which is supported at the central level by Recreation Sub-committee.

The public library service in Mizoram has been one of the means of instrument to develop and educate the community. It provides reading materials to the community and has been an institution for the society in their formal and non-formal education through its various collections and programs. It is not only that it also helps the society in various kinds of activities by providing knowledge and information through its services and activities. The state has many developments and changes from the library services and the next chapter will describes the role of public libraries, i.e. State and District Libraries for the socio-cultural development of Mizoram.

REFERENCES

Census of India 2001. Series 16 - Mizoram; Primary Census Abstracts. Aizawl : Directorate of Census Operations, Mizoram.

Jayaswal, P.K.(1997). Dr. B P Barua; *An Assessment of his Role in Institution-Building*. Public Libraries in Developing Countries: Status and Trends edited by P K Mahapatra and V K Thomas. New Delhi: Vikas.

Lalropuia,C. (1985). YMA Chanchin (YMA Golden Jubilee 1935-1985 Nghilh loh nan). Aizawl: Central YMA.

Mizoram. Department of Information and Public Relations. (2004). Aizawl.

Ngurtinkhuma, R.K. (2007). *Rural Library in Mizoram: Problems and Prospects*. Rural Libraries in the North East India; Problems and Prospects edited by Narendra Lahkar. Kolkata: Central reference Library.

RRRLF (1997). Books for the Millions at their Doorsteps; Information Manual. Calcutta: RRRLF.

Sharma, N.N. (2007). *The Growth and Development of Rural Libraries in Assam*. Rural Libraries in the North East India; Problems and Prospects edited by Narendra Lahkar. Kolkata: Central Reference Library.

Thanhlira, R. (1990). When Aizawl Refused to Fall. Aizawl Centenary.

Vanlallawma, C. 998). YMA History 1935-1995. Aizawl: Central YMA.

YMA Chanchinbu. A monthly journal of CYMA. April 2004.

Public Library in India : 143-167
R. K. Ngurtinkhuma
Today and Tomorrow's Printers & Publishers, New Delhi-110 002 (India)

Chapter 5

LIBRARY ASSOCIATIONS

The term 'association' is used to denote a group or body of individuals or institutions associated with a common purpose revolving generally for the two main purposes, viz.,

a. advancement of the service oriented goals of the association, and

b. protection of the interests of the members.

Association may be of different kinds with different objectives and categories, professional or non-professional. However, by considering its nature, Pandey S.K.Sharma defined library associations as 'a group or body of libraries or librarians and users of libraries formed with the common purpose of advancement of library profession including service and also for protection of interests of the members including raising their capabilities to serve more effectively'. (Sharma;1985;16)

There are more than seventy professional organizations and associations at state level in India. William A Borden went to Baroda in 1910 at the invitation of Maharaja Sayajirao Gaekwar of Baroda and organized the first professional organization of librarians in the country, the Baroda Library Club in 1912. (Patel; 2004;199) Other professional associations came up afterwards and some of the national level associations worth to be mentioned for their contributions in public library developments in the country.

1. The Indian Library Association (ILA)

The Indian Library Association (ILA) was founded on 13 September 1933 at Calcutta at the First All India Library Conference attended by a galaxy of intellectuals, educationists, librarians, and eminent citizens of Calcutta. (Khanna; 1987;319). A.C.Woolner, Vice Chancellor of Punjab University and K M Asadullah, Librarian of Imperial Library was the first Chairman and Secretary of the association respectively. The headquarters of ILA was shifted to Delhi in August 1964 and at present is housed in its own flat. It was decided that the Association would work for development of libraries and library movement, improvement of status of librarians and stressing for better training for librarians. (Sharma;1987;144). It can therefore, be traced that ILA will work as representatives of Indian librarians and libraries for the cause of libraries.

1) Objectives

The objectives of the Association laid down in the constitution are:

a) Promotion of library movement and improvement in library service in all its aspects in India;

b) Promotion of library science education and the improvement in the training of librarians in India;

c) Promotion of bibliographical study and research in library science;

d) Improvement in the state and conditions of service of librarians;

e) Affiliation of the state and other library associations with Indian Library Association and co-operation with international organization with similar objectives;

f) Publication of bulletins, periodicals, books, etc. which will help in the realization of the objectives of the Association;

g) Establishment of libraries, documentation centers and assistance in their establishing and working;

h) Promotion of appropriate library legislation in India;

i) Providing a common forum to all persons engaged or interested in library and information work by holding conferences and meetings for discussion of professional, technical and organizational issues;

j) Accreditation of institutions imparting library and information science education and training;

k) Promotion as well as formulation of standards, norms, guiding for management of library and information systems and services; and

l) Carrying out all such other activities as are incidental or conducive to the attainment of the above-mentioned objectives.

2) Organization

The ILA has a president, six vice presidents, a general secretary and an executive committee. It is organized to operate through the following twenty-tree Central Sectional Committees:

- Agricultural Libraries
- Government Department Libraries
- Engineering and Technology Libraries
- Health Science Libraries
- Education in Library & Information Science
- University Libraries
- Library Legislation
- Libraries & Information technology
- Adult Education & Neo-Literates
- Status & Pay scales of Library Professionals
- Oriental Libraries
- Public Libraries
- School Libraries
- Copyright & Intellectual; Property Right
- Special Libraries
- College Libraries
- Library History
- Documentation & Information Services
- Preservation & Conservation
- Women in Library & Information Services
- Libraries for Special groups
- Distance Learning in Library & Information Science

- Training & Development Programmes

3) Activities

All India Library Conference is organized every year at some places in the country hosted by either a university or an institution or a local library association. Other important activities include organization of workshop, seminars, convention and other activities, which can promote libraries and librarianship in India. Some the topics in such activities include *Library Legislation; School Children Libraries; Library cooperation/Resource Sharing; Library Personnel; Reading Materials/Collection Development; Bibliography and Documentation; University Libraries - Their Functions and Problems; Research Libraries in the Country; National Pay Policy for Libraries and Information Centers; National Information System; Computerization and Library Networks; Library Research; and Library Education.* (Vashishth;1991).

The Indian Library Association is a member of International Federation of Library Associations (IFLA) and the Commonwealth Library Association (COMLA). The association hosted IFLA Conference of 1992 in New Delhi. The Association also drafted Model Public Library Bill and arranged advanced training and internship for Indian librarians with the British Library Association in London.

4) Publications

The Association started publishing Library Bulletin since 1942, though its publication was suspended in 1946 and was published again as ABGILA from 1949 to 1953. This title was changed to the Journal of the Indian Library

Association in 1955, the Indian Library Association in Bulletin in 1965, and ILA Bulletin in 1975 till today. (Patel;2004;183). The bulletin is published quarterly, which includes professional articles on different topics on library and information science and librarianship as a whole. The Association also published ILA Newsletter every month to disseminate current information about the latest trends in the filed of library and information science. Another important publications includes *the proceedings of the All India Library Conferences since 1978, Indian Library Directory, A Survey of Public Library Services in India, Year's Work on Indian Librarianship, 50 Years of Indian Library Association; 1933-1983 and others.*

2. The Indian Association of Special Libraries and Information Centre (IASLIC)

The IASLIC was founded on 3 September 1955 at the lecture hall of the Indian Museum, Calcutta on initiatives and inspirations of librarians, documentalists, information scientists, scientists and technologists. It is much recognized by professionals in the field.

1) Objectives

Keeping in view the importance of inter-communication of facts and ideas among scientists, technologists and research workers, and of the collection of specialized information among them, IASLIC formulated the following objectives: (Sharma; 1987;145-146).

1) to encourage and promote the systematic acquisition, organization, and dissemination of knowledge;
2) to improve the quality of library and information science services and documentation work;

3) to co-ordinate the activities of an co-operation and assistance among special libraries, scientific, technological and research institutions, and learned societies, commercial organizations, industrial research establishments, as well as other information centers to the fullest extent;

4) to serve as a field of active contact for libraries, information bureaus, documentation centers, specialists, and other having common interests;

5) to improve the technical efficiency of the workers in special libraries, information and documentation centers, and to look after their professional welfare;

6) to act as a centre of research in special library and documentation technique;

7) to act as a centre of information in scientific, technical and other fields;

8) to take such action as may be incidental or conducive to the attainment of the objects of the association, or any of them;

9) to act as a nucleus of research in special librarianship and documentation techniques, and to provide forum for libraries in India.

2) Organization

The General Body of the Association elects a President, six Vice Presidents, a General Secretary, a Treasurer, two Joint Secretaries, two Assistant Secretaries, a Librarian, and 25 Council Members for a period of two years. The Association is organized in six divisions, namely, Documentation Service, Education, Publications and Publicity, Library Services, Documentation Reproduction and

Translation, and Cooperation and Coordination of Libraries. It has formed four special interest groups, such as, Special Interest Group on Industrial Information, Special Interest Group on Social Science Information, Special Interest Group on Computer Application, and Special Interest group on Humanities.

3) Activities

IASLIC has been organizing seminars and conferences at different parts of the country, which are usually, hosted by university libraries, department of library and information science, institutions, associations, and other information centers. Discussions in the seminars and conferences included different areas of current issues on *Mechanization of Library Services, Training of Special Librarianship in India, Rendering of Indic Names, Bibliographical Control of Special Libraries, Methods of Scientific Communication, Decentralization of Library and Information Services, Users and Library and Information Services, Education for Librarianship in India, General versus Special Classification Scheme, Bibliometric Studies, Marketing of Library and Information Services in India, Document and Data Processing, Problems and Prospects of Library Associations in India, Indexing and Abstracting Services in India, Translation Services, and others.*

The Association also provided a program titled, "Training in Special Librarianship and Documentation" from 1964 to 1970. The Association also conducted language courses in German, French, and Russian from 1958 to 1963 for translators for special libraries. (Patel; 2004;187). The Association is affiliated with the International Federation of Library Associations and Institutions (IFLA) and the International Federation for Information and Documentation

(FID) and plays an important role for the international cooperation of the two federations.

4) Publications

The IASLIC Bulletin, its official organ, has been published quarterly since 1956 and devoted to the advancement and dissemination of the fundamental and applied knowledge of library and information science in an accessible form to professional colleagues who have a common interest in the field in this country and abroad. The IASLIC Newsletter has been a bimonthly publication of the association since 1966 carrying important information and news about the activities of library and information services. Other important publications includes, *Directory of Special and Research Libraries in India, Glossary of Cataloguing Terms in (Indian) regional Languages, Education for Librarianship in India; A Survey, Draft General Code for Interlibrary Loan, Methods of Scientific Communication, IASLIC; Perspective, Performance, and Promise-A Silver Jubilee Commemorative Volume, Indexing Systems, and Library Architecture.*

3. Mizoram Library Association

A single person or institution cannot perform all the functions and services in his/her professional field. But collective action by interest groups in a particular profession serves a forum to coordinate efforts for the developmental work as a whole. Mizoram being developed in different ways, library has also been one of the development areas. Besides the establishment of government, public and academic libraries, NGOs have played an important role in establishing local libraries to cater the local community information needs. For the growth and development of libraries and services to the users, library professionals have shown keen interest to establish a professional association within the state namely Mizoram Library Association.

1) Meeting of Library Professionals

Under the initiative steps taken by C.Lianzama, State Librarian, the first meeting of local library professionals was held at State Library, Aizawl on 17th. July 1987, and the following library professionals attended the meeting;

i) Mr. C.Lianzama, Librarian, State Library, Aizawl

ii) Mr. Lalmakthanga, Librarian, Pachhunga University College, Aizawl

iii) Mr. K.M.Zakhuma, Asst. Librarian, NEHU, Mizoram Campus, Aizawl

iv) Mr. Vanhmingmawia, Librarian, Sub. Divisional Library, Aizawl

v) Mr. Ramzauva Ralte, Librarian, Mizoram Hindi Training Institute, Aizawl

vi) Mr. Hmingdailova, Librarian, Mizoram Institute of Education, Aizawl

vii) Ms. P.C.Laltlani, Librarian, Aijal Theological College, Aizawl

viii) Mr. Liansailova, Librarian, Mizoram Board of School Education, Aizawl

The meeting was presided over by Pu C.Lianzama and Pu Liansailova acted as Recording Secretary. Following are the important points that were discussed in the meeting relating to the promotion of library services within the state:

- The present library professionals play vital role for the promotion of the status and development of library services within the state; and there are no others to take these responsibilities other than us.

- Individual efforts did not bear fruit and hence, this resulted the need of collective efforts of the library professionals.

- It is essential to take steps for the library user education among the general public as a whole.

The meeting, after a prolonged discussion, resolved to establish an association. Mr. C.Lianzama, Mr. K.M.Zakhuma, Mr. Ramzauva Ralte and Mr. Liansailova (Convener-Secretary) were authorized to take necessary steps and to prepare draft constitution and henceforth, further decided that library professionals meeting may be convened within the month of October to discuss about the matters relating to establishment of library association by inviting library professionals of public, academic and special libraries within the state.

2) Establishment of Mizoram Library Association

As a result, another round of meeting was held on 23 October 1987(Friday) at 11;30 a.m. at the MBSE Conference Room, Khatla. The following library professionals within the state attended the meeting;

i) Mr. K. M. Zakhuma, Librarian, NEHU, Mizoram Campus, Aizawl

ii) Mr. C. Vanlalhluna, Library i/c, Mizo Cultural Club, Thingsulthliah

iii) Mr. Chawngthankima, Sr. Library Attendant, Pachhunga University College, Aizawl

iv) Mr. Lalramliana, Semi-Professional Assistant, Pachhunga University College, Aizawl

v) Mr. R. Engrothanga, Library i/c, YMA, Kawnpui South

vi) Mr. K. Laldawngliana, Library i/c, Joint YMA, Kawnpui

vii) Mr. Rotluanga, Librarian, Sub. Divisional Library, Kolasib

viii) Mr. Liansailova, Librarian, Mizoram Board of School Education, Aizawl

ix) Mr. Thanrehlova, Library i/c, Sihphir Public Library, Sihphir

x) Mr. R. K. Ngurtinkhuma, Deputy Librarian, Lunglei Govt. College, Lunglei

xi) Mr. Ramzauva Ralte, Librarian, Mizoram Hindi Training Institute, Aizawl

xii) Ms. P. C. Laltlani, Librarian, Aijal Theological College, Aizawl

xiii) Mr. C. Lianzama, State Librarian, State Library, Aizawl

xiv) Mr. Hmingdailova, Librarian, Mizoram Institute of Education, Aizawl

xv) Mr. C. Lalropuia, Office Secretary, Central YMA, Aizawl.

The meeting was presided over by Mr. K.M.Zakhuma and Ms. P.C.Laltlani conducted devotion. The meeting unanimously resolved to establish Mizoram Library

Association with the following objectives:

- To unite all persons engaged in library works or interested in library service in Mizoram.
- To provide, establish and improve libraries and library services.
- To improve the standard of librarianship and status of library profession.
- To promote better administration of libraries.
- To encourage the establishment, development and use of libraries in Mizoram.
- To encourage professional education and training for librarianship.

The meeting approved the draft constitution. On the spot, Mr. P.C.Lalropuia and Mr. P.C.Laltlani were appointed as Returning Officer and Polling Officer respectively to conduct election and the following persons are declared elected as the first MLA Office Bearers for 1987-89:

President	: Mr. C. Lianzama, Librarian, State Library, Aizawl
Vice President	: Mr. K. M. Zakhuma, Asst. Librarian, NEHU, Mizoram Campus, Aizawl
General Secretary	: Mr. Liansailova, Librarian, MBSE, Aizawl
Assistant Secretary	: Mr. Hmingdailova, Librarian, MIE, Aizawl
Treasurer	: Ms. Lalremsiami, Deputy Librarian, Aizawl College, Aizawl.

The first meeting of the Office Bearers was held on 26.10.1987 at the Mizoram State Library, Aizawl. The meeting appointed the following 7(seven) persons as an Executive Committee members:

i) Mr. Lalmakthanga, Librarian, Pachhunga University College, Aizawl

ii) Mr. Ramzauva Ralte, Librarian, MHTE, Aizawl

iii) Mr. Rotluanga, Librarian, Sub. Divisional library, Kolasib

iv) Mr. Lalramliana, Semi-Professional Assistant, Pachhunga University College, Aizawl

v) Mr. Lalchatuana, Librarian, Hrangbana College, Aizawl

vi) President, Central YMA, Aizawl

vii) Mr. C. Lalropuia, Office Secretary, Central YMA, Aizawl

The association was registered under the Registration of Societies Act having Registration No. SR.27 of 1987.

4) Activities

Mizoram Library Association, since its inception, has been actively engaged to achieve its aims and objectives, particularly for the promotion and development of library services within the state. Some of the activities undertaken by Mizoram Library Association are explained below:

i) Library Seminar-cum-Training

The Association in collaboration with the Department of Art & Culture, Government of Mizoram and Raja

Rammohun Roy Library Foundation (RRRLF) organized Library Seminar and Training Programmes in alternate years for the recognized libraries in Mizoram since 1989 on different topics.

- The first Library Seminar-cum-Training Programme was held on 19-20 October 1989 at the Hrangbana College Hall, Aizawl. Dr. H.Thansanga Education Minister of Mizoram was Chief Guest. Mr. R.K.Ngurtinkhuma and Mr. K.M.Zakhuma presented seminar paper on "Library Pawimawhna (The Importance of Library)", and "Mizoram Library tihhmasawn dan leh Chhawr tangkai dan (Impact of Library for Development and its usefulness)", respectively. The second day was devoted for training conducted by Mr Lalramliana. Total participants were 103 from different parts of the state.

- The second Library Seminar-cum-Training Programme was held on 14-15 November 1991 at Aizawl. The first day was observed as celebration of Children's Day and opening of the programme. Ms. Lalremsiami and Mr C.Lianzama presented seminar paper on, "Laws of Library Science", and "Ram hmasawn nan Library - Library Legislation (Library for National Development - Library Legislation)", respectively. The Training Programme was organized at Hrangbana College Hall on the second day and Mr. R.K.Ngurtinkhuma acted as resource person. 135 participants attended this programme from different corners of the state. It was followed by Mizoram Library Association Conference and passed the following resolutions:

  a) The State Legislative Assembly may pass Mizoram Public Libraries Bill.

b) The association may publish a Newsletter.

c) The government immediately may construct Library Building.

d) The Association may have library visit in collaboration with the government.

- The third Seminar-cum-Library Training Programme was held on 14-16 November 1993 at Aizawl. The first day was for the inaugural and seminar programme. Mr Liansailova presented seminar paper on, "Growth and Development of Libraries". The last two days were devoted for Library Training. Banner was displayed at different places under the caption of, "Lehkha chhiar hi finna a ni" (Reading is Wisdom)"; "Mizoram Public Libraries Act 1993 tih hlawhtlin thuai nise(Mizoram Public Libraries Act 1993 may be implemented immediately)"; "Library Act siam a ni hi kan lawm(We Welcome Mizoram Public Libraries Act)"; and "Mizoram than len nan Library a pawimawh (Library for the Development of Mizoram)".

- The Fourth Seminar-cum-Library Training Programme was held on 14-16 November 1995. Mr C.Lianzama and Mr. C.Vanlalruaia presented Seminar paper on, "Mizoram Public Library Act 1993", and "Information technology in Modern Libraries", respectively. Ms. Carol VLMS Dawngkimi and Mr. C.Lawmzuala conducted the Library Training.

- The fifth Seminar-cum-Library Training Programme was held at Aizawl on 18-20 November 1997. Mr. Lalchatuana presented seminar paper on, "Zirna atan Library (Library for Education)". Mr. Zomuana Joute and Mr. C.Lawmzuala conducted library training.

Local library visit programme was also conducted for the participants. This programme was followed by the Mizoram Library Association Conference and passed two resolutions;

a) Mizoram Public Library Act 1993 may be implemented by the State Government immediately (Mizoram Public Library Act 1993 hi Mizoram Sawrkarin ĥmang tawh rawh se).

b) State and District Library Building may be constructed by the State Government immediately (Mizoram Sawrkarin State Library leh Sub. Divisional Library building nei lo te sak thuai rawh se).

- The sixth programme under the caption of, "Mizoram State Library Silver Jubilee Celebration" coinciding with "National Book Week-cum-Library Seminar and Training" was held at Aizawl on 17-19 November 1999. Ms. Carol VLMS Dawngkimi presented seminar paper on, "Hmasawn nana Library Pawimawhna (Importance of Library for Development)". Mr. R.K.Ngurtinkhuma and Mr. F.Lalenga were the Resource Persons in the Library Training.

- In 2001 Library Training Programme was held at different district headquarters as below:

a) On 3 - 4 October 2001, it was organized at Kolasib for recognized libraries in Kolasib District.

b) On 17 - 18 October 2001, it was organized at Mamit for recognized libraries in Mamit District.

c) On 23 - 24 October 2001, it was organized at Lunglei for recognized libraries in Lunglei District.

d) On 6 - 8 November 2001, it was organized at Champhai for recognized libraries in Champhai District.

e) On 13 – 14 November 2001, it was organized at Aizawl for recognized libraries in Aizawl District.

- The eighth Library Seminar-cum-Training was held at Aizawl on 14-15 January 2004. Mr. C.Lianzama presented Seminar paper and Mr. P.L.Ringliana was the Resource Person in Library Training. Mr. C.Lianzama presented seminar paper on, "Mizoram Public Libraries Act 1993", and Library Training was conducted by Mr. P.L.Ringliana on, "Village Library enkawl dan tha (Best Practices for the Village Library Administration)". Mizoram Library Association organized this programme.
- State Level Library Seminar and Training Programme was held at Aizawl on 22-23 March 2006 and attended by 344 participants from different corners of the state. Mr. C.Lawmzuala presented seminar paper on, "Collection Development for Libraries", and Mr. Thankima and Mr. Zothanglawra conducted Training Programme on, "Preservation and Maintenance of Library Materials".

2) Library visits

The association has taken keen interest to visit libraries to know the ground realities with regard to establishment, functioning, services and organizations as well as to provide on-the-spot training to the local librarians. The professionals belonging to the Association visited libraries of different parts of the state under the sponsorship of the Department of Art & Culture, Government of Mizoram. Some of them are presented below:

a) In 1992, the association visited forty-two recognized village libraries at different areas of the state and twenty-seven in Aizawl. The visits were organized in five phases dividing the association members in five groups.

b) In 2003, twenty-one recognized libraries were visited to assess on the spot condition of the library.

c) Based on suggestions received from the recognized libraries, Special Library Training were given on different topics to the library staff of the following libraries:

- Zotlang Branch YMA Library,
- Chanmari West Branch YMA Library,
- Chaltlang Branch YMA Library,
- Hunthar veng Branch YMA Library, and
- Zotlang Presbyterian Church Library

3) *Certificate Course*

The association in collaboration with the Department of Art & Culture, Government of Mizoram organized Certificate Course in Library Science at Aizawl during August to December 1997. Classes were held at the Hrangbana College building at evening. Structure of the

Course was designed to cater the need of present library professionals within the state. Six Library Professionals who are working in different organizations on various capacities are engaged to give lectures at the Course. Out of 24 admitted students, 20 students successfully completed the course and the course was subsequently recognized and approved by the North Eastern Hill University, Shillong vide No.AC.34/88.5;02(B).

4) Best Library Award

In order to motivate, promote and develop village/ local libraries, selection of Best Library was conducted amongst the Recognised Libraries in 2003. Out of the 418 Recognized Libraries, twenty libraries participated in the fray. After careful consideration and verification, the following libraries were selected as Best Libraries in Mizoram:

First	:	Bethlehem Vengthlang Branch YMA Library, Aizawl
Second	:	Chanmari Branch YMA Library, Aizawl
Third	:	Bungzung Branch YMA Library, Bungzung
Fourth	:	Kanan Branch YMA Library, Aizawl
Fifth	:	Lungpher Branch YMA Library, Lungpher

Dr. R.Lalthangliana and Pu Aichhinga, Ministers of Mizoram donated Rs. 10000/- and Rs. 5000/- for the Best library Award respectively. The above selected "Best Libraries" were given the following prizes at the Mizoram Library Association Conference 2004:

First Prize : Rs.10, 000.00 with Citation;

Second Prize : Rs. 7,000.00 with Citation;

Third Prize : Rs. 5,000.00 with Citation;

Fourth Prize : Rs. 3,000.00 with Citation; and

Fifth Prize : Rs. 2,000.00 with Citation.

5) *Publications*

The Mizoram Library Association felt the need of publications as a means and measures for the development of library services in Mizoram in general and in rural areas in particular. It has the following publications so far which can be treated as a tool for the village/local librarians:

i) Library Education Booklet

ii) Compilation of Proceeding of Seminar Papers held in 1989, 1991 and 1993 under the title of, "Library Hmasawnna (Library Development)".

Iii) "Library Kaihhruaina (Library Guide)" which contains about the management and organization of libraries.

6) *Other professional activities*

Apart from the above activities, the following points may be added in brief:

- The Association, in 1999, organized essay competition on "Library Services for National Development". Besides, Radio talk and Television Programmes were also had to educate and serve the public on the impact of libraries in the socio-cultural, economic and education development.

- The Association met Chief Minister and his Cabinet and his colleagues in connection with the development of library services in the state particularly to implement Mizoram Public Libraries Act 1993 and construction of State and District Libraries at Aizawl and other district headquarters as well.

The Association organized felicitation programme for those who completed Degree Course in Library & Information Science from Mizoram University and manu LIS graduates attended such programmes. It is a time for discussion and interaction among the LIS persons in connection of the promitin and development of library and informations centres to meet the challenges of the world in an infoamtion age.

4. Other Associations

India is one of the most advanced countries in the world in the field of knowledge and information sciences. Many national and regional associations are coming up in the field of library and information sciences. All-India Public Library Association, being the first national level association in the field came into being in 1920 following the result of the first All-India Public Library Conference held in Madras in November 1919 under the sponsorship of Andhradesa Library Association, the first state library association in the country established in 1914. (Patel; 2004;193) Many professional associations have come up at the national and regional level and now all the states have established state library associations. These professional associations organized seminar, workshops, training and other important activities for the advancement and development of public libraries in the country.

Some of the national and state level professional associations that have contributed for the cause and development of public libraries are:

1) National Level Library Associations

There are different library associations at the national level. The main objectives of these national level library associations are to develop and maintain library services in their area of operations. Some of the national level library associations are:

1) All India Public Library Association, 1919;
2) Indian Library Association, 1933;
3) Government of India Library Association, 1933;
4) All India Rural Library Service Association, 1933;
5) All India Manuscript Library Association, 1944;
6) Library Field Worker Association, 1951;
7) Indian Association of Special Libraries and information Centers, 1955; and others.

2) State Level Library Associations

Most of the states in India have their own state library association having objectives to work and develop library services within their states. Some of such associations are:

1) Andhra Pradesh Library Association, 1914;

2) Maharashtra Library Association, 1921;
3) Bengal Library Association, 1925;
4) Madras Library Association, 1928;
5) Karnataka Library Association, 1929;
6) Punjab Library Association, 1929;
7) Samastha Kerala Pustakalaya Samiti, 1931;
8) Bihar Library Association, 1936;
9) Assam Library Association, 1938;
10) Utkal Library Association, 1944;
11) Kerala Library Association, 1945;
12) Hyderabad Library Association, 1951;
13) U.P.Library Association, 1951;
14) Delhi Library Association, 1953;
15) Gujarat library Association, 1953;
16) Madhya Bharat Library Association, 1957;
17) Gomantak Library Association, 1961;
18) Rajasthan Library Association, 1962;
19) Jammu & Kashmir Library Association, 1966
20) Tripura Library Association, 1967;
21) Manipur Library Association, 1987;
22) Mizoram Library Association, 1987;
23) Meghalaya Library Association, 1994;
24) Nagaland Library Association, 1996; and others.

REFERENCES

Khanna, J K (1987). Library and Society. New Delhi: Ess Ess Publications.

Patel, Jashu and Krishan Kumar (2004). Libraries and Librarianship in India. Westport: Greenwood, 2004.

Sharma, Pandey S.K. (1985). Public Libraries in India. New Delhi: Ess Ess.

Sharma, Pandey S K (1987). Libraries and Society. New Delhi: Ess Ess.

Vashishth, C.P. (1991). Indian Library Association. Quoted by Jashu Patel and Krishan Kumar. *In.* Libraries and Librarianship in India. Westport: Greenwood Press, 2004. p.183.

Public Library in India : 169-196
R. K. Ngurtinkhuma
Today and Tomorrow's Printers & Publishers, New Delhi-110 002 (India)

Chapter 6

PUBLIC LIBRARY IN SOCIO-CULTURAL DEVELOPMENT

Man is human by distinctive culture within the society. 'Without culture, we would not be human at all'. (Giddens;1997;18). Society and culture are two complementary terms that go hand-in-hand. It is difficult to separate one from the other. There can be different sub-cultures within a society that may change from time to time. Culture is not changed by itself but by certain factors that influence the society. Library is one of the factors that changed the culture of certain groups within a society. Impact of State and District libraries on Socio-cultural development particularly on Mizo society is being discussed below to aware the importance of library services for the community.

1. Meaning of Socio-Culture

Men, as social animal, have always sought to examine themselves and their social life. Several intellectual disciplines such as theology, economics, political science, history, psychology and ethics were developed to explain different aspects of human enterprises. In the mean time, Auguste Comte (1798-1857), known as father of sociology, felt the need to create new discipline to deal with social institutions as marriage, family and community as well as the numerous social structures and processes. Thus, Comte combined two terms 'socius', Latin for society, and 'logos', Greek for studying, and coined 'sociology' which literally means 'study of society'.

He suggested that sociology's most important job would be to study the small unit of society such as the family and community to find out how these groups produce self-sacrifice, loyalty, mutual respect, and all the other basic kinds of social bonds needed to tie members of a large, complex society together. (Denisoff and Wahram; 1983;17). Some other theorists on sociology, namely, Karl Marx(1818-1883); Herbert Spencer (1820-1903); Emile Durkheim (1858-1917); and Max Weber (1864-1920) came up after Auguste Comte having coined their views and ideas on sociology. Many development have came up under sociology but not devised far from its original path. It can be argue that sociology is one of the groups of social sciences, that studies human groups and societies concerning social interactions, social groups, and social behavior. Society and culture are very important phenomena of sociology and as such sociological knowledge is a knowledge of causal connections, or connections of interdependence among wide range of phenomena such as the conduct of individuals in institutions like families, churches and sects, workshops, armies, civic and political associations, territorial, ethnic and national communities; the patterns of relationship among individuals; the role of structure and authority in the working of institutions and communities; the stratification of societies; communities and institutions with respect to income and status or difference; the role of cognitive and normative beliefs in the actions of individuals and in the functioning of communities, institutions and societies. (Kuper and Kuper; 1985; 799-800).

All human societies have a religion, a spoken language, a kinship system, and considerable technology. Edward B.Taylor defined culture as, 'The complex whole which includes knowledge, belief, art, morals, law, custom, and any other capabilities and habits acquired by man as a member of society'. (Abraham; 2006;53). Culture covers the way of life of a social group consisting of belief, values, standards, practice, language, and technology shared by members of a social group. Culture refers to the ways of life of the members of a society, or of groups within a society. It includes how they dress, their marriage customs and family life, their patterns of work, religious ceremonies and leisure pursuits. (Giddens;1997;18). A society may be big or small, but the social group may have distinct culture within the society. Culture is not static; but elements of culture change from time to time. The society has abandoned many belief systems and cultural practices which are not consistent with the present scientific evidence. Many myths and numerous superstitious are now exploded and the way of life, like cooking and eating habits, dress and marriage system are also changed. 'No cultures could exist without societies. But equally, no societies could exist without culture'. (Giddens; 1997;18).

A socio-cultural approach is the roles of different ethnic groups, gender and the culture; with all these elements combined it forms a personality. Socio-culture is the way of people act and develops based on around their surroundings. Socio-cultural factors involve self-concept and self-esteem. It is based upon people's belief and what they stand for. There can be many different things that can make a person popular. Such things can be a persons' values, belief, language, norms or technology. These entire factors are part of culture. They may be small but influence personal life of a society. Therefore, socio-culture is the actions that we choose to do, to become what we are.

2. Role of Public Library in the Socio-cultural Development

The purpose of a library in modern society is to educate the community in the widest sense. Society consists of various groups of community belonging to one or other social group, such as shopkeepers, businessmen, technicians, bureaucrats, clerks, students, educationists, teachers, engineers, doctor, intellectuals, mechanics, agriculturists, farmers, labours, etc. The interest of knowledge of these different groups of people within the society is very much varied according to their human needs. The primary role of public library, such as State Library, District Library, Block Library, Tehsil Library, Taluka Library, Village Library and others is to provide the best information facilities to all those library users in the community. Library and society are interlinked and interdependent. Society without libraries has no significance, and libraries without society has no origin….it is regarded as 'social institution', a product of society for its cultural advancement. (Khanna;1987;7). IFLA/UNESCO Public Library Manifesto 1994 stated that:

> "The Public library is the local center of information, making all kinds of knowledge and information readily available to its users. The services of the public library are provided on the basis of equality of access for all, regardless of age, race, sex, religion, nationality, language or social status".

Public library as a local center of information has to be organized effectively by the authority by ensuring its accessibility to all the sections of the society. "The public library service acts as an intellectual catalyst for socio-cultural development by providing facilities for the purposes of acquiring education and information as well as recreation, aesthetic appreciation and research". (Rath;1996;15). It should serve the users with free of cost to all age groups at everywhere with the best possible means. The collection of public library should focus all the sections of the society to provide their information needs in educating their personal life and social attitudes as well. G.L.Trehan stated that, "It is the social function of the library to provide book service to the community. Library is the only organized social institution which fosters the reading of books". (Trehan:1980;44).

Public library exists to serve the community. It has a very important role to play in the future development of the country particularly in the socio-cultural and educational enlightenment. Role of public library on social-cultural development can be narrate as below:

1) Cultural Center for the Society

A public library functions as a cultural center of the society. It provides and focuses for cultural and artistic development in the community and helping to shape and support the cultural identity of the community. Public Library Mission stated that, "promotion awareness of cultural heritage, appreciation of the arts, scientific achievements and innovations". The public library collects all documents related to different cultural fields and promotes awareness of cultural heritage, appreciation of arts and scientific innovations through its services. It does not only preserve documents of cultural heritage, but also organized cultural programmes through its audio-visual services and inter-cultural activities as well. It also provides access to cultural expressions of all visual and performing arts. These can be achieved by collaborating with other organizations or partnership within the local, national or international level by organizing cultural programmes and by ensuring the interest of the local community. Rath said that, "If national and university libraries are the barometer of a country's erudition, public libraries are the barometer of its general culture". (Rath:1996:26). The description of library as 'mind of society', the 'community's intellectual center' reflects its influence in moulding the life of the community. (Khanna:1987:xxii). It should be a key agency in the local community for the collection, preservation and promotion of local culture in all its diversity. Public libraries in a developing society should:

- preserve cultural heritage;
- provide access to all form of cultural expression;
- make efforts to foster inter-cultural dialogue;
- favour cultural diversity; and
- support oral tradition. (Venkatappaiah;2007;72-73).

2) Community Information Center

In an information age, the key function of the public library is to provide up-to-date facts and information to all the sections of the community. The Public Library Manifesto 1994 mission stated that, "ensuring access for citizens to all sorts of community information". Information needs of various citizens may vary from person to person, but public library by its nomenclature should serve its best to provide and quench the users information desire. Some of the roles in providing information are:

- providing access to information at all levels;
- collecting information about the local community and making it readily accessible, often in co-operation with other organizations;
- training people of all ages in the use of information and the associated technology;

- guiding users to the appropriate information sources;
- providing opportunities for disabled people to have independent access to information; and
- acting as a gateway to the information world by making it accessible to all, thus helping to bridge the gap between 'the information rich' and 'the information poor. (IFLA/UNESCO;2001;30-31).

Public library, besides its reference and information services, may organize community information service considering the local situation. In organizing community information service, social, cultural, economic, educational level, racial, employment opportunities, religious differences, etc. may be considered since it may different from one community to the other within the locality. The community information services attend the following two types of information requirements of the society:

1) Information requirements of an individual related to food, clothing, health, shelter, education savings, investment, material problems, legal right, employment, travel, environment, business, etc.

2) Information related to social, economic and political responsibilities and duties of citizens, functioning of local self-government, pollution control, developmental project, etc.

3) Information related to birth control, childcare, nutrition, immunization, infertility, sanitary and health care services and special training on cooking, interior decoration, embroidery, sewing, social and ethical responsibilities, etc. may be organized for local women. (Kaula; 2006; 12).

Public library is for the community and is the community agency to provide local information needs in various forms. It should provide those information by documents or oral, printed or electronic devices. For arranging free access to information, the public libraries should:

- provide basic information for the down trodden people;
- provide access to all citizens for all types of information at all levels;
- develop local histories;
- develop community information service;
- utilize the service of National Informatics Centers; and
- introduce computer skills for achieving speed, accuracy and bulk in service.

Diana Formway, who lives in New York and organizes a stack of multicolored children's novel said that, "Libraries showed me what was out there in the world as well as connected me to other people and places outside my small town in upstate New York". (McVey and Long;2006;2). This simple statement affirmed that library give us information about what's happening in and around the world.

3) Recreation Center

Public library services provide creativity development to the children and local young adults by providing recreational reading books for their personality development and spiritual growth in their leisure time. Recreation in library discussion denotes 'such of leisure time as will promote personal happiness and social well being'. (Khanna;1987;39). Public Library Manifesto 1994, in its mission stated that, "stimulating the imagination and creativity of children and young people". Children and young adults basically need special care in their personality development to meet the challenges of the challenges of the society. "Young people between childhood and adulthood develop as individual members of the society with their own culture". (IFLA/UNESCO; 2001;27). The library should know their information needs and should develop good collection for leisure readings like biographies, sports and games, travel books, religious books, audio-visual materials, magazines, popular novels, etc. including electronic information resources. Story hours, puppet shows, dramas, and other events like book discussion may also be organized in a library. Collection of reading materials that suffice local youth information needs may help them to feel that the library is mean for them and help them to overcome a feeling of alienation from the library or even from the society as well.

In order to facilitate local youths by this library service, special training may be essential for the library staff to cover customer care service. Young adults are feel shy and need care and help in different areas of activities. This is the best period to guide them in the right direction to become good citizen and sociable in the society. Children's Club or Youth Club may also be formed to organize cultural programmes, such as, art competition, concerts, film shows, story hour, etc. The public library must aware of the cultural and social changes in the community and develop flexible services to meet the challenges in these situations.

4) Knowledge Center for Disadvantaged People of the Society

Public Library Manifesto 1994, in its missions statement stated that, "Specific services and materials must be provided for those users who cannot, for whatever reason, use the regular services and materials, for example linguistic minorities, people with disabilities or people in hospitals or prison". The public library services have no limitation. It covers even the remotest area of the country. All people in the society should have equal opportunity to access information from the library to develop their knowledge in one way or the other. Prisoners, patients in the hospital bed, blind persons, inmates of the rehabilitation centers, etc. should also have an opportunity to access information at their respective places with free of charge. This accessibility can be achieved by extension services. Book-mobile/mobile library, audio-visual programme, concerts or extension lending services may be adopted to provide such facilities to those disadvantaged persons. Special training programmes on information and communication technology may also be organized to the physically handicapped persons for their rehabilitation.

5) Creativity Center for Children

One common saying is that, "Children are the future leader of the nation". This depicts importance of care and teaching to the children. The Bible says, "Train a child in the way he should go, and when he is old he will not turn from it". (Proverbs 22:6). We cannot ignore our children to guide and give training for their future in the society. Children borne with different creativity mind that needs to be explore and developed. The children's section of the public library is organized and operated in such a manner that it takes special care for creating and reading habits in children from an early age. This section may be equipped with picture, children book, toys, etc. that can develop and stimulate children's attitudes and personal growth and programmes, like film shows, fancy dress, story hours, dramas, recitation, etc. may be organized to bring awareness among children. If our children are provided with their creativity developmental sets, they will bear in mind and will follow when they grow old and can behave as good citizen of the community. They have the same right to access library services sine they are within the society. We can, therefore, organize public library as a play center as well as creativity development center of the child.

6) Center of Communal Harmony and National Integration

A nation's prime role is cordial relationship among the citizens of different cultures within the society. No country stands with single community, race, religion, caste, rituals, etc. As common saying stated, 'United we stand, divided we fall', every nation want to have united citizen in every respect. At the same time, every country has its own diplomacy to the other to construct cordial relationship in one way or the other.

As communal harmony and national integration are prime problems of today, meeting between the social leaders and local community in order to build up confidence and remove misunderstandings and prejudices would be advisable. Library could arrange such meetings by its own or in collaboration with other organizations providing wholesome recreation to all. Public libraries having served the nation with equal treatment play an important role for the unity, co-operation and national integration of a country. Through its provided services it can lead the people to the common front. There may be different castes/tribes within in a society having their own culture, but library services may bring together to the same integrity. This service is very clear in the case of India. India is a vast country, comprising different culture, religion, castes/tribes, etc. It is said that India is a land of diversity. In this situation, the prime importance of India is national integration. Library is the best agent for the national integration in India through its innumerable services.

7. Community Resource Center

Former Prime Minister, Mr. P V Narasimha Rao, while inaugurating the first "Chief Ministers Conference on Rural Development" on 8 October 1992, he urged the Chief Ministers to take personal interest in rural development programme by stating there is "no other programme which is more important than rural programme. Out of Rs.30,000 crores outlay during Eight Five Year Plan, 6-8 was to be earmarked for the establishment and maintenance of Rural Library and Community Resource Center(RLCRC). The local community can develop their personal intellects through the library services, namely, reading, film shows, seminars/ workshops, lectures, etc. Public library is the best institution of the society to learn and disseminate their knowledge. It is nit only a center of information and knowledge, but also to educate and train the other citizens to become resourceful and intellect to the society as well.

8) Bridging the Digital Divide of Local Community

Digital divide means the unequal and disproportionate pace of development in society having access to digital information, infrastructure (ICTs) and other ICT-based service. There is a wide division between those who have real access to ICT and are using it effectively, and those who don't. Some of the factors that lead to digital divide are due to:

- poor physical infrastructure;
- unstable government;
- lack of strong ICT policy;

- higher in rural population;
- gender disability;
- poverty;
- low literacy rate; and
- linguistic diversity.

Access of the right information at the right time at the least cost is the search of a person at this information age. Research and development increase new areas of knowledge but tainted one's idea. New development in Information, Communication and Technology (ICT), though it is a new way of development in science & technology, it creates certain problems between the community, 'information rich' and information poor' or 'who have' and 'who have not'. The community consists of various localities, rich and poor or educated and uneducated, all need to have the same skill to access their personal information requirements. This diversification creates exclusiveness to those who have not of the latest technology to access their information needs. Exclusiveness in the society may result anti-social activities of the people.

Public library is the only institution that can provide equal chance to the society to access information need by the latest technology with free of cost. (Ngurtinkhuma;2005;78). By accessing information need through public library services, local community can have the same opportunity and their exclusiveness may be conquered. In other words, the public library services can bridge the digital divide through its ICT services to the community with free of cost.

3. Mizoram Perspective

Historically, Lushai or Mizo are intelligent tribe of

Mongoloid Hillman inhabiting parts of the wild forest-covered mountainous region forming the watershed between India and Burma. 'The ancestral home would appear to have been somewhere in the neighborhood of S.E.Tibet and Western China, whence, by slow degrees through the centuries, they have passed southward and westward to their present habitat'. (Lorrain;1940;v).

During the administration of District Council in Mizoram, the first public library, i.e. District Library was established in Aizawl in 1968 and afterwards State Library and other four District Libraries were established during the UT Administration to serve the people of Mizoram through library services. And afterwards, the State Legislative Assembly passed the Mizoram Public Libraries Bill in 1993. The Government of Mizoram had been contributing Rs.1, 57,20,000 to the RRRLF Matching Scheme during the last twenty-six years, 1982-83 to 2007-08; average annual contributions is Rs.6,04,615.38, and 424 village/NGO libraries were also recognized.

The tribal community of Mizo has distinct social and cultural life from the rest of the people of India. There have been many changes in the socio-cultural life of the people through the ages. The researcher have conducted personal interview on the socio-cultural development of Mizoram; and describes impact of State and District Libraries on socio-cultural development of Mizoram with the support of respondents and personal interview held on various occasions; but the responses were more or less the same and stated as below:

1) Impact on Social Life

The contributions of the Christian Missionaries for the development of Mizo society are very wonderful. Sixty-two Christian Missionaries from United Kingdom worked in Mizoram during 1894-1977. They did not come only for Gospel evangelical work but also for social evangelism to support and strengthen the people in different ways of life. As a result, 87% of the total populations are Christian in Mizoram. According to the Scheduled Castes and Tribes Lists (Modification) Order, 1956 and as inserted by Act 81 of 1971of Indian Parliament, Mizo belongs to the Scheduled Tribe, and as such out of the total population of the state, 94.46% are Schedule Tribe, 0.03% Scheduled Caste and 5.51% are other social groups in 2001.

A Mizo village was independent and governed by its own chief, known as *Lal,* who was a despot in his own jurisdiction. His words were law in his territory, all that was in the village belong to him, and he could call upon his subjects to furnish him with anything that he needed. All disputes and cases were to be decided by him. (Sangkima;1992;35). His *Upa,* who formed his council of advisers, assisted the Chief. The villagers had to pay taxes to the Chief called *fathang*. In a village, there are *Ramhual,* who are an agriculturist, had to pay more taxes than commoners. There were also free citizens, known as *zalen,* they were exempted from taxes. *Zalen* were respected and were friends to the chief who helped him whenever he needed to entertain guests. (Darchhawna;2007;2).

Family is one of the oldest institutions in human society. As such family occupies an important and prominent place in the history of the Mizo society. Father is head of the family, who exercise family administration. At mealtime head of the family normally gave instructions, what they should do and not to do to the other members.

(Siama;1978;30). It is also an important occasion to teach manners and etiquettes.

Mizo unmarried men are supposed to stayed at *Zawlbuk* (a bachelor's dormitory). Men are responsible to the society, being guards of the village from enemies; so that they should be at one place at night for emergency circumstances. *Zawlbuk* being an important social institution has three fold functions; such as:

- It served as a sleeping place and recreational center for unmarried as well as young married men;
- It imparted training and taught discipline to young boys and even the rude people in the village were disciplined and put under control; and
- It also served as an inn for a man from another village. (Sangkima;1992;39).

Another institution in Mizo society there exists since immemorial was *bawi.* A person who surrenders himself to a Mizo Chief for any reason was commonly called a *bawi.* There are four kinds of *bawi,* such as,

(1) *Inpuichhung bawi* –Those who had been driven by starvation to take refuge in the chief's house. Widows, orphans and other who were unable to support themselves and had no relatives willing to do so formed the bulk of this type of *bawi.*

(2) *Chemsen bawi* – Those criminals who, to escape from the consequences of their ill deeds took refuge in the chief's house. Murderers and debtors who were unable to pay their creditors were in this category.

(3) *Tuklut bawi* – Those persons who, during war, had deserted the loosing side and joined the

victors by promising that they and their descendents would be *bawi.*

(4) *Sal* – Those persons captured in raids are called *sal.* They performed works for the *bawi* and their children were treated as *bawi.* The price of their release depended entirely on the goodwill of the owners. (Darchhawna;2007;3).

The Mizo have three important festivals, signifying different occasions, like *Chapchar Kut, Mim Kut* and *Pawl Kkut. Chapchar Kut* is spring festival celebrated after the clearing of jungles for their jhum cultivation. Particularly it is a festival of youth, to which boys and girls look forward. *Mim Kut* is especially reserved for the dead persons. The first corn of the year was offered to the dead body by his/her relatives. *Pawl Kut* is harvest festival, held at the end of harvest. It is especially for the children though grown-up people also take part in the festival. But, only *Chapcha Kut* is celebrated today, which is also very different from the original celebrations. This is due to the development of the society in various ways of life through certain means of communications and informations.

All these social impact of Mizo society has no longer existed today. Now, the elected persons representing the people of the state administered the state and villages democratically. *Zawlbuk* do not existed, there were no *bawi* system and no taxes were given to the village administrators directly.

The social life of Mizo has been changing and developing towards the progressive livelihood. In this course of time, the State and District Libraries of Mizoram also have an impact towards the development of the society. The researcher has described the following points in this regard:

1. Collections of State and District Libraries give the community information about the life and standards of other societies. The reader may have educated himself to have better livelihood and style of living through such documents. Library is a center of such information for the local communities since many people are not afford to buy such documents from their own resources. It helps us to know social life of other community, which makes us sociable to other community.

2. The reading materials provided by the libraries has been giving knowledge and wisdom to the society. Through its provided reading materials we can learn about health, beauty care, manners, legal activities, etc.

3. It gives us awareness of other societies that brings changes of the social life of the community. It is also a center of national integration by its various services rendered to different societies of the state.

4. Man's social life in influence by its environments. Likewise, library changes social life in positive or negative way through its various kinds of information provided to the readers. Good books impart good moral, which build societal development in the right way of livelihood.

5. It also builds up knowledge and wisdom to develop the society. Documents we read in the library changes our mind set, which may influence the society. One can have high thinking from the developed societies.

6. Library books bring good results for our day-to-day works and educational field as well, which is an important agent to develop and changes social life.

7. Library gives how a society should be and the value of different cultures. It motivates to do something useful for the society and it gives confidence in running and organizing social and cultural activities.
8. Library is the best available information center to retrieve and disseminate informations to the society and preserves cultural heritage. Library directs social life of the society. Library builds up human character and since we have these libraries, our social life has been changing in various directions.
9. Gives us environmental awareness to adapt our livelihood accordingly.
10. It gives us political awareness though its collections from which we can understand bout the political situations of other nations/states. It directs us to the political consciousness of the society.

2) Impact on Cultural Life

Like other human communities, Mizo have their own distinctive culture, quite different from the Buddhists, Hindu and Islamic cultures. The Mizo had very little contact with the outside world prior to the coming of the British, as such the influence of other cultures and religion upon them was very limited. (Darchhawna;2007;2).

The Mizo have their own customary law, in which marriage occupies the central point of the law. In the Mizo society, free mixing of boys and girls is permitted, and the young man, in advance, can obtain the tacit consent of a girl to a marriage and thus pave ways for a smooth negotiation with his parents through *Palai* (mediator). Then the bride's price will be fixed; basically the girl's parents can demand anything for the brides' price, which have two categories. *Manpui* and *Mantang*. *Mantang* is sub-divided into different heads, like *Sumhmahruai, Pu sum, Pa lal, Ni ar, Naupuakpuan,* and *Sumfang* that will be distributed to the relatives of the girl accordingly.

The treatment and disposal of dead bodies was another culture of the society. Before the coming of the British, the dead body was disposed of by *kuangur*, but it was stopped and dead body were buried in a common burial ground known as *thlanmual*. (Sangkima;1992;141). If a person die, all the villagers will go to the dead man's house to condole the bereaved family and will them in different ways.

The Mizos, blessed as they are with a beautiful environment and rich culture, are a vibrant and sociable people. They love to dance, and can boast a number of folk and community dances which have been handed down from one generation to the other through the ages. Famous dances of Mizo are, *Cheraw*, colorful dance with the help and support of bamboo; *Khuallam,* normally performed by men of distant relatives attending *Khuangchawi* dressed with *Pawndum; Chheih Lam,* usually performed by men with some friend normally at evening; *Chai,* is a community dance at the time of merry making; *Rallu Lam,* is a warriors' dance; *Solakia,* a victory dance over an enemy; and *Par Lam,* colorful dance usually performed by girls to show happiness.

The department of Art & Culture occasionally organized programs, like seminar and workshop on different aspects of Mizo culture and society, like folk song competition, Mizo traditional song competition, cultural dance competition, drama competition based on Mizo stories, music festival, etc. having invaluable contribution for the preservation of Mizo culture. Most of these competitions are organized among the cultural clubs and Branch YMA. As a result, Mizo culture is rooted in the minds of the community. Mizo dress and other traditional items have become known to the generations.

As stated above, Mizo have their own culture since immemorial, but some of these cultural life were no longer existed due to certain developments within the society. These changes are basically takes place after the coming and influence of the British and other world. The establishment of State and District Libraries gave various knowledge about the culture of the other states/nations, and its impact on Mizo culture is stated below:

1. The marriage arrangement has been changing due to the influence of the other societies. In this course of time, State and District Libraries may act as center to educate the people through its collection of documents and other organized programs, like cultural exhibition, lectures, workshops, etc.

2. The cultural dances of Mizoram has been modified to be more beautiful but without losing its originality. Cultural identity is an important aspect of modern life, and the libraries can preserved our cultural identity through its services and preservation of documents in this regards.

3. Library documents gave its readers about the culture of other societies. If we know some similarities with our cultures, we can feel that our culture is not very far from them and which can give us sociable with those societies.

4. State and District Libraries acted as inventories and depositories of cultural activities through its collection of documents and extension services. It is the best means for the preservation of our culture through its collections.

5. Frequent library users equipped themselves with informations and knowledge, which help them exercise their logical thinking positively. This in turn brings gradual change in the lifestyle as well as cultural ethos.

3) Impact on Economic Condition

Economic condition is one of the factors for the development of a society. To have decent society a country must be economically developed but a societal development solely determined by its economic development. (Sangkima;1992;93). Before the coming of the British, the people used only barter economy and the economic condition was very poor. Consequent upon the coming of the British, people began to use money as well as earning it through selling of their goods especially to the English people as a result of introduction of money and traders also entered from abroad mostly Bengalis. Major H.W.G.Cole, Superintendent of Lushai Hills, started Aizawl bazaar in 1910(Liangkhaia;2002;159). This had been one of the factors that change economic conditions of the state, and as a result, now Aizawl became one of the most important market place in North East of India.

Mizoram economy had been relied on agriculture. Agriculture is the main occupation with more than 80% of the population depending upon agriculture and allied sector, and as such, most of the households engaged in jhum cultivation. Horticulture has been developing and the main products are orange, banana, pineapple passion fruit, and lemon. Due to the increase of population and growth in various fields of developments, the economy of Mizoram has been developing in Co-operative movement and industries. According to the census report of 2001, Cultivators in Mizoram are 58.1% of the total population, Agricultural laborers are 5.9%, Household industry workers are 1.5% and other workers are 34.5%. The state per capita income (at current prices) is Rs.21,327 in 2003-04. Library, through its various collection, can act as means for taking stock of informations for the economic development of a society. The impact of State and District Libraries on the economy of Mizoram, through its various services is stated below:

1. The economy of a society depends on what the society is. As it has impact on social life of the society, its impact on economy cannot be ignored. The library books provide various information on the economy of others and from which we can learn many valuable lesions in regard to our own state economy.

2. Each family has their own management. The library is the source for the study of home economics through its collations on such kind of information materials.

3. Through the library books, self-employed persons can have right direction in their employment and that helps them for the economic condition of their family.

4. Library are very helpful to provide instructions on cooking, health, gardening, weaving, and looking after of children which is taken care by women in Mizo society. These services have an important impact on he family of the society or could change family earnings.

4) Impact on Religion and Belief

The Mizos believed in a supreme God whom they called *Pathian*, but it was not believed that He had much to do with them in their daily life. (Lloyd;nd;19). He was good God, never doing any harm to human beings. Therefore, they conceived the idea that they need not offer sacrifices to him. When they were blessed with good fortunes, they said *Pathian a tha* (God is good) and when they were in a state of fear they uttered, *Pathian in zah a ngai ang chu* (God will mercy upon us). But when misfortunes frequented them, they said, *Pathian a thin ur* (God is angry with us). (Challiana;1978;29,30).

The Mizo believed in the existence of evil spirits, commonly known as *Ramhuai.* This evil spirit is the source of all illness and misfortunes and were terribly afraid of it and hence, utmost care was taken to avoid cursing of these spirits. They worshiped big trees, stones, mountains and water, since they believe that the evil spirit dwelt in it. They can take different form they liked, as tiger, fire, wind, etc. Therefore, they frequently offered sacrifices to please these evil spirits. (Sangkima;1992;53). There are different kinds of sacrificial ceremonies depending upon the circumstances.

The Mizo believed in life after death at *Mitthi Khua* (dead man's village) and *Pialral* (paradise) somewhere beyond this world. The people who earned *Thangchhuah* in this world go to Pialral where life was luxurious, plenty to eat and no work to do, but others go to *Mitthi Khua,* where life was dull and colorless and a shadowy existence and they continue work and toil like they do in this world. (Darchhawna;2007;7). This belief in *Pialral* and *Mitthi Khua* was instrumental in shaping the norms and values of the Mizo. (Hluna;1992;19).

Mizo are very superstitious. They are afraid of dried skull of many things, like dried skull of monkey, big banyan tree, separating a family member to north and south on the same day, cutting of nails at night, etc. They belief that the superstitious acts can cause ill-fated to oneself or the other family member.

But the coming of the Christian Missionaries changed the religious belief of the people of Mizo. In no time, they converted into Christianity and observed Christian ways and celebrations, while abandoning their former religious rite, beliefs and rituals. (Lalrimawia;1995;129). The Christian Missionaries has contributed tremendous developmental works for the Mizo society. Consequent upon their work, Mizo used to have one common language, known as Mizo Tawng (Mizo Language), which unite different tribes of the society. Accordimg to the Census of India 2001, the main religious communities of Mizoram are given with Table 7.1 below.

Table 7.1: Religious Community of Mizoram

Religions	*Total*	*%*
Christians	7,72,809	87.0%
Buddhists	70,494	7.9%
Hindus	31,562	3.6%
Muslims	10,099	1.1%
Sikhs	326	0.0%
Jains	179	0.0%
Others	2,443	0.3%
Religion not stated	661	0.1%

On the influence of the Christianity and the Missionaries, the government established social institutions, including State and District Libraries. These Libraries has also play roles for the development of the people of the state in one way or the other and hence, the researcher described impact of State and District Libraries on religion and belief as follows:

1. The State and District Libraries collected different documents concerning religious belief and other related materials which can illustrated the primitive religious acts of the society.

2. The library users could understand about the religious activities of various religions through the collected documents of the libraries. This can caused changes in the religions and belief of the society. They are the most important institutions to collect and serve the society through its services on religion.

3. The superstitions of Mizo are now being driven out due to the information and knowledge provided by libraries from various sources. Library changes various belief and superstitions of the Mizo society.

Mizo are very fond of books and reading. But due to the low economic condition, many persons are not afforded to buy books from their own resources. The most important resources are library books. One of the respondents said that I saw many persons borrowing library books. During 1980s, I visited State or District libraries at least twice in a week, but now I have no much acquainted with these libraries, however. I am confident that local libraries run by YMA/NGO are very useful for the local communities. If you go to the villages, you will see that one book will be read by at least three persons in a week. None of the books in their local libraries are lying idle; at least five or six persons have gone through it. Books supplied by RRRLF though State Library Committee is very resourceful to them.

Many readers might not feel that the books they read had influence their socio-cultural life, but from the above arguments given by the respondents it is true that the library materials of State and District Libraries of Mizoram has some impact in the society. The political consciousness, social life, work culture, family life, cultural consciousness, religious belief, etc. are influence of the environment. These libraries, therefore, touch the heart of its readers and influence their livelihood. Culture has become one of the most important aspects of any community considering in terms of economy. Most of the tourist interests are culture of the society; traditional items and cultural differences form the others. By considering the economy of the society, library plays an important role in the economy of the country through its holdings and services.

The State and five District Libraries in Mizoram are treasure for storing and serving important materials to the community. These libraries collect, preserved and conserved documents relating to socio-cultural aspects of the society for future generations. They acted, as center of accessing local information needs relating to the social life of Mizo and other societies. The role played by these libraries for socio-cultural development of the society also has contributed to the educational development of the state that is explained in the next chapter in detailed.

REFERENCES

Abraham, M. Francis (2006). Contemporary sociology: An introduction to concepts and theories. New Delhi: Oxford University Press.

Challiana (1978). Pi Pu Nun. Aizawl: Trio Book House.

Darchhawna (2007). Socio-cultural and Religious History of the Mizo. *In*. PLANNER 2006 Souvenir. Aizawl: Department of Library & Informatin Science, Mizoram University.

Denisoff, R.Serge and Wahram, Ralph (1983). An Introduction to Sociology. 3rd. ed. New York: Macmillan.

Giddens, Anthony (1997). Sociology. 3rd. ed. Cambridge: Polity Press.

IFLA/UNESCO (2001). The Public Library Service. IFLA/UNESCO Guidelines for development. Munchen: K.G.Saur

Kaula, P.N. (2007). The need, structure and development of rural libraries. Proceedings of National Seminar on Legislation Based Rural Library service in India. Organised by Ranganathan Society for Book Culture, Library and Information Studies, North East Chapter on 8-10 Sept.,2007 at Imphal.

Khanna, J.K. (1987). Library and Society. New Delhi: Ess Ess Publications.

Kuper, Adam and Kuper, Jessica, *eds*. (1985). The Social science Encyclopedia. London: Rouledge.

Lalrimawia (1995). Mizoram: History and Cultural Identity(1890-1947). Guwahati: Spectrum

Lloyd,J.Meirion (nd). On Every High Hill. Liverpool: Foreign Mission Office.

Liangkhaia (2002). Mizo Chanchin. 5th.ed. Aizawl: LTL Publications.

Lorrain, James Herbert (1940). Dictionary of the Lushai Language. Culcutta: The Asiatic Society.

McVey, Kaitlin R. and Long, Laurindda Keys.(2006). Libraries in America. Span. Jan./Feb. 2006. New Delhi: American Embassy.

Ngurtinkhuma, R.K.(2005). Public Library for bridging the digital divide in Mizoram. Proceedings of 'Bridging the Digital divide". Public Library Services in North-East Region: Opportunities and Challenges. Organized by Department of Library & Information Science, Mizoram University and Raja Rammohun Roy Library Foundation, Kolkata on 19-21 May 2005 at Aizawl.

Rath, Pravakar (1996). Public Library Finance. Delhi: Pratibha Prakashan.

Sangkima(1992). Mizos: Society and Social Change. Guwahati: Spectrum.

Siama,V.L. (1978). Mizo History. Aizawl: Lalrinliana & Sons.

Trehan, G.L.(1980). Library services for a developing society. ILA Bulletin. Vol.XVI (1-2), Jan.-Jun., 1980.

Venkatappaiah, Valega.(2007). Need for a state policy for public library and information system and services. Proceedings of National Seminar on Legislation Based Rural Library service in India. Organized by Ranganathan Society for Book Culture, Library and Information Studies, North East Chapter on 8-10 Sept., 2007 at Imphal.

Public Library in India : 197-239
R. K. Ngurtinkhuma
Today and Tomorrow's Printers & Publishers, New Delhi-110 002 (India)

Chapter 7

PUBLIC LIBRARY IN EDUCATIONAL DEVELOPMENT

Library and education are two related institutions, depending on each other that cannot be separated, as book and pen or table and chair are interrelated. The State and District Libraries in Mizoram are wonderful institutions that play an important role to acquire educational information to its clients. The IFLA/UNESCO Public Library Manifesto 1994 believes in the public library as a living force for education, culture and information, and as an essential agent for the fostering of peace and spiritual welfare through the minds of men and women. Public library services are provided on the basis of equality of free access, regardless of age, race sex, religion, nationality, language, religion, or social status. All have equal opportunity to access resources provided to the entire society.

1. Meaning of Education

Idealists, the pragmatists, the naturalists, and the realist philosophers have defined education differently. Dewey defined education as, 'Education is the development of all those capacities in the individual which will enable him to control his environment and fulfill his possibilities' and Foebel also defined it as, 'a process by which child makes its internal external'. (Rai;1999;1). M.K.Gandhi expressed the meaning of education as, 'by education I mean an all round drawing out of the best in child and man, body, mind and spirit. Literacy is not the end of education not even the beginning. It is one of the means whereby man and woman can be educated. Literacy in itself is no education'. (Chandra;2004;1). Most widely accepted in the west is propounded by Plato. The meaning of education is initially available with the works of Plato. He defined education as a life-long process starting, 'from the first years of childhood and lasting to the very end of life'. Education not only provides knowledge and skills but also inculcates values, training of instincts, fostering right attitudes and habits. In his Republic, Plato pointed out that, 'true education, whatever that may be, will have the great tendency to civilize and humanize them in their relation to one another and to those who are under their protection'. (Chandra;2004;1). All the definitions of education have stated that education is the process of development. This development is most probably concern about the gradual and continuous progress of mind and body from cradle to grave, which involves character development, development of social virtues, personal creativity development, control and sublimation of basic instincts, development of a sense of community, progress of cultural and civilization, preparation for adult life, use of leisure and synthesis of national as well as international consciousness.

Education is a three-fold process of imparting knowledge, developing skills and inculcating proper interests, attitudes and values. (India.Ministry of Education). It can be, therefore, mention the three important roles of education as:

(1) Imparting of knowledge and skills,

(2) Inculcation of values, and

(3) Imparting of vocational skills.

Education is a comprehensive concept, which comprehends the knowledge obtained through different means. Education can be broadly classified into three divisions, namely, formal, informal and non-formal education. These three kinds of education can be state as below:

1) Formal Education

Formal education is provided in educational institutions according to a particular pattern by enrolling an individual for a particular course of study. (Sharma; 2004;25). The educator educates the educands according to a particular programme following a prescribed predetermine syllabus. In this formal kind of education, the educands has to attend the class to receive education at a fixed time and place and has to complete the course within a specific given period fixed in terms of years. It is a teacher-student contact education where students receive direct teaching from the teachers. The merits of formal education can be outlined as:

1) Planned with a particular end in view;
2) Limited to a specific period;
3) Well defined and systematic curriculum;
4) Given by specially qualified teachers;
5) Includes activities outside the class-room; and
6) Observes strict discipline.

2) Informal Education

Informal education complements the formal

education, without which formal education remains incomplete. Education of this type has no specific time or place at which it is provided. There is no fixed educator, syllabi, rules, and formalities. Under this kind of education, one can receive his/her education while playing in the field, talking to the family members at homes, chatting with friends, in short, everywhere. It has no end, but teaches the individual more than he can learn through formal education. An expert defined it as, 'the process by which a person imbibes attitudes, develops skills, cultivate values and acquires knowledge, without there being any organization or system about it. This would include the deliberate attempts of parents and elders in the family and community to help the young ones grow and adapt themselves to the environment. Informal education would also include all incidental learning that takes place while at work or at play and during travels- as well as spontaneous learning through films, radio, and television'. (Sharma;2004;27-28). The merits of informal education are:

1) Incidental and spontaneous;
2) Not pre-planned nor deliberate;
3) Not imparted by any specialized agency; and
4) No prescribed timetable curriculum.

3) Non-Formal Education

After the World War II, in the post colonial period new nations, one after another, scrambled for expanded and improved formal education. By the late sixties, there was a growing uneasiness that the formal education was not enough to educate the communities as the traditional two fold categories of formal education and informal education leaves a big gap. Studies by Philip Coombs and other revealed that as societies developed a third kind of education emerged which could be labeled as non-formal education. Coombs and Ahmed defined non-formal education as, 'any organized, systematic, educational activity carried on outside the framework of the formal system to provide selected types of learning to particular sub-groups in the population, adults as well as children'. (Chandra;2004;23). In non-formal education there is no institutional base for education; one educate himself/herself through courses offered by distance education mode, with the help of either other methods of learning or through self study. The three main objectives of Non-formal education are:

1) Immediate objective is the removal of illiteracy;
2) The middle range objective is the application of 'new' knowledge to resolve economic, cultural, and social problems; and
3) The long-range objective it to provide life-long education.

Non-formal education is an important aspect of educational system that can help the local youths in continuing education without disturbing their daily works. Non-formal education can be taken up in different types, such as: (Sharma; 2004;35).

1) Adult Functional Literacy Programmes;
2) Correspondence Courses;
3) Open School Studies;
4) Satellite Instructional Television Programme; and
5) Programme for the dropouts in the age group 6-14.

In India, the Central Board of Secondary Education, New Delhi started the Open School in July 1979, the first of its kind in the country. It is an institution set up to bring the flexibility and openness in the educational system and to extend educational opportunities to the weaker and disadvantaged sections of the society. The main objectives of the Open School are:

1) To offer a parallel non-formal system as an alternative to a formal schooling;

2) To provide the opportunity of education to out-of-school learners, school drop-outs, working adults, housewives and learners from disadvantaged section of the society living in remote areas of the country;

3) To offer bridge/preparatory courses for enabling learners to take up secondary level courses;

4) To offer Secondary, Senior Secondary Technical Vocational and Life-enrichment courses through distance teaching methods; and

5) To promote an open distance-learning system of education through research, publication and information dissemination.

2. Introduction of Education in Mizoram

Before the coming of the Christian Missionaries, formal education was practically not available for the Mizos. There was no written communication among the Mizos but stone inscriptions by pictures or diagrams. The missionaries started formal education and their advent to this land is the basic step for the development of the people as a whole, and without which our work will also be in complete.

1) The Coming of Christian Missionaries

The British expeditions had paved the way for the coming of the Christian missionaries to Mizoram. Even before the coming of the missionaries there had been a prophecy made by some people that the white people across the ocean would come over and that their message would be obeyed and accepted. Darphawka was one of those who prophesied this. He further said that all his daughters would have got married by the time the missionaries arrived in Mizoram. The Christian missionaries made their appearance into Mizoram not long after this vision, and by that time all of Darphawka's children were already married. (Zatluanga;1966;17). Miss Bowser also wrote that, "One Mizo from the south, Darphawka heard a voice in his dream. The voice spoke to him by saying, a great light will come from the wet and shine upon Mizo land; follow the light, for the people who bring it will be the ruling race. In the morning the man gathers his sons and friends and told them of his dream and advised them. This light may not shine in my life time, but when it comes, follow it- follow it". (Hminga;1987;44).

The Christian missionary who first set foot on Mizoram was Rev. William Williams. He came from Shella and arrived Aizawl on 20 March 1891 and returned home on 17 April 1891. He asked some of the Mizo boys to join him for education at Khasi Hills but not success. (Remthanga;1990;239). During his short stay at Aizawl for 29 days, he had an opportunity to speak to the Mizo people. He distributed cards bearing the picture of Jesus Christ and tried to influence them. He was a Welsh Calvinistic Methodist Foreign Mission working in the Khasi and Jaintia Hills. Hearing a bout the people he came to Mizoram to survey the inhabitants and to see if there would be any chance of preaching the Gospel there. (Sangkima;1992;81).

In England, a wealthy Christian, Robert Arthington, hearing of Winchester's death in the Lushai raid, became greatly burdened to send the Gospel to the fierce headhunting tribes of northeast India. So he established the "Arthington Aborigines Mission" in 1889 for this purpose. At the same time, Mr. James Herbert Lorrain, an English youth, was deeply impressed by an artist's pictorial illustration of the kidnapping of Mary Winchester, and prayed to God that he might be sent as a missionary to this tribe. (Hluna;1992;41). He left his job in December 1890, as telegraphist in London Post Office, and joined the mission and sailed towards Calcutta to work among the fierce tribes. His chum and life-long comrade and friend, Rev. Frederick W. Savidge, joined him in the following year at Brahmanbaria, a New Zealand Baptist Mission station. Rev. F. W. Savidge was a graduate and a schoolmaster before he joined the Arthington Mission. (Hminga; 1987;47). The military authorities did not allow them to enter Mizoram because the land had recently been brought under the British administration and the land was still in a very unsettle state. They waited for almost three years and during this course of time they learned some of the Mizo vocabulary and folklore by heart.

At last, the Chief Commissioner of Assam gave permission to enter the North Mizo Hills division 'entirely on their own risk'. First they came to Silchar, the headquarters of Cachar, from there they took a country boat on Boxing Day (the next day of Christmas) 1893 for Mizoram. (Lewin;1912;316). After seventeen days journey they reached Sairang, a village in Mizoram and entered Fort Aijal (now Aizawl, the capital of Mizoram state) on the 11th. January 1894 and still observed in the state as 'Missionary Day'. They settle down at Thingpuihuan tlang (now, Mizo Higher Secondary School Field).

The missionaries found Mizos very friendly, hospitable, honest, sincere, warm-hearted, intelligent, painstaking and with plenty of initiatives. (Hluna;1992;45). They are very kind and affectionate to the Mizo people and they were called as *Zo Sap* and gave Mizo name to each one of them, Rev. James H. Lorrain as *Pu Buanga* and Dr. Frederick W. Savidge as *Sap Upa.* The two missionaries, Rev. James H. Lorrain *(Pu Buanga)* and Rev. Frederick W. Savidge *(Sap Upa)* stayed for almost four years in Mizoram. Rev. David Evan Jones, a Welsh Presbyterian Mission, known as *Zosaphluia* by Mizos who arrived Aizawl on 31st. August 1897, relieved them and worked here till 1927. The second Welsh Presbyterian missionary, Rev. Edwin Rowlands, known as *Zosapthara* by Mizos, arrived Aizawl on 31st. December 1898 to join the mission work Rev. D. E. Jones and worked here till 1928. (Sangzuala;1994;49). After staying for four years together, *Pu Buanga* and *Sap Upa* left Mizoram in the same year. (Saiaithanga;1969;11). Thirty-seven Christian Missionaries worked in northern area from 1894 to 1968 and twenty-five in southern area from 1903 to 1977. The missionaries not only worked for the evangelization of the people but also for the development in other fields like education, medical, social and cultural activities as well. Their contribution for the development to the Mizo will remain. They lead the people from darkness to the light.

2) Introduction of Mizo Alphabets

In their missionary zeal, Rev. J. H. Lorrain and Rev. F. W. Savidge gave attention for the transformation of Mizo languages into a written form. Rev. James Herbert Lorrain wrote: "When we first came into contact with the Lushais at Kassalong in the Chittagong Hill Tracts in 1892, and settled amongst them at Fort Aijal in January 1894, the tribe had no written language. Years before in 1874, Lt.Col. (then Capt) Thomas Herbert Lewin, Deputy Commissioner of the Chittagong Hill Tracts, had published his 'Progressive Colloquial Exercises in the Lushai Dialect', and in 1884

Assistant Surgeon Brojo Nath Saha, Civil Medical Office of the same district, had published his 'Grammar of the Lushai Language', both of which we found extremely useful in our earliest efforts to learn words and phrases". (Lorrain; 1982;v). Their first and foremost task was to translate the Mizo language in a written form and strived to prepare Mizo Alphabets in the form of Roman scripts with the phonetic form of spelling based on the well-known Hunterian system of orthography as closely as possible. (Lorrain;1982;viii). The first Mizo Alphabets prepared by them in 1894 was as follows: (Saiaithanga;1969;9)

AW	A	B	D	E	F	G
NG	H	I	J	K	L	M
N	O	P	R	S	T	T
U	V	Z	CH			

Later, Rev. Edwin Rowlands *(Zosapthara)*, a highly qualified person, in charge of education, modified the first Mizo alphabets developed by J. H. Lorrain during their missionary work in Abors and Miris.(Lorrain;1982;viii). In *Mizo Zirtir Bu*, second edition, published in 1901 and in *English Primer-Lushai Translation* prepared by *Zosapthara*, the present Mizo alphabets was already published. The Mizo Alphabets was, however, altered by *Zosapthara* in the earlier period of his work in Mizoram from its original devised by Rev. J. H. Lorrain as follows: (Lalhruaitluanga Ralte; 2007;47).

	A	AW	B	CH	D	E	F
G	NG	H	I	J	K	L	M
N	O	P	R	S	T	T	U
V	Z						

3) Establishment of Schools

There was no formal system of education among the

Mizos before the coming of the British. The only system was 'oral education' or information passing orally from father to son or the like. *Zawlbuk,* a bachelors' house, in which all unmarried young men of the villages slept was the main center of social education. Here all men of different ages imparted education from the elders. *Zawlbuk* play an important role for the informal education in Mizo society.

The formal education was introduced to the Mizos only some years after the British occupied the land. A. Porteaus, the Political Officer, northern Mizoram wrote in 1897 that, "I desire to point out that, although it is now seven years since Aijal was occupied, nothing whatever has yet been done by Government in the way of commencing to educate the Lushais". (Sangkima;1992;85). Both the government and missionaries try to impart education among the Mizos simultaneously but later on education was taken over by the missionaries from the government for sometimes.

1) Elementary Schools

The first formal school was started at Aizawl on November 1893. This school is meant for the children of sepoys and the teacher was engaged from the Military Police havildar who received a staff allowance of Rs. 5/- per mensem in addition to his pay. It was taught in Hindi and was not available for Mizo children. (Sangkima; 1992;85). A school was also established in the southern area, Lunglei and Demagiri, in 1894 based on the contributions of Military Police and Rs. 100/- received annually from the Chittagong Hill Tract Primary Education Fund. The salary of the School Master was Rs. 25/- per month with Rs. 3 annas 8 as ration money from the school fund. (Lianzawna;1996;9).

The two Christian missionaries, Rev. J. H. Lorrain and Rev. F. W. Savidge, who had accepted education as their part of ministry, started a primary school on 2 April 1894 at Aizawl with two pupils. The school was run successfully for sometimes, but was soon closed, as they want to complete their translation work for they had to be replaced by the Welsh Missionary. (Sangkima;2002;86). Rev. D. E. Jones (Zoaphluia), who succeeded the two pioneer missionaries and taking over their works, began his work by gathering a few children and young men together, and taught them how to read and write. Sooner or later, he intended to start a school and accordingly, celebrated his twenty-eight birthday by reopening a school started by his predecessors on the 28th February 1898. (Lloyd;n.d;34). The school built with poles of solid trees, walls of bamboos, and thatch could accommodate about 50 pupils, but only 15, most of them boys, came at the beginning. The teaching was very simple and confined to the art of writing and reading. The attendance was very irregular. Some of them are coming from distant villages, carrying enough rice to last for sometimes and stayed in a small hostel build by Maj. Shakespeare, the Superintendent of the Lushai Hills. Several boys were self-support and earned their livelihood by cleaning the sepoy's utensils in their free time. The pupils after acquiring their lessons, they returned to their homes and taught the knowledge they had acquired to their friend. The statistical report submitted by Rev. D. E. Jones at the end of 1899, the number of pupils in the mission school was 56, of whom 50 were boys and 6 girls. In January 1900, Rev. Edwin Rowlands, one of the Welsh Missionaries, a gifted musician and an experienced teacher who taught for some time at Taxas in the United States took over the school from Rev. D. E. Jones. Earlier in 1899, he organized two temporary schools, one at Chhingchhip and another at Thompawnga village for a month. Modon Gopal, a Khasi missionary, who had earlier resigned from a government job and joined the mission at Mizoram, conducted a school at Thompawnga village. (Hluna;1992;54).

The missionaries wanted their pupils to run schools at different villages on trial basis. In 1901, they started schools with their pupils and appointed Thanga at Khawrihnim, Chawnga at Phulpui and Tawka at Chhingchhip. The concerned villagers on voluntary basis constructed the schools. They got their food by public contribution of many tinful of rice from the villagers as their salary. In 1902, some of the mission schoolboys started Night Schools on voluntary basis at Aizawl, Muallungthu and Chaprasi village. Consequent upon the policy of the government, the first regular village school was opened by the missionaries at Khandaih(now Phullen) in 1903, followed by other eight schools in the month of October of the same year at Khawrihnim, Phulpui, Zukbual, Luangtan, Biate, Khawreng, Hmunpui and Maite.At the end of 1903, there were 15 Lower Primary Schools in the district and Mizos on roll reached well over 400. The school was in two levels, elementary school and the advanced or training school. This division became a regular feature and in 1903, the elementary section became Lower Primary Section that had up to Class III and the advanced section became the Upper Primary section with Class V as the highest class. (Hluna; 1992; 54).

Rev. Edwin Rowland conducted the first examination in 1898 to test on knowledge of the pupils in their lessons. In 1901, Mr. Protheo, the officiating Director of Public Instruction, Assam, suggested that Garo Hills Lower Primary Examination system with certain modifications should be adopted in Mizoram for starting classes and conducting Lower Primary Examination. Major Shakespeare, the Superintendent of the Lushai Hills, of the view that the advanced system of examination may not be suitable for the infant Mizo pupils and on the line of suggestions made by Mr. Protheo, he set the second examination for the students in 1901 on the subjects of Lushai Reading and Composition and Arithmetic. Seven students attempted this examination and all of them did fairly well. (Hluna;1992;64).

Increase of primary schools and scholars resulted greater demand for the establishment of higher educational system automatically. In 1907, there were 22 primary schools with 781 students in Mizoram, and consequently, the Upper Primary School was upgraded to the status of Middle English School. By understanding the demand, Rev. Edwin Rowlands re-arranged the educational system in Mizoram as follows(Rowlands;1907;118); but, Upper Primary School was discontinued and absorbed into Middle English School making into three years course in 1929. (Laltawnga;2005;24).

Lower Primary School	-	4 years course
Upper Primary School	-	2 years course
Middle English School	-	2 years course.

Following the resolution of the Educational Officers Conference in 1913, the second middle school in Mizoram, known as Serkawn Middle School, was opened in 1913. Till 1944 only two Middle English Schools were opened in Mizoram, one at Aizawl under the Welsh Presbyterian Mission and another at Serkawn under the Baptist Mission of U.K. It is, therefore, acknowledged that the Government of Assam did not take keen interest for the establishment of Middle Schools in Mizoram.

2) Secondary Schools

There had been great demand for the opening of High School in Lushai Hills since 1926 because the door of higher education was completely closed for those who could not go out of the state for their education. By understanding the local situation, missionaries intended to open in 1929, but the Government did not permit to do so. (Lalhmuaka;1981;24). In April 1931, the Lushai Chiefs made an appeal to the Commissioner of Surma Valey and Hill Districts, Mr. J. Hezlett, to open High School at Aizawl, but he made a note in his school inspection as: (Hluna; 1992; 142)

> "I have had petition from the Lushai chiefs as king that a High School should be established in Aijal. I hardly think that it is required at present as there is undoubtedly a danger that more Lushai will be educated upto the Matriculation standard than can find employment in the district".

Mr. A.Macdonald, the new Superintendent of Lushai Hills was very pleased with the participation of Mizo people during the World War II and took initiatives for the opening of High School in Aizawl. At last, Rev. E. L. Mendus, a senior missionary, inaugurated the long awaited of High School on the 25th. February 1944 at the Young Lushai Association (YLA) Hall, Mission veng, Aijal with Rev. J. M. Lloyd as Headmaster. The school began with 56 students of Class VII. (Lalvunga; 1994;16). Depending on the transformations it had passed through, this school had been called by different names and the school was known as Mizo Higher Secondary School since 2006. The first batch of 25 students appeared at the Matriculation Examination from this School in 1948, and of whom 20 came out successfully. (Lalhmuaka: 1981:85). Later on, other High Schools were opened at Lunglei and Champhai in 1948 and 1950 respectively. (Lianzawna;1996;20). In 1996, Pre-University Course of the University was taken up by the School Education and made it as higher secondary course, Class XI and XII. Consequently, Higher Secondary Schools were started in various existing High Schools of Mizoram.

3) Higher Education

The history of higher education is Mizoram is very recent spanning over a period of less than half a century. It started with the establishment of Aijal College (now, Pachhunga University College) on 15 August 1958. It was founded and managed by a group of Mizo elders. Pu Pachhunga, the leading entrepreneur of the day donated a substantial amount of money for the college and the college was thereafter named as Pachhunga Memorial College. On April 19th. 1979, the North-Eastern Hill University adopted as a Constituent College and since then it was renamed as Pachhunga University College. Thereafter, Mizoram has a tremendous growth in higher education and colleges have been established in different areas of the state. Now, there are 25 affiliated colleges to Mizoram University. (Ngurtinkhuma;2006;21). Training Institutes, like Polytechnic, Women Polytechnic, College of Teachers Education, Industrial Training Institute, District Institute of Education and Training and Mizoram Hindi Training College were also established by the Government of Mizoram.

The Government of India and underground Mizo National Front signed the Mizoram Peace Accord on 30th June 1986, provided for a separate University in Mizoram. Subsequently, the Parliament of India passed the Mizoram University Bill in 2000 and the President of India gave his consent to it on 25th April 2000. Thereafter, the Mizoram University came into being on the 2nd. July 2001 with the joining of its first Vice-Chancellor, Prof. A..K.Sharma. From this day, the NEHU, Mizoram Campus that had functioned since October 1979 with the constituent Pachhunga University College, was automatically transferred to the Mizoram University vide the Mizoram University Act of 2000.

By re-organizing the educational system of Mizoram, the state follows the national pattern of 10+2+3. The first ten years of education comprise three stages, namely, Primary, Middle and High School. (Mahajan;1994;12). Classes I to IV constitute Primary School stage, Classes V to VII Middle School stage, Classes VIII to X High School stage. Classes XI and XII is Higher Secondary School stage and Under-graduate course, Collegiate Education, is of three years. Class IV is Primary School Leaving Certificate Examination, whereas Class VII is Middle School Leaving Certificate Examination. Class X and Class XII are High School Leaving Certificate Examination and Higher Secondary School Leaving Certificate Examination respectively. The Mizoram Board of School Education conducts these Examinations. The University conducts under-graduate and Post-graduate courses examinations. These educational stages may be shown in table 8.1 as below:

Table 8:1 : Educational stages of Mizoram

Level	*Stages*	*Classes*	*Duration*	*Examination*
Elementary	Primary School	I	One year	Promotion
		II	One year	Promotion
		III	One year	Promotion
		IV	One year	Board
	Middle School	V	One year	Promotion
		VI	One year	Promotion
		VII	One year	Board
Secondary	High School	VIII	One year	Promotion
		IX	One year	Promotion
		X	One year	Board

	Higher Secondary School	XI	One year	Promotion
		XII	One year	Board
Collegiate	Degrees	Under-graduate	Three years	University
University	Degrees	Post-graduate	Two years	University

4) Training Institutes

The Christian Missionaries worked with their full efforts for the development of the state in education. After establishing several schools, they started training schools to train the teachers with high hopes of developing their teaching skills. One-month course of training programme for the teachers was carried out in Aizawl from 1914 to 1925. Such kind of training school was also started Serkawn in southern area in 1934. These training schools were later named as Guru Training (Diploma Course), and continued until the establishment of Basic Training Center in 1953 by the Government. (Laltawnga;2005;25). Basic Training Center for the Primary School teachers and Normal Training School established in 1970 for the Middle English School teachers were upgraded into the District Institute of Education and Training in 1988. Apart from this, the Government also established some training institutes like Polytechnic, Women Polytechnic, College of Teachers' Education, Industrial Training Institute and Mizoram Hindi Training College for different training purposes.

The scenario of Mizoram Educational Institutions, teachers and students during 2005-06 is shown in the following table 8.2: (Mizoram Statistical Handbook 2006):

Table 8.2 :Mizoram Educational Institutions, Teachers and Students.

Sl.No	*Institutions*	*No. of Institutions*	*No. of Teachers*	*No. of Pupils*	*Average of Pupils per Teacher*
1	University	1	159	414	2.6
2	Colleges	25	663	7,964	12.01
3	Higher Secondary School	75	854	10,555	12.39
4	High School	484	3,700	41,610	11.24
5	Middle School	1,121	7,983	88,044	11.02
6	Primary School	1,688	5,210	1,32,046	25.34
7	Training Institutes	9	135	1,983	14.68
	Total	3,403	18,704	2,82,616	15.1

4) Administration and Organization

The Chief Commissioner of Assam, Sir J. B. Fuller visited Aizawl in February 1904. He was very much pleased by the result and administration of the Mission Schools. He, therefore, instructed the Superintendent to submit proposals for handling over of the education of Lushai Hills to the missionaries. In consultation with the Welsh Missionaries, the Superintendent's proposal was approved and from 1st April 1904, the government schools and the teaching staff were transferred to the Mission. The mission, therefore, took over the administration and supervision of primary schools from 1904 to 1952. (Lianzawna;1996;15). Subsequently, Rev. Edwin Rowlands was appointed as the Honorary Inspector of School. In 1903, Rev. J. H. Lorrain and Rev. F. W. Savidge settled at Lunglei as missionary under the Baptist Missionary Society and took up the southern area of Mizoram from the Welsh missionaries. Consequent upon the separation of Mizoram in two areas, Rev. Edwin Rowlands and Rev. F. W. Savidge took over the responsibility of Honorary Inspector of Schools for northern area and the southern area respectively. (Hluna;1992;78-79). During this period, from middle standard to upwards are under the supervision and controlled of the government.

The educational administration of Mizoram had passes through different stages. From 1952 to 1972, it was under the District Council administration of Assam with Inspector of Schools as its head. During 1972 to 1987, it was under the administration of the Union Territory Government and since 1987 to till date, under the administration of the state Government with Director as its head. The coverage of Education Department was, at the beginning, very vast. During the UT administration three departments, viz., Social Welfare, Sports & Youth Services and Industrial Training Institute had separated from this department and in 1989, the department was further trifurcated into three departments, viz., Art & Culture, Higher & Technical Education, and School Education departments. The departments of Higher & Technical and School Education departments will be further elaborated here.

1) School Education Department

The School Education Department of Mizoram covers from Primary to Higher Secondary Schools with other training institutes. Minister of School Education was the highest decision making authority and was supported by the Commissioner/Secretary to the Government of Mizoram, School Education Department and other supporting staff at the administration. For the supervision, control and direction, a Director headed the department. Joint Directors, Deputy Directors, Physical Education Officer, Research Officer,

Finance & Accounts Officer and other staff supports the Director. Further, there is District Education Officer in each of the districts to look after the Secondary Schools; and Sub-Divisional Education Officer to look after the elementary schools supported by Circle Education Officers.

i) SCERT

Mizoram SCERT was established in 1980 with Officer-on-Special Duty as its head, but its head was designated as Joint Director since 1989. The objectives of SCERT are as follows:

i) To act as an agent of change in school education and teacher education by organizing in-service training of teachers and orientation of education officers dealing with all stages of education;

ii) To act as nodal agency for all kinds of educational programmes and schemes with an aim with bringing about qualitative improvement of education at the school level;

iii) To develop curricula, instructional materials, textbooks, teacher's handbooks, teaching aids, educational films, tape slides, etc. for use in educational institutions;

iv) To provide academic support and supervision toward educational and vocational education programmes;

v) To give technical guidance and support to the District Institute of Education and Training (DIETs);

vi) To conduct research studies investigation on various educational problems;

vii) To act as clearing house for new ideas and educational practices and innovations in the state;

viii) Documentation, publication and dissemination of various educational books and journals; and

ix) To develop inter-sectoral, inter-departmental, inter-state linkages and relationships with state and educational level institutions and organizations.

ii) District Institute of Education and Training (DIET)

Presently known as DIET was established on 1st. September 1953 under the name of Basic Training Center to give training facilities for the Primary School Teacher. Another training center, known as Normal Training School for the Middle School Teachers was also established on 4th. February 1970. BY amalgamating these two training institutes, it had its name as Under Graduate Teachers Training Institute (UGTTI) on 19th. September 1974. It was renamed as Teachers Training Institute (TTI) on 1st. July 1980 and bears its present name District Institute of Education and Training since December 1988. (Sailo;1999;106).

There are two DIETs in Mizoram, one each at Aizawl and Lunglei. Since 2006, another six DIETs, known as Mini-DIET were established in another district headquarters, one each at Kolasib, Mamit, Champhai, Serchhip, Lawngtlai and Saiha. The main purpose is to provide training facilities to the working teachers of Elementary schools as well as pre-service trainees.

iii) Mizoram Board of School Education (MBSE)

The Mizoram Board of School Education established

by an Act of the Legislative Assembly in 1975 has the authority to recognized institutions/schools under the jurisdiction of School Education Department. It also prescribed and prepared textbooks for the elementary and secondary schools. It has been conducted different public examinations, such as:

a) Primary School Leaving Certificate Examination;

b) Middle School Leaving Certificate Examination;

c) Middle English School Leaving Certificate Examination;

d) High School Leaving Certificate Examination;

e) Higher Secondary School Leaving Certificate Examination;

f) District Institute of Education and Training Examination; and

g) +2 Vocational or Proficiency Certificate Examination.

The following table illustrates an abstract of HSLC and HSSLC Examination result conducted by MBSE for the last five years by Table 8.3 below:

Table 8:3: Abstract of result - HSLC & HSSLC

Sl.No.	*Name of Examination*	*Discipline*	*Year*	*No. of Candidates*	*No. of Passed*	*Passed percentage*
1	HSLC		2003	7150	2213	30.95
			2004	11414	3422	29.98
			2005	12562	5750	45.77
			2006	8787	3358	38.21
			2007	11401	5867	51.46

2	HSSLC	Arts	2003	5735	2128	37.1
			2004	5742	1919	33.42
			2005	6982	2941	42.12
			2006	3393	1968	58.01
			2007	4605	2535	55.04
		Science	2003	730	320	43.83
			2004	837	340	40.62
			2005	1408	690	49.01
			2006	1026	605	58.96
			2007	1279	691	54.02
		Commerce	2003	218	115	52.75
			2004	269	127	47.21
			2005	379	203	53.56
			2006	261	185	70.88
			2007	296	187	63.17

Consequent upon the dissolution of the Mizo District and creation of Mizoram as a Union Territory in 1972, Pawi-Lakher Region Council was split into three District Councils, namely, Lai District Council, Mara District Council and Chakma District Council. The Councils were provided with certain powers by the Sixth Schedule of the Indian Constitution and have full authority over the management of primary education within their jurisdiction. However, the education department continues to play significant administrative and academic roles in the field of primary education in the district councils, like recognizing primary schools, prescription of textbooks, curricula and syllabi, conduct of examinations, finance, etc. In fact, though the council had their own primary educational boards, the department also makes all educational rules and regulations and the powers of the district councils are restricted since the State Education Department exercises control over the final allocation of fund. (Mahajan;1994;67).

2) Higher & Technical Education Department

The department came into existence since 1989 by separating from the Education department. It looks after:

1) University and Collegiate education;

2) Teacher education at the postgraduate level;

3) Post-matric scholarship and research fellowship;

4) Hindi education;

5) Technical education; and

6) Quality education at the higher education level.

The Commissioner/Secretary to the Government of Mizoram, Higher & Technical Education supports the highest decision making authority, Minister of Higher & Technical Education, with other Officers and staff at the secretariat level. The Director of Higher & Technical Education is responsible for administration, supervision and coordination of all educational activities related to higher and technical education. Joint Director, Deputy Director and other Officers and staff assisted him. (Mahajan;1994;59).

There are nine Government Colleges (including one Teachers' Training College), twelve Deficit Colleges, one Private College, one Law College and one Nursing College under this department. These colleges are affiliated to the Mizoram University. A number of students qualified to receive their degree certificates in various disciplines from these colleges. The following table may depict number of graduates from these colleges since Mizoram University conducted various examinations of higher education within the state by Table 8.4 below:

Table 8.4 : Abstract of Under-graduate Examinations

Courses	*Category*	*2003*	*2004*	*2005*	*2006*	*2007*	*Total*
BA	Appeared	1350	1246	1164	1460	1805	7025
	Passed	801	1018	976	1214	1188	5197
	Passed %	59.33	81.7	83.84	83.15	65.81	73.97
BCom	Appeared	70	41	68	55	130	364
	Passed	49	33	64	31	27	204
	Passed %	70	80.48	94.11	56.36	20.76	56.04
BSc	Appeared	102	72	110	60	77	421
	Passed	77	56	81	57	58	392
	Passed %	75.49	77.77	73.63	95	75.32	93.11
BSc(HSc)	Appeared	16	9	13	8	24	70
	Passed	16	9	13	8	23	69
	Passed %	100	100	100	100	95.83	98.57

3. Library for Educational Development

Library service is the service to the people of a community regardless of caste, creed, religion, age, sex, language, status of education and attainment. Library and education are sister services that cannot be taken out one from the other, but go hand in hand. The primary purposes of the public library are to provide resources and services in a variety of media to meet the needs of individuals and groups for education, information and personal development including recreation and leisure. They have an important role in the development and maintenance of a democratic society by giving the individual access to a wide and varied range of knowledge, ideas and opinions. (IFLA/UNESCO;2001;2). Richard Thau, Director of Pennsauken Free Public Library stated that, "The library should be the learning place for a vibrant and diverse community, it should inspire people of all ages with the love of books, learning, reading, advancing the pursuit of knowledge, and enhancing the quality of life for all who use the library. The agency must remind itself that it is an educational, informational, and recreational entity where service is the most important variable in the give and take between library and patron". It is being increasingly realized that self-education permeates the entire life of the individual from cradle to the grave. And the most appropriate agency of continuing education for people of all ages is a public library. (Khanna;1994;9). An important institutional relationship for a public library is that with the local schools and the educational system in the service area. Types of linkages and/or forms of co-operation include: (IFLA/UNESCO;2001;38).

- Sharing resources
- Sharing staff training
- Cooperative collection development
- Co-operative programming
- Co-ordination of electronic services and networks
- Co-operation in the development of learning tools
- Class visits to the public library
- Joint reading and literary promotion
- Programme of web-awareness fro children
- Sharing of telecommunications and network

infrastructures

- Jointly arranged authors' visits

The reason for the foundation of public library is to act as an agent, which provides access to knowledge in printed and other formats to support formal and informal or non-formal education as a whole. As long as the world exists, there will be an enormous development in various fields of education due to the on going research and development. The impact of public libraries on education can be summarized as follows:

1) Self-education Center

Education has no limits. It is a universal nature, being expanded its area in different fields of studies due to the progress of research and developments. As the Bible says, "Man does not live on bread alone"(Bible); no body has enough resources for his/her formal education but needs to have free access to the resources of a library for improvement and expansion of his/her acquired education at all levels. Formal education alone is not sufficient for an overall development of one's educational pursuits. Informal education or self-education is a lifelong process and public public library should supports the continuous self-education program by providing services to the people free of charge. As an educational center, the public library has to support and promote all types of education, formal, non-formal, adult and life-long, by keeping adequate stock of documents and other information materials, print or electronics, hard or soft, and makes them available to all sections of the community. The IFLA/UNESCO Public Library Manifesto 1994 stated in its missions as, "supporting both individual and self conducted education as well as formal education at all levels". Pravakar Rath also stated that, "Some of the facets relevant to the educational impact of public libraries are – Book reviews/Book talks, Concerts (live or recorded), Craft demonstrations, Cultural exhibits, Field trips, Film showing, Formal courses, Lectures, Literacy tutorials, Reading improvement classes, Story hours, Training of volunteers. (Rath;1996;10). It should also provide opportunity for personal creative development being the social institution for life-long learning and independent decision-making. The library service as a self-education center may be observed from the words of Ms. Usha Mujoo-Munshi, Fulbright Scholar, 1996-97 as, "I was asked to make a presentation. I went to the reference desk of the library at the UMCP and asked the librarian for help. She listened to me carefully, and said 'I will see what I can do'. Next morning, before entering my room, I checked the pigeonhole to pick up any communication for me. I was amazed to find an envelope containing reprints and some references that were exactly what I was looking for. After my presentation I went to thank her personally".

2) Supporting Literacy Activities and Continuing Education

Public libraries, State or District Libraries, plays a vital role in literacy activities and movements. "Public libraries are best suited for post-literacy and continuing education programmes". (Kumar;1992). J.K.Khanna also stated that, "The most appropriate agency of continuing education for people of all ages is the public library". (Khanna;1987;9). Such libraries help literates and neo-literates to prosper their literacy developments by providing reading materials. The IFLA/UNESCO Public Library Manifesto 1994 also stated in its missions as, "supporting and participating in literary activities and programmes for all age groups, and initiating such activities if necessary".

The positive roles played by public libraries in post-literacy programmes are:

- A good collection of reading and audio-visual materials related to the life and living of neo-literates;
- A separate reading room for neo-literates, wherever possible, with good and attractive collection of reading and audio-visual materials;
- Regular provision in the library budget for procurement of reading and audio-visual materials for neo-literates;
- Competent staff with proper orientation to attend the needs of neo-literates;
- Close line with nearby literacy centers, supplying reading materials to the neo-literates through these literacy centers at the initial stage. This will help to attract the neo-literates to the regular library service;
- Group discussions and reading with neo-literates to develop reading habits among them;
- Information services to the neo-literates related to their live and living;
- Oral services to the neo-literates and illiterates to attract them to literacy and library activities.

3) Developing Reading Habits

The IFLA/UNESCO Public Library Manifesto 1994 stated in one of the missions of public library services as, "creating and strengthening reading habits in children from an early age". Adolescence are in a phase of building their personality and their interests are very varied and changeable, and need to give them to achieve their full development as individuals and citizens. "Adolescence needs special attention as many of them voluntarily stop reading at this stage of their lives. Librarians and professionals who understand the psychological and emotional growth of adolescents need to introduce them to reading through a wide range of books that are compatible with their changing interests. J.K.Khanna stated that, "Library must encourage reading at all levels and for different purposes.... Library must inculcate in the minds of individuals that reading is of far greater significance for the creation of intellectual, moral, aesthetic, social and political values, and in the context of reading, a book represents a social relationship between writer and reader, and the library has the clearest view of this relationship being a social agency'. (Khanna;1987;11).

Reading and writing are the two best means of communication techniques that can be carried out in promotion of reading habits and literacy programmes. It is a prerequisites to being and integrated and active member in the society. The public library may support such activities to promote literacy activities by making the best use of modern technology. This can be achieved by: (IFLA/ UNESCO;2001;34)

- Promoting reading
- Providing appropriate materials for those with poor literacy skills
- Working with other agencies in the community involved in combating illiteracy
- Participating in campaigns to combat illiteracy and improve numeracy
- Organizing events to promote an interest in reading, literature and media culture

- Promoting and providing training in the use of computer technology
- Promoting awareness of new developments in the media market
- Helping people to find the information they need in the appropriate format
- Co-operating with teachers, parents and other contact persons to help new citizens acquire the necessary educational skills that will help them to manage their loves in the new context.

Public libraries may serve with different priorities and qualities with special collections to the community to provide best reading materials to its clients, particularly to the young groups by serving them to have reading habits of their interests. Monica Medina Blanes stated that services for adolescents should:

1) Facilitate the transition from children's to adults' service;
2) Stimulate lifelong learning through reading and libraries;
3) Encourage the habit of reading for information and pleasure;
4) Provide instruments and skills for using information;
5) Provide collections and services for all the young adults in the community with the aim of addressing their educational, information, cultural, and leisure need.

There is a need to implement reading habits to the young adults for their educational and future livelihood. To encourage them, library services can take different steps, like collection of specialized reading materials, organizing readers club, literary club, symposia, etc.

4) Personal Creativity Development

Men are born free but in a limited way. All men need to develop his own personal creativity and pursue new interests for his survival. A library is to 'providing opportunities for personal creative development'. To achieve this, people need access to knowledge and work of the imagination. Nobody can access his information needs from his own resources but the public library can provide access, in a variety of different media, to a rich and varied store of knowledge and creative achievement, which individual cannot acquire on their own behalf. (IFLA/ UNESCO;2001;5). The contributions of a public library by colleting and disseminating information, including the community's own literature, has been a unique and still a vital function rendered for the personal development of an information seekers.

God makes man with different purposes of creativities and one has to develop in meaningful recreational activities by accessing information. The public library services can make fundamental contribution to daily survival and educational development by being directly involved in providing information to people in developing communities; for example, environment awareness programmes, AIDS awareness programmes, adult education programmes, etc. The local libraries can act as a center of personal creativity development to the local communities by giving education on different topics of their interests and local needs.

5) Research Activities

Research is an endeavor, to discover, and verify knowledge". (Khanna;1994;12). Research is the basic principle of development expanding the horizons of knowledge that is carried out generally in educational institutions. The primary basic information for a research activity is information that can be mostly accessed in a library. IFLA/UNESCO Public Library Manifesto 1994 stated that "The public library networks must be designed in relation to national, regional, research and special libraries as well as libraries in schools, colleges and universities". The public library supports lifelong learning, working with schools and other educational institutions to help students of all ages with their formal education. (IFLA/ UNESCO;2001;29).

Research activities needs basic as well as correct information from various sources that may be in primary, secondary, and tertiary to the scholars. Such information may be available in various forms; namely, books, journals, geographical sources, microfilms, Internet, etc. An individual scholar due to high cost or the other way may not acquire such documents, but library serves the user to access their information needs in various forms. A public library that serves the general public in various information materials added support to the research actions in various fields by providing their required information data. The library offers many types of specialized services to help in the advancement of research in society, such as:

1) identifying, accumulating, processing for use needed and pertinent materials speedily;

2) preparing and circulating list of latest additions;

3) evaluating an interpreting new documents and providing to the right users requisite information contained in them in the form of reviews, abstracts, tables of contents, and photocopies of excerpts;

4) maintaining highly specialized reference files and indexes;

5) conducting literature searches;

6) providing accurate, factual and relevant information to inquirers;

7) preparing bibliographies;

8) translating publications wholly or in part;

9) providing cheap and rapid means of photocopying;

10) providing quick reference and referral services; and

11) extending the limitations of its own resources by interlibrary loan, co-operative acquisitions and through such methods of bibliographical co-operation as union lists, and catalogues and the exchanging of catalogues and bibliographies. (Gates;1987;13).

6) Computer Literacy Skill and Electronic Networks

The rapid development of information technology brought huge amount of information playing a key role for the promotion of library services in an electronic environment. One of the missions of the Public Library Manifesto reads that, "Facilitating the development of information and computer skills". The notion of library has been growing very fast, automated library, Electronic library, digital library, and virtual library. Library has no limit for its growth and services, being known today as library without walls. IFLA/UNESCO Guideline for Development stated that, "Public libraries are instruments of equal opportunity and must provide a safely-net against alienation and social exclusion from technological advance by becoming the electronic doorway to information in the digital age". (IFLA/ UNESCO;2001;40).

The library should provide access to the resources of the library and other information centers through effective electronic networks at all levels from local to international. Access to the internet/world wide web should be free to the public regardless of economic means to have access to information available in an electronic form. The world is facing a digital divide, who have and have-nots or the information rich and the information poor, but library serves as a bridge by providing digital forms of information in its services to the community. The world's facing problems of an information age, such as, information explosion, price escalation of library documents, and increased cost of library documents (Sridevi; 2005;113) can be overcome through the library services. Library co-operation, Resource sharing or Internet resource sharing in the field of an education can be provided by libraries at local, regional, national or international level to access required information by the users. Libraries, therefore, by giving electronic resources and computer literacy skills can greatly enhanced services to their users by providing them with access to the collection of other libraries or information centers.

Besides, a public library service to the cause of education is extended to the special user groups. Since education has no end or limit, all men need to acquire education by one kind of educational means. Those people, who are potential users may not use library services regularly but have right to access information through its services in one or the other. They may not come to the library to access their required information, but the library services may be extended to reach those persons so that they can avail equal opportunity with others. The library should, therefore, establish ways of making library materials and services accessible to these users. Those services may include: (IFLA/UNESCO;2001;32).

- Special transport, e.g., mobile libraries, book-boats and other forms of transport to serve those living in isolated areas
- Services taken to the home of those people who are housebound
- Services taken to the factories and industrial premises for employees
- Services for those confined in institutions, e.g., prisons and hospitals
- Special equipment and reading materials for those with physical and sensory disabilities, e.g., hearing impaired and visually impaired people
- Special materials for people with learning difficulties, e.g., easy-to-read material and cassettes
- Services for immigrants and new citizens to help them to find their way within a different society and to provide access to media of their native culture
- Electronic communication, e.g., Internet catalogues.

4. State and District Libraries on Mizoram Education

Mizoram has remarkable progress in education. A Mizo alphabet was devised in 1894 and it was only 113 years since the establishment of the first school in the area. But the educational institutions have been increasing and in all together, from primary to university, there are 3403 institutions in the state. The average growth of educational institution is 30.11 per annum. By the coming of Christian missionaries, education started in one or the other. Schools established by them were soon closed down, but to support and supplement their evangelical work, Rev. D.E.Jones, one of the missionary, started Sunday school in 1898 and was affiliated to All India Sunday Sunday School Union in 1906 (Hluna;1992;198). The spread of the Gospel brought in its stride the desire for learning so that in each village where Church was planted, Sunday Schools were started initially for learning reading and writing. This immensely contributed to the rapid growth of literacy among the Mizos. (Laltawnga: 2005:24). The Sunday School played an important role in the promotion of education among the Mizos and had been the main center of learning till 1922. (Lalhmuaka;1981;53).

As a result of the contribution of the Church and the Government towards the progress of literacy, Mizoram became the second highest state in literacy following Kerala of Indian states. According to 2001 census, there were 14,841 persons of literate without educational level as a result of adult education programme, Church contribution for the educational programme and other related services rendered by the society at different levels. The following table depicts the growth of literacy in the state by Table 8.5:

Table 8.5: Literacy of Mizoram

Year	*Population*	*Literates*	*Literacy %*	*Growth rate %*
1901	82,434	771	0.93	-
1911	91,204	3,635	3.98	371.46
1921	98,406	6,183	6.28	70.09
1931	1,24,204	13,320	10.70	115.45
1941	1,52,786	29,765	19.48	123.46
1951	1,96,202	61,093	30.57	105.25

1961	2,66,063	1,17,097	44.01	91.67
1971	3,32,390	1,78,793	53.79	52.68
1981	4,93,757	2,95,685	59.88	65.37
1991	6,89,756	4,61,930	82.27	56.22
2001	8,88,573	6,61,445	88.8	43.19

Mizoram is not very much aware of library services. There were no library services at the elementary school level practically. But, the schools sometimes have library hours by visiting local libraries, particularly State and District Libraries at the District headquarters, by having story hours, by organizing art work periods or organizing quiz, etc. These programmes and sessions gave competitive mind and love of books to the students. However, some secondary schools organized school library in their school campuses. The school library was established from the Government funds or contribution of the staff and students from their library fees. But, such libraries were not managed and organized properly because of different reasons, such as:

- Lack of fund;
- Lack of trained/qualified/professional staff;
- Improper facilities;
- Inadequate collection of reading materials;
- Inadequate support/interest of the Government;
- Inadequate equipment; and
- Ignorance of library services.

Classroom teaching is not sufficient anywhere to impart further knowledge and challenge in their educational activities. Students could not gather all their educational materials from their own resources but rather need help from other institutions like libraries. As the school libraries were functioning properly due to some reasons, they have to depend on public libraries, State and District Libraries and its extension services to collect their daily information needs at maximum level.

The researcher conducted personal interview to various person on the impact of State and District Libraries in the Educational development of Mizoram and also circulated open-ended questionnaires to the respondents. Most of the opinions are of the same and such responses were given as below:

1. State and District Libraries might act as important institutions to give reading materials to the poor students by creating textbook section and providing reading materials for their educational developments. One of the respondents commented "I have seen many students in these libraries reading some books which may help them in their lessons. Some schools gave assignments or projects to their students to prepared on the basis of library materials only. This practice make the students comfortable in the library use and promote in their learning habits as well". These libraries are center of learning to the students by providing reading materials for their various components of studies. One of the respondents commented that District library provides reading materials that build his/her mental and physical development, which helps him/her in educational aspects.

2. It is an important center of learning, particularly for non-formal education system. These libraries collected various documents dealing different

subjects, which is advantage for the community as a whole. On educational aspects, State and District Libraries acted as a source of educational information, particularly in non-formal education system.

3. State and District Libraries are very important institution for the education of Mizoram by providing reading materials of different areas which students could not buy from their own resources, like General Knowledge Books, Encyclopedias, Yearbooks, etc.

4. Libraries are center of learning particularly for the research scholars. They collected various documents, which deals with culture of the society. It is the best important research center on Mizo culture and society.

5. Education as overall development of human beings. Its collections and services provide to the community is part and parcel of education and it is very purposeful for the development of livelihood.

State and District Libraries serving the people of Mizoram through its various service provided valuable documents for the educational development of the people. Since their establishment, they act as source of information for the local community to grasp ignorance. They have been providing invaluable services in the field of education and the next chapter of this study will present data analysis from the respondents of the questionnaires serve to various persons with findings out of it, which may also include about the contributions of State and District Libraries on educational development of Mizoram.

REFERENCES

Bible (1985). The Gospel according to St. Luke.4: 4 (NIV). Grand Rapids: Zondervan.

Chandra, S.S. and Sharma, Rajendra K.(2004). Principles of Education. New Delhi: Atlantic. Quoted from Platos' Republic.

Gates, J.K. (1987) Introduction to Librarianship. Quoted by J.K.Khanna. Library and Society. New Delhi: Ess Ess Publications.

Hluna, J.V. (1992). Education and Missionaries in Mizoram. Guwahati: Spectrum.

Hminga, C.L. (1987). The Life and Witness of the Churches in Mizoram. Serkawn: Literature Committee, Baptist Church of Mizoram.

IFLA/UNESCO (2001). The Public Library Service: IFLA/UNESCO Guidelines for Development. Munchen: K G Saur.

India. Ministry of Education. Education and National Development. Report of the Education Commission 1946-66. Vol.2 (8.02). New Delhi: National Council of Educational Research and Training, 1966.

Khanna, J.K. (1994). Library and Society. 2nd ed. New Delhi: Ess Ess Publications.

Kumar, Krishan.(1992). Role of Public Libraries in the Promotion of Literacy. *Library Herald,* 30(2-4), Jul.1991 -- Jan.1992.

Lalhmuaka (1981). Mizoram Zirna lam Chhinchhiahna (The records of Zoram education). Aizawl: Tribal Research Institute.

Lalhruaitluanga Ralte.(2007). A AW B Tobul. *Lengzem,* March 2007.

Laltawnga, R.(2005). Landmarks in the (early) Development of Education in Mizoram. SCERT Silver Jubilee Souvenir Magazine 1980 – 2005. Aizawl: SCERT.

Lalvunga, K.C.(1994). Mizo High School. Government Higher Secondary School, Aizawl - Golden Jubilee Souvenir (1944-1994).

Lewin, Lt.Col.Thomas H. (1912). A Fly on the Wheel. Aizawl: Tribal Research Institute.

Lianzawna. C. (1996). Mizoram Education Chanchin. Aizawl: H.Rokhumi.

Lloyd, J. Merion (n.d). On Every High Hill. Liverpool: Foreign Missions Office.

Lorrain, James Herbert (1982). Dictionary of the Lushai Language. Calcutta: Asiatic Society.

Mahajan, Baldev, Majumdar, Srilekha and Lallura, F (1994). Educational Administration in Mizoram: Structures, Processes and Future Prospects. New Delhi: NIEPA.

Ngurtinkhuma, R.K.(2006). College Library Scenario in Mizoram. Fourth Convention of PLANNER Souvenir 2006. Aizawl: Department of Library & Information Science, Mizoram University.

Rai, B.C. (1999). Theory of Education: Sociological and philosophical basis of education. Lucknow: Prakashan Kendra.

Rath, Pravakar (1996). Public Library Finance. Delhi: Pratibha Prakashan.

Remthanga, H and Lalbiaktluanga (1990). Kohhran Chanchin. Aizawl: Synod Publication Board.

Rowland, Rev. Edwin. (1907).School Thu- Middle English. *Chanchinbu,* July 1907.

Saiaithanga (1969). Mizo Kohhran Chanchin. Aizawl: Regional Theological Literature Committee.

Sailo, Pasena.(1999). District Institute of Educational and Training. Mizoram Literacy Souvenir 1999. Aizawl: Directorate of School Education.

Sangkima (1992). Mizos: Society and Social Change 1890-1947. Guwahati: Spectrum.

Sangzuala, Upa C.(1994). Kohhran Chanchina Hunbi Pawimawh te. Mizoram Gospel Centennial Jubilee -1994 Souvenir. Aizawl, Mizoram Presbyterian Church Synod.

Sharma, Sashi Prabha (2004). Basic Principles of Education. New Delhi: Kanishka Publishers.

Sridevi, J and Vyas, Shalini (2005). Library and Society. New Delhi: Shree Publishers and Distributors.

Zatluanga (1966). Mizo Chanchin. Aizawl: Khuma Printing Press.

Public Library in India : 241-289
R. K. Ngurtinkhuma
Today and Tomorrow's Printers & Publishers, New Delhi-110 002 (India)

Chapter 8

DATA ANALYSIS AND FINDINGS

1. Data Analysis

Analysis of data is one of the most important mechanisms to find out the result of any research work. To wind up research problems, researcher has to organize and collect various data from various sources, which can lead to logical findings and conclusion. Data collection can be done by various methods depending upon the research problem. Analysis of data should be scientific in nature and easily understandable in presentation, so that there will be no fallacious or inappropriateness in the research result. This chapter presents the analysis of data collected from various sources of information that could match with the research problems and objectives so as to derive reasonable findings. On the basis of the received questionnaires, the researcher could carry out the analysis of data with the help of tables and charts/graphs as explained below.

The following data is basically analyzed on the research activities carried out through structured questionnaires covering different areas and most of the respondents belong to various levels, such as:

1) Users of State Library, Aizawl;

2) Users of District Libraries at Aizawl, Lunglei, Saiha, Kolasib and Champhai;

3) Students of University, College and Secondary Schools; and

4) Academicians and intellectuals of the state.

The scheduled questionnaires were sent to various corners of the state. All together, 600 questionnaires were circulated to different type of users and out of which 404 responses were received which constitutes 76.33% in total. Therefore, the total population of this questionnaire is, unless otherwise mentioned specifically, 404 and the present study is carried out in various approaches. Some of the questionnaires were served at premises of the State and District Libraries, particularly among the library users. Collection of data through questionnaire was carried out during the month of March-April 2007. The respondents have been classified into different categories and analyzed to find out the problems of the research on different heads, viz., by age group, by gender, by educational qualifications, by occupation, by library membership.

The study covers altogether six public libraries, viz., one State Library and five District Libraries serving the people of Mizoram. Table 9.1 as below has been illustrated covering six public libraries under study along with their year of establishment.

Table 9.1: Name of Library and Year of establishment

Sl.No.	*Name of Libraries*	*Year of establishment*
1	State Library, Aizawl	1974
2	District Library, Aizawl District, Aizawl	1969
3	District Library, Lunglei District, Lunglei	1975

4	District Library, Saiha District, Saiha	1975
5	District Library, Kolasib District, Kolasib	1980
6	District Library, Champhai District, Champhai	1982

Data is analyzed with the help of five different categories to get the correct corresponding findings of the study. The five categories by which data are analyzed are:

1) Age group;
2) Occupation;
3) Educational Qualifications; and
4) Gender.

1. Library Membership

Generally library serves the members to locate their required information on different areas. In the case of public libraries, it covers all the community irrespective of race, caste, religion, sex, and age. Books are issued to the library members only.

1) Library Membership by Age :

The data from the questionnaire in regards to the Members of State and District Libraries by age group has been reflected in Table 9.2 supported. Library membership is presented in various categories to get the proper situation of the study. In this data analysis, N= 404, where 'N' signifies the total respondents.

Table 9.2: Members of State and District Libraries by age group

N=404

Age group	*State Library*	*District Library*	*Both*	*None*	*Total*
Below 18	-	24(5.94%)	-	82(20.29%)	106(26.24%)
19 – 30	7(1.73%)	48(11.88%)	21(5.19%)	72(17.82%)	148(36.63%)
31 – 40	14(3.46%)	31(7.67%)	6(1.48%)	29(7.17%)	80(19.81%)
Above 41	7(1.73%)	20(4.95%)	5(1.23%)	38(9.40%)	70(17.32%)
Total	28(6.93%)	123 (30.44%)	32(7.92%)	221(54.7%)	404(100%)

While analyzing the above table it was revealed that, out of the total population of 404, only 6.93% were the members of the State Library, while 30.44% of District Library and 7.92% as members of both State and District Library. It is further revealed that, 54.7% were none of the library member from the respondents. Hence, it could be seen that more than half of the populations were not the members of either of the libraries.

State Library members are 6.93%, this is due to the fact that it is located at Aizawl and its members are from Aizawl City only. The services rendered by State Library were not reaching other parts of the state, as there is no extension service to the rural areas. Again, 30.44% are members of the Five District Libraries of Mizoram, who utilizes the services of the library for their information through books or documents.

Going by age group, 36.63% members were between 19-30 years of age while 26.24% of library members were below 18 years of age, whereas, 19.81% members belong to the 31-40 age group and 17.32% members belong to above 41 years of age.

2) Library Membership by Gender:

Library membership by gender group has been tabulated under Table No.9.3.

Table 9.3: Library membership by gender group

N=404

Gender Group	*State Library*	*District Library*	*Both*	*None*	*Total*
Male	20	78	32	130	260
	(4.95%)	(19.30%)	(7.92%)	(32.17%)	(64.35%)
Female	8	45	-	91	144
	(1.98%)	(11.13%)	-	(22.52%)	(35.64%)
Total	28	123	32	221	404
	(6.93%)	(30.44%)	(7.92%)	(54.7%)	(100%)

Table 9.3 was analyzed in respect of Library membership by gender group and it was revealed that, there are more male members than female. The male membership has gone up to 4.95% in State library and 19.3% in District Libraries whereas only 7.92% were in both libraries. In the case of female, 1.98% was State Library members and 11.13% in District Libraries, but there were no library members in both of the libraries. Altogether, 6.93% were State Library members and 30.44% of District Libraries and 7.92% belong to the members of both the categories of libraries whereas 54.7% do not belong to the members of either of the library out of the total respondents.

3) Library Membership by Occupation:

Membership of various occupations has also been analyzed from data received. The library membership by occupation has been depicted in Table 9.4 below

Table 9.4: Library membership by occupation

N=404

Occupation	*State Library*	*District Libraries*	*Both*	*None*	*Total*
Student	2	47	10	121	180
	(0.49%)	(11.63%)	(2.47%)	(29.95%)	(44.55%)
Service	20	48	10	66	144
	(4.95%)	(11.88%)	(2.47%)	(16.33%)	(35.64%)
Sefl-employed	-	12	4	14	30
		(2.97%)	(0.99%)	(3.46%)	(7.42%)
Others	6	16	8	20	50
	(1.48%)	(3.96%)	(1.98%)	(4.95%)	(12.37%)
Total	28	123	32	221	404
	(6.93%)	(30.44%)	(7.92%)	(54.7%)	(100%)

By occupation, out of the 404 respondents, 11.63% are District Library members, 2.47% are both the library members and 0.49% are State Library members from students. 11.88% of service personals are District Library member and 4.95% are State Library members, whereas only 2.47% are member of both the libraries. Service persons claim the highest number in library membership in District Libraries, followed by student having 11.63%. Self-employed and other category of persons were not very fond of library membership, which can be assumed that they have no time to access information from the libraries that may be due to their daily works or engagements.

The Total membership of State and District Libraries from the above Graph may be illustrated with the help of the following Graph No. 9(1).

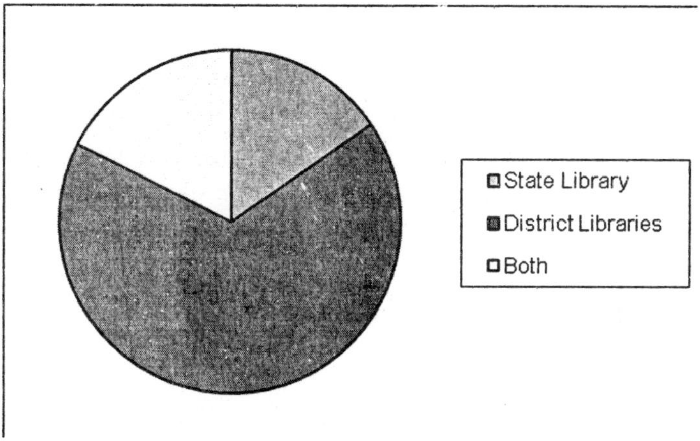

Graph 9(1): Library membership

By analyzing the State and District Library membership in Mizoram, it can be concluded that in comparison of the state literacy, i.e. 88.8% being the second highest in Indian states, library membership is very low. Some of the principal reasons of poor membership of State and District Libraries in Mizoram are as follows:

1) Lack of library awareness programs to the general community and students as well;

2) Poor facility of library services to provide user interests at different levels of information;

3) Inadequate library services to meet the present challenge in terms of ICT and other related communication era;

4) Ignorance about the services of the public libraries to the local community;

5) Poor collection of libraries to access local information needs;

6) Library location and building; etc.

However, State and District Libraries, being local information gateways, the next point will discuss about the frequency of library visits by different community of the society to access information needs which can be shown in table and charts.

2. Frequency of Library Visit

One of the most important criteria for the evaluation of a library services can be carried out from its visitors. A library may have big and sophisticated infrastructure with good collection of documents and other materials or with the latest ICT applications but if there are no library users or visitor, all those materials do not carry of much importance. Library users are one of the trinity of libraries, viz., books, staff and users/readers. Users/readers play a crucial role to study the impact or importance of a library for the peoples it serves. If library serves very well to its clients, the users will visit frequently and they will not turn away from it. To assess the impact of State and District Libraries for the local community, it is adequate to know the frequency of library visit by the local community to access their information needs is essential.

1) Frequency of Library Visit by Age Group:

Frequency of library visits by age group has been presented in Table 9.5 as below.

Table 9:5: Frequency of library visits by age group

N=404

Age Group	*Daily*	*Weekly*	*Monthly*	*Occasionally*	*Total*
Below 18	4(0.99%)	26(6.43%)	13(3.21%)	63(15.59%)	106(26.23%)
19 - 30	10(2.47%)	42(10.39%)	13(3.21%)	83(20.54%)	148(36.63%)
31 – 40	9(2.22%)	22(5.44%)	10(2.47%)	39(9.65%)	80(19.8%)
Above 41	4(0.99%)	14(3.46%)	6(1.48%)	46(11.38%)	70(17.32%)
Total	27(6.68%)	104(25.7%)	42(10.39%)	231(57.17%)	404(100%)

The above Table 9.5 depicts that among the total number of library users, 57.17% visits the library occasionally while 25.7% visit weekly and 10.39% visit monthly. Further, while analyzing the above data with respect to age group, the users in between 19 to 30 and 31 to 40 constitute 2.47% and 2.22% respectively visiting library daily while, 0.99% are age group of above 41 and below 18 years. It is interesting to note that, the age group in between 19 to 30 is the highest i.e, 10.39% visit the library weekly.

2) Frequency of Library Visit by Gender:

The library visitors by their gender group have been represented in the following Table 9.6:

Table 9.6: Frequency of library visit by gender group

N=404

Gender	*Daily*	*Weekly*	*Monthly*	*Occasionally*	*Total*
Male	20 (4.95%)	80 (19.80%)	28 (6.93%)	131 (32.42%)	260 (64.36%)
Female	7 (1.73%)	24 (5.94%)	14 (3.46%)	100 (24.75%)	144 (35.64%)
Total	27 (6.68%)	104 (25.7%)	42 (10.39%)	231 (57.17%)	404 (100%)

While making a comparison to male with female gender group, it could be revealed that the male visitors are higher than the female visitors in all the frequency of library visits, such as, daily, weekly and monthly. When 4.95% male visits library daily, only 1.73% female visit library; 19.8% male visit weekly, 5.94 female visit library; further, when there are 6.93% monthly visitor of male, there are 3.46% female and 32.42% are male occasional visitor, 24.75% are female occasional visitor. The analysis reveals that, frequency of library visit is more in male visitors than female visitors, which affirm that male readers have more accessibility of information provided by State and District Libraries in Mizoram than female readers.

3) Frequency of Library Visit by Educational Qualification:

The frequency of library visits by users has been also shown in Table 9.7 with respect to their educational qualifications.

Table 9.7: Frequency of library is by educational qualifications

N=404

Qualification	*Daily*	*Weekly*	*Monthly*	*Occasionally*	*Total*
Under Metric	6 (1.48%)	18 (4.45%)	4 (0.99%)	30 (7.42%)	58 (14.35%)
HSLC	14 (3.46%)	45 (11.13%)	24 (5.94%)	51 (12.62%)	134 (33.17%)
Graduate	5 (1.23%)	21 (5.19%)	6 (1.48%)	90 (22.27%)	122 (30.2%)
Post-Graduate	2 (0.99%)	20 (4.95%)	8 (1.98%)	58 (14.35%)	90 (22.27%)
Total	27 (6.68%)	104 (25.7%)	42 (10.39%)	231 (57.17%)	404 (100%)

Educational qualifications have been categorized into four groups, such as, Under-matric, HSLC, Graduate and Post-Graduate. On analysis, it could be established that, HSLC pay the highest among the other groups visiting libraries daily by 3.46%, weekly by 11.13%, and monthly by 5.94%. By taking the whole analysis, only 6.68% respondents' visit State and District Libraries daily, this is very low in comparison to 57.17% of occasionally visitors. The monthly visitors of libraries are 10.39%, which can be considered as reliable being one-fourth of the total population.

The frequency of library visits depict that library users are very little in the government run six public libraries in Mizoram. Frequency of library visits by total respondents may be shown with the help of the following Graph 9(2).

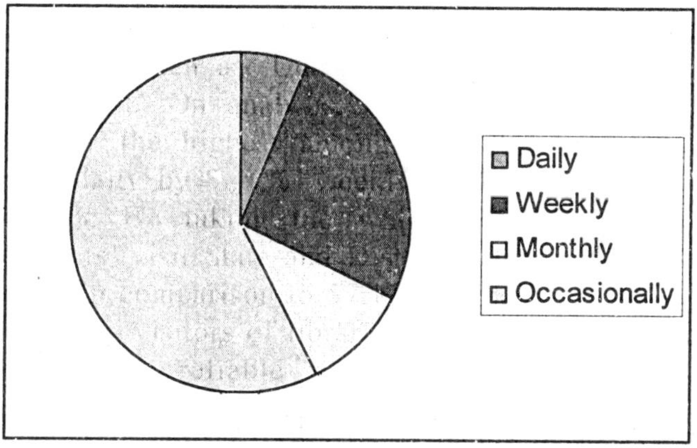

• *Graph 9(2): Frequency of library visits by respondents*

3. Purpose of Library Visits

Public library, State or District Libraries, is a place where all local community persons can access their information needs through different means of services. Library members or non-members of the locality have the opportunity to access the library services irrespective of race, culture, sex, religion or caste.

1) Purpose of Library Visit by Gender:

The purpose of library visits by gender groups has been illustrated with the help of the following Table 9.8:

Table 9.8: Purpose of library visit by gender

N=404

Gender Group	*To read books*	*To read periodicals*	*To borrow books*	*Others*	*Total*
Male	96	36	102	26	260
	(2.37%)	(8.91%)	(25.24%)	(6.44%)	(64.36%)
Female	24	10	101	9	144
	(5.94%)	(2.47%)	(25%)	(2.22%)	(35.64%)
Total	120	46	203	35	404
	(29.7%)	(11.39%)	(50.24%)	(8.66%)	(100%)

From the above table, it is clearly describe that for male and female readers the main purpose of library visit is to borrow book both constituting 25.24% and 25% respectively, and is followed by 8.91% in the case of male to read periodicals and 5.94% to female to read books. There are more female visiting library for the purpose of books in the library.

2) Purpose of Library Visit by Educational Qualifications:

The purpose of State and District Library visit by

educational qualifications can also be analyzed from the following Table 9.9:

Table 9.9 Purpose of library visit by educational qualification

N=404

Educational Qualification	*To read books*	*To read periodicals*	*To borrow books*	*Others*	*Total*
Under-Matric	17 (4.2%)	8 (1.98%)	23 (5.69%)	10 (2.47%)	58 (14.35%)
HSLC	51 (12.62%)	16 (3.96%)	48 (11.88%)	19 (4.7%)	134 (33.17%)
Graduate	28 (6.93%)	8 (1.98%)	86 (21.28%)	-	122 (30.2%)
Post-Graduate	24 (5.94%)	14 (3.46%)	46 (11.38%)	6 (1.48%)	90 (22.27%)
Total	120 (29.7%)	46 (11.39%)	203 (50.24%)	35 (8.66%)	404 404(100%)

The above table depicts that 4.2% of under-matric, 12.62% of HSLC, 6.93% of Graduate and 5.94% Post-graduates visitors go to the state and district library to read books. HSLC have the highest percentage due to the fact that books are the main sources of their educational information. Out of the total respondents, there are only 11.39% visiting libraries for the purpose of periodicals whereas 29.7% are to read books. Among the graduates, 6.93% are to read books, 1.98% for periodicals, and 11.38% to borrow books. Most of the post-graduate users visit libraries to borrow books having 11.38% and only 3.46% are to read periodicals in the library.

3) Purpose of Library Visit by Occupation:

The following Table 9.10 represents data of purpose of library visit by occupation and the same has been analyze below:

Table 9.10: Purpose of library visit by occupation

N=404

Occupation	*To read books*	*To read periodicals*	*To borrow books*	*Others*	*Total*
Student	54	8	100	18	180
	(13.36%)	(1.98%)	(24.75%)	(3.96%)	(44.55%)
Service	42	20	65	17	144
	(10.39%)	(4.95%)	(16.08%)	(4.2%)	(35.64%)
Sefl-employed	10	14	6	-	30
	(2.47%)	(3.46%)	(1.48%)		(7.42%)
Others	14	4	32	-	50
	(3.46%)	(0.99%)	(7.92%)		(12.37%)
Total	120	46	203	35	404
	(29.7%)	(11.39%)	(50.24%)	(8.66%)	(100%)

The above table illustrates that out the total respondent, 13.36% of students visit the State and District Library to read books, which is 30% among the student respondent. Consultation of periodicals is low, only 1.98% of total respondent (4.44% of students group) are for periodical consultations. 24.75% student of total respondents visit library to borrow books. Clearly we can see that service persons more consulted periodicals than students. Out of the total respondents only 4.95% of service persons visit library for periodicals. This shows that service persons are much interested in the latest information through periodicals than students. Other categories of persons that may include pensioners, politicians, social workers, etc. visit libraries mainly to borrow books constituting 7.92%; some of them to read books in the library and only few of them, 0.99% consulted periodicals. The overall data of the above table is represented by Graph 9(3) below:

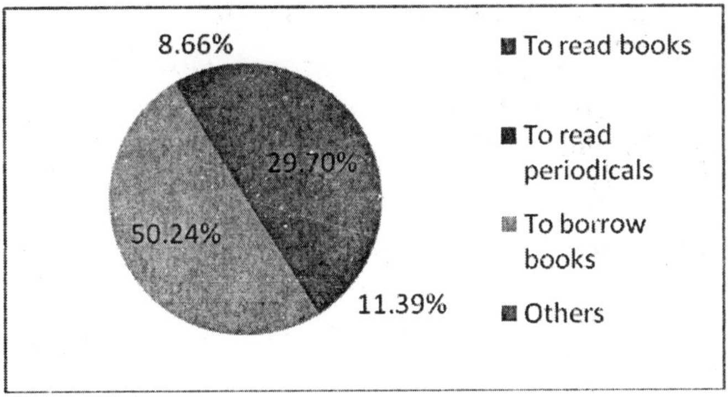

Graph 9(3): Purpose of library visit by respondents

4. Approaches of the Library

Public libraries are regarded as local gateway of information, which can be accessed by local community to quench their information thirst. At the same time, human beings have different information needs depending upon their personal interests. Library users are of different approaches in the library to locate or accessed their interest through different means of documents. The approach of the entire library users are of different, but their approaches are to quench their information needs in one kind or the other.

Library users are of different in nature, works or business, but, in an information age, all have to acquire certain kind of information, which can help him in his/her personal field. The approaches of student and businessman, military person and professional officer may be different in nature. Therefore, all library users, married or unmarried, student or research scholar, children or adult have their information needs and hence the following tables depict the different approaches of the State and District Library users.

1) Approaches of Library by Age Group:

The approaches of State and District Library by various age group is presented by data received from the respondents and is illustrated in Table 9.11:

Table 9.11: Approaches of library by age group

N=404

Age group	*Social Inform.*	*Cultural Inform.*	*Educational Inform.*	*Recreation/ Leisure*	*Others*	*Total*
Below18	3	2	49	38	14	106
	(0.74%)	(0.49%)	(12.12%)	(9.4%)	(3.46%)	(26.23%)
19 - 30	23	8	81	20	16	148
	(5.69%)	(1.98%)	(20.04%)	(4.95%)	(3.96%)	(36.63%)
31 - 40	20	8	22	13	17	80
	(4.95%)	(1.98%)	(5.44%)	(3.21%)	(4.2%)	(19.8%)
Above41	22	-	26	15	7	70
	(5.44%)	-	(6.43%)	(3.71%)	(1.73%)	(17.32%)
Total	68	18	178	86	54	404
	(16.83%)	(4.45%)	(44.06%)	(21.28%)	(13.36%)	(100%)

The above table, supported by Graph, represents approaches of various library users by their age group. Below 18 years of age approaches the State and District Libraries generally for their educational information being they are in school going children. The approaches for social or cultural information are only 0.49% of the total respondents to below 18 years. Among the 19-30 years of age, 20.04% are for educational information, whereas 4.95% are for recreation or leisure. Between 19-30 years of age, 5.69% library users approach for social information, which is high enough in comparison to below 18 years of age. 6.43% of above 41 years of age approaches library for educational information that is highest in this group and followed by 5.44% of social information. To 31-40 age group, 5.44% approach for educational information and is highest in this group.

2) Approaches of Library by Gender:

The following Table 9.12 demonstrates the approaches of State and District Library by gender group and data has been analyzed:

Table 9.12: Approaches of library by gender group

N=404

Age group	*Social Inform.*	*Cultural Inform.*	*Educational Inform.*	*Recreation/ Leisure*	*Others*	*Total*
Male	61 (15.09%)	13 (3.21%)	94 (23.26%)	42 (10.39%)	50 (12.37%)	260 (64.36%)
Female	7 (1.73%)	5 (1.23%)	84 (20.79%)	44 (10.89%)	4 (0.99%)	144 (35.64%)
Total	68 (16.83%)	18 (4.45%)	178 (44.06%)	86 (21.28%)	54 (13.36%)	404 (100%)

Out of the total respondents, 15.09% of male approaches State and District Libraries for social information, whereas only 1.73% female approaches for the same information. The approaches of these two levels of public libraries, i.e. State and District Library by male and female are quite in balance. It is affirm that male is more interest for social information than female. Male are more interested in public libraries to access their information needs in educational (23.26%) than female (20.79%). More female group approaches libraries for recreation/leisure (10.89%) than male users (10.39%).

3) Approaches of Library by Educational Qualifications:

The next Table 9.13 illustrates data of State and District Library approaches by educational qualifications as receive from respondents and the same has been analyzed below to get clear picture in this regard.

Table 9.13: Approaches of library by educational qualification

N=404

Educatinal qualifications	*Social Inform.*	*Cultural Inform.*	*Educational Inform.*	*Recreation/ Leisure*	*Others*	*Total*
Under-Matric	10 (2.47%)	4 (0.99%)	17 (4.2%)	9 (2.22%)	18 (4.45%)	58 (14.35%)
HSLC	27 (6.68%)	4 (0.99%)	42 (10.39%)	36 (8.91%)	24 (5.94%)	134 (33.17%)
Graduate	20 (4.95%)	4 (0.99%)	67 (16.58%)	17 (6.68%)	4 (0.99%)	122 (30.2%)
Post Graduate	11 (2.72%)	5 (1.23%)	52 (12.87%)	14 (3.46%)	8 (1.98%)	90 (22.27%)
Total	68 (16.83%)	18 (4.45%)	178 (44.06%)	86 (21.28%)	54 (13.36%)	404 (100%)

Among the four groups of State and District Library approaches, educational information has the highest purpose from various occupations. Out of the total respondents, 4.2% of Under-matric, 10.39% of HSLC, 16.58% of Graduates and 12.87% of post-graduates visit libraries for the purpose of educational information. In total, only 4.45% visit Public libraries for the purpose of cultural information. Again, 6.68% of HSLC and 4.95% of graduates approached for social information. The approaches of total respondents in illustrated with Graph 9(4) below:

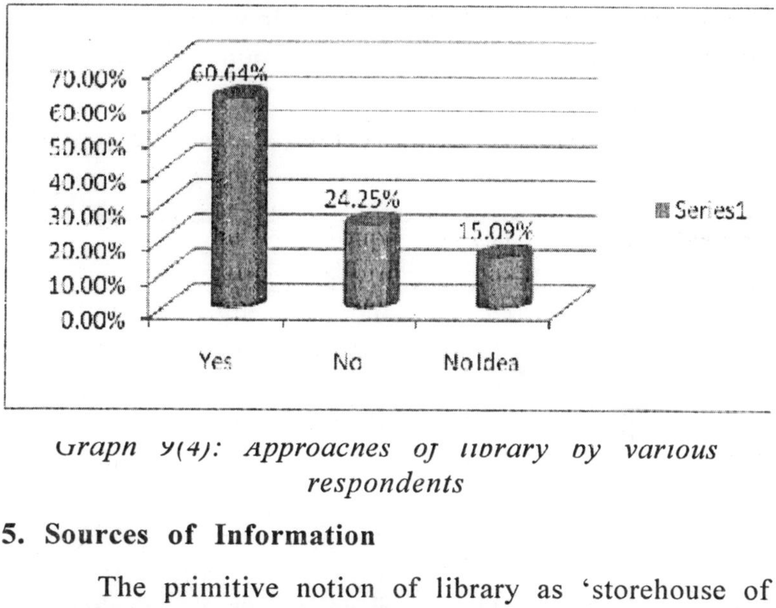

Graph 9(4): Approaches of library by various respondents

5. Sources of Information

The primitive notion of library as 'storehouse of books' is also now considered as 'source of information'. We should not think of a library, being public, academic or special, to hold only books and some periodicals and journals. Library being a source of information for its client collect and arranges different means of communication materials for the users. Latest ICT equipments are also part of the means of accessing information in a knowledge society. Books, viz., reference books, textbooks, novels, etc., periodicals and journals, newspapers, computer files, VCD/DVD, microfiche/microfilms, Audio-Visuals, etc. are part and parcel of information materials that are suppose to be available in the libraries.

1) Source of Information by Age Group:

To understand the main sources of information of State and District Library users, the researcher analyzes data from questionnaire on five points, viz., books, journals, Audio-visual, and others. The following Table 9.14 represents data on sources of information by age group:

Table 9.14: Sources of Information by age group

N=404

Age Group	*Books*	*Journals*	*Audio visual*	*Others*	*Total*
Below 18	76	17	4	9	106
	(18.81%)	(4.2%)	(0.99%)	(2.22%)	(26.23%)
19 - 30	90	45	3	10	148
	(22.27%)	(11.13%)	(0.74%)	(2.47%)	(36.63%)
31 – 40	52	25	-	3	80
	(12.87%)	(6.18%)		(0.74%)	(19.8%)
Above 41	34	30	-	6	70
	(8.41%)	(7.42%)	-	(1.48%)	(17.32%)
Total	252	117	7	28	404
	(62.37%)	(28.96%)	(1.73%)	(6.93%)	(100%)

The above table, supported by graph, depict that book is the main source of information in the State and District Libraries to the age group of below 18 years. Out of the total respondents, 18.81% of this age group use library books for their main source of information, which is very high in comparison to the second source, Journals being only 4.2%.

To the age group of 19-30 years of age, books is again the main source of information being 22.27% and followed by Journals being 11.13%, that is only half of the later. Again, for 31-40 age group, book is still the main source of information in the library, being 12.87% and followed by Journals, 6.18% only. But, for the age group of 41 above, books and Journals have contributed as source of information from the library constituting 8.41% and 7.42% respectively. Hence, the researcher avows that books are the main source of information to all those age groups in State and District Library as a whole.

***2) Source of Information by Educational Qualifications*:**

The following Table 9.15 and also represented data collected from the respondent on sources of information in State and District Library by educational qualifications:

Table 9.15: Sources of Information by educational qualifications

N=404

Edicatopmal Qualifi.	Books	Journals	Audio visual	Others	Total
Under Matric	30 (7.42%)	23 (5.69%)	2 (0.49%)	3 (0.74%)	58 (14.35%)
HSLC	96 (23.76%)	24 (5.94%)	3 (0.74%)	11 (2.72%)	134 (33.17%)
Graduate	58 (14.35%)	52 (12.87%)	2 (0.49%)	10 (2.47%)	122 (30.2%)
Post Graduate	68 (16.83%)	18 (4.45%)	- -	4 (0.99%)	90 (22.27%)
Total	252 (62.37%)	117 (28.96%)	7 (1.73%)	28 (6.93%)	404 (100%)

The above table affirms that 7.42% of Under-matric mainly depends on books for their source of information and is followed by journal constituting 5.69% out of the total respondents. By taking HSLC, 23.76% depend on books and 5.94% of journals; among the graduates, 14.35% on books and 12.87% on journals; and to post-graduates, 16.83% on books and 4.45% on journals form the total respondents. By analyzing data, all the categories of educational qualification mainly used books as their main source of information having 62.37% and is followed by journal constituting 28.96%.

3) Source of Information by Occupation:

The following Table 9.16 represent data received from respondents on sources of information in State and District Library by occupation is analyzed as below:

Table 9.16: Sources of Information by occupation

N=404

Occupation	*Books*	*Journals*	*Audio Visual*	*Others*	*Total*
Student	128 (31.68%)	28 (6.93%)	7 (1.73%)	17 (4.2%)	180 (44.55%)
Service	84 (20.79%)	50 (12.37%)	-	10 (2.47%)	144 (35.64%)
Self employed	10 (2.47%)	19 (4.7%)	- -	1 (0.24%)	30 (7.42%)
Others	30 (7.42%)	20 (4.95%)	-	-	50 (12.37%)
Total	252 (62.37%)	117 (28.96%)	7 (1.73%)	28 (6.93%)	404 (100%)

The above table depicts that 31.68% of students form the total respondents used books as the main source of information in the State and District Libraries, whereas only 6.93% used journals; and to the service persons, 20.79% used books and 12.37% on journals. To self-employed persons, 4.7% relied on journals and is followed by books constituting 2.47% and to other group of respondents, 7.42% on books and 4.95% on journals. In all these categories of information, a book mostly provided information to the library users and is followed by journals. The whole data may be represented with the following Graph 9(5):

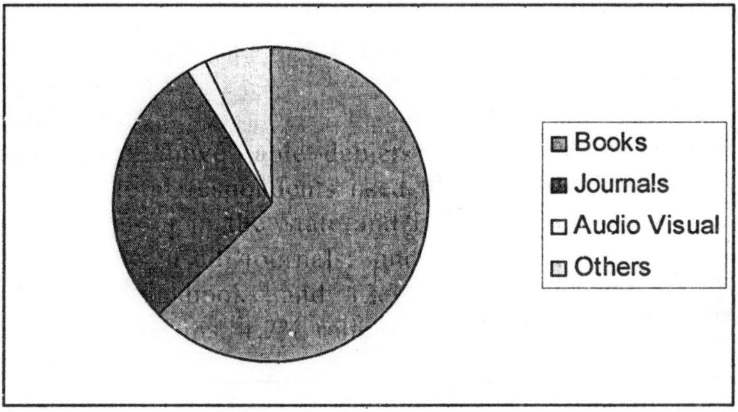

Graph 9(5): Sources of Information by library users

6. State and District Libraries as Local Information Center

State and District Libraries as local center of information has purpose to serve the community in their pursuit of knowledge. The services of these libraries are provided on the basis of equality of access for all, irrespective of age, race, sex, religion, nationality, language or social status. Under this topic the researcher is going to present the services provided by the state and district libraries of Mizoram from the data collected from questionnaire provided for the purpose. The presentation and analysis will be in the form of table and charts and interpretation of the same will follows.

The State and District Libraries has also a particular responsibility to collect local information and make it readily available. It also acts as memory of the past by collecting, conserving and providing access to material relating to the history of the community and of individuals. The State and District Libraries, therefore, has a key role in collecting, organizing and exploiting information, as well as providing access to wide range of information sources. In advanced countries, some of the public libraries provide space for information kiosks and telecentres, organizes seminars and workshops on how to use Internet. State and District Libraries as local center of information is to serve its clients in providing their information queries.

Table 9.17: State and District Libraries as local information center by occupation

N=404

Occupation	*Yes*	*No*	*No Idea*	*Total*
Student	94(23.26%)	46(11.39%)	40(9.9%)	180(44.55%)
Service	94(23.26%)	31(7.67%)	19(4.7%)	144(35.64%)
Self-employed	25(6.18%)	5(1.23%)	-	30(7.42%)
Others	32(7.92%)	16(3.96%)	2(0.49%)	50(12.37%)
Total	245(60.64%)	98(24.25%)	61(15.09%)	404(100%)

The above table clearly depict that 23.26% of student group are of the opinion that State and District Library as local center of information, but 11.39% do not agree, whereas, 9.9% have no idea. To service persons, 23.26% agree and 7.67% are against it from the total respondents. 6.18% of self-employed persons do also agree and to other group of occupants, 7.92% agree and 3.96% do not agree. All the categories of occupations, agree that public library as local information center.

2) State and District Libraries as Community Information Center by Gender:

Date received from respondents on State and District Libraries as community information center by gender is given under Table 9.18 below:

Table 9.18: State and District Libraries as local information center by gender

N=404

Gender	*Yes*	*No*	*No Idea*	*Total*
Male	165(40.84%)	58(14.35%)	37(9.15%)	260(64.35%)
Female	80(19.8%)	40(9.9%)	24(5.94%)	144(35.64%)
Total	245(60.64%)	98(24.25%)	61(15.09%)	404(100%)

The above table declared that out of the total respondents, 40.84% male affirms State and District Libraries as local information center; but 14.35% do not agree and 9.15% have no idea. To male respondents, it is undoubtedly clear that public library is the local center of information. By taking female responses, 19.8% agree; 9.9% do not agree and 5.94% have no idea in this respect; however, it is avow that female respondents agree State and District Library as local center of information.

By taking the whole respondents, 60.64% affirms

State and District Libraries as local center of information, 24.25% do not agree and 15.09% have no idea. This declaration is shown under Graph 9(6) as below:

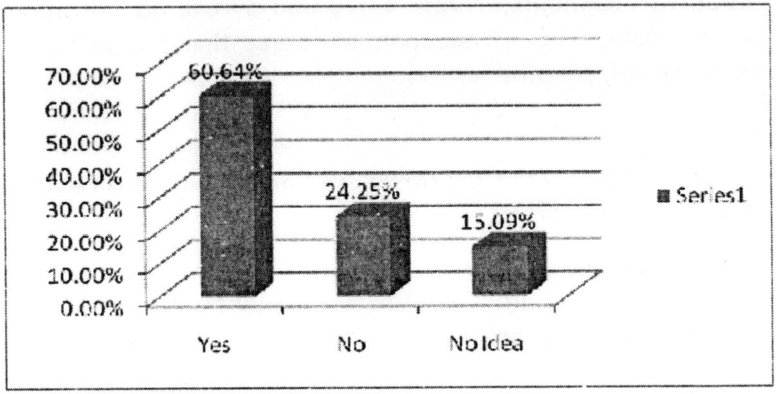

Graph 9(6): State and District Libraries as local information center

7. State and District Libraries as Depository of Local Information Needs

The services of the state and district libraries, being a part of public library, are designed to facilitate and invite use of resources and satisfy the reading goals of individuals of all ages and groups. The services provided, for the best result, should provide resources to cater information needs of the users for the benefit of the community in one way or the other.

1) Depository of Local Information Needs by Age Group:

The following Table 9.19 demonstrates data from received respondents on State and District Library as local information need by age and has been analyzed accordingly.

Table 9.19: Libraries as depository of local information needs by age group

N=404

Age group	*Yes*	*No*	*No Idea*	*Total*
Below 18	34(8.41%)	40(9.9%)	32(7.92%)	106(26.23%)
19 – 30	47(11.63%)	86(21.28%)	15(3.71%)	148(36.63%)
31 – 40	34(8.41%)	30(7.42%)	16(3.96%)	80(19.8%)
Above 41	24(5.94%)	32(7.92%)	14(3.46%)	70(17.32%)
Total	139(34.4%)	188(46.53%)	77(19.05%)	404(100%)

The above table clearly shows that available resources in the state and district libraries in Mizoram are not much beneficial to cater local information needs for 19-30 years of age. To this age group, 21.28% declared that they do not deposit enough information, but 11.63% are happy with the collections. But, for age group 31-40, 8.41% avow that they provide enough information whereas 7.42% do not agree. To the above 41, 7.92% are not happy with the deposits of State and District Libraries, but 5.94% are happy with the collections. By taking the total data of respondents, 46.53% stated that public library deposits are not sufficient for local information, whereas 34.4% agree of the deposits provided to its clients.

2) Depository of Local Information Needs by Gender:

The following Table 9.20 show data of State and District Library as depository of local information needs by gender:

Table 9.20: Libraries as depository of local information needs by gender

N=404

Gender Group	*Yes*	*No*	*No Idea*	*Total*
Male	105(25.99%)	114(28.21%)	45(11.13%)	260(64.36%)
Female	34(8.41%)	74(18.31%)	32(8.91%)	144(35.64%)
Total	139(34.4%)	188(46.53%)	77(19.05%)	404(100%)

The above table affirms that 25.99% male of the total respondents declared State and District Libraries do not deposit local information needs whereas 28.21% do not agree to. By taking female respondents, 18.31% seconded male gender group by stating public library do not deposit local information needs, and only 8.41% are against to this statement. By taking the whole data, 46.53% follow the above declaration.

3) Depository of Local Information Needs Occupation:

Table 9.21 of the following data represents declaration of various occupants on State and District Library as depository of local information needs and the analysis is below:

Table 9.21: Libraries as depository of local information needs by occupation

N=404

Occupation	*Yes*	*No*	*No Idea*	*Total*
Student	53(13.11%)	87(21.53%)	40(9.9%)	180(44.55%)
Service	59(14.6%)	60(14.85%)	25(6.18%)	144(35.64%)
Self employed	6(1.48%)	21(5.19%)	3(0.74%)	30(7.42%)
Others	21(5.19%)	20(4.95%)	9(2.22%)	50(12.37%)
Total	139(34.4%)	188(46.53%)	77(19.05%)	404(100%)

The above table illustrates the statement of the various occupants on State and District Libraries as depository of local community information center. Among students, 13.11% of the total population agreed State and District Libraries deposit local information needs whereas 12.53% do not agree. To self-employed persons, 5.19% do not agree and 1.48% is against them. The gap among the other group of occupants that 5.19% of the total respondents feel public library deposits local information needs whereas only 4.95% do not agree.

By taking the total responses, 34.4 % of the total population agrees State and District Libraries as depository of local community information needs, whereas 46.53% do not agree and 19.05% have no idea. This is illustrated with the following Graph 9(7):

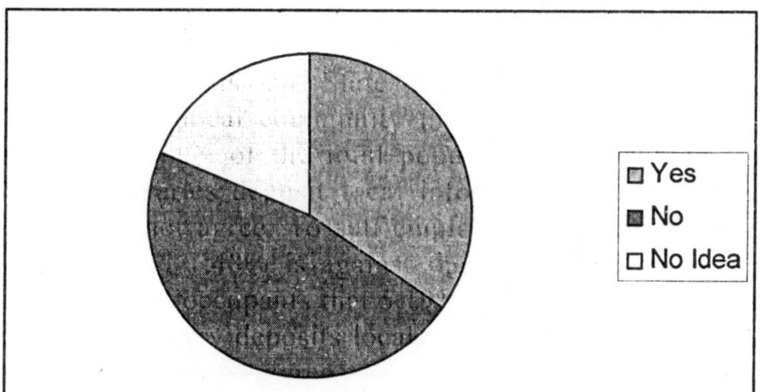

Graph 9(7): Libraries as depository of local information needs

8. State and District Libraries on Educational Development

It is earlier stated that education has no ends. Life

is full of education from cradle to grave. The learning process may be through formal or informal education, by which one can impart knowledge in one field or the other. In this sense, scholars argue it that education and libraries are the two side of the same coin, one cannot be separated from the other. Library is the basic principle and root of education. Educational systems are, sometimes, changing and the present study will confine to the present system.

1) Life Long Learning Center by Age Group:

Table 9.22 that illustrates data on State and District Libraries as life long center by age has been analyzed:

Table 9.22: Library supports life long learning by age

N=404

Age Group	*Yes*	*No*	*No Idea*	*Total*
Below 18	50(12.37%)	42(10.39%)	14(3.46%)	106(26.23%)
19 - 30	48(11.88%)	76(18.81%)	24(5.94%)	148(36.63%)
31- 40	32(7.92%)	27(6.68%)	21(5.19%)	80(19.8%)
Above 41	37(9.15%)	28(6.93%)	5(1.23%)	70(17.32%)
Total	167(41.33%)	173(42.82%)	64(15.85%)	404(100%)

From the above table, it can be declared that 12.37% of below 18 years of age agree State and District Libraries as life long learning center whereas 10.39% of the total respondents against them. Likewise, 31-40 age group declared that State and District Libraries as life long learning center, constituting 7.92% 'Yes' and 6.68% 'No' and above 41 age have the same conclusion having higher percentage of respondents 'Yes' to 'No'. But, for age group 19-30, State and District Libraries cannot be regarded as life long learning center; 18.81% of the total respondents against the later while 11.88% support the later statement.

***2) Life Long Learning Center by Occupation*:**

The following Table 9.23 illustrates data of State and District Libraries as life long learning center by occupation:

Table 9.23: Library supports life long learning by occupation

N=404

Occupation	*Yes*	*No*	*No Idea*	*Total*
Student	77(19.05%)	76(18.81%)	27(6.68%)	*180(44.55%)*
Service	54(13.36%)	64(15.85%)	26(6.43%)	*144(35.64%)*
Self-employed	6(1.48%)	20(4.95%)	4(0.99%)	*30(7.42%)*
Others	30(7.42%)	13(3.21%)	7(1.73%)	*50(12.37%)*
Total	167(41.33%)	173(42.82%)	64(15.85%)	404(100%)

The above table described that 15.85% of service persons do not agree State and District Libraries as life long learning center, whereas 13.36% agree and 6.43% have no idea. 4.95% of self-employed persons also do not agree as life long learning center while 1.48% agree. On the contrary, 7.42% of other categories of occupants agree and 3.21% do not agree State and District Libraries as life long learning center. The whole data can be supported and represented with the following Graph 9(8):

9. Formal and Non-formal Education Center

Public library, as peoples' university and local gateway to knowledge, provides basic condition for life long learning independent-decision making to the community. It is a living force for education, and an essential agent for fostering of peace and spiritual welfare among people. State and District Library, being public library system serves the community by providing knowledge to the general and specific in both formal and non-formal education.

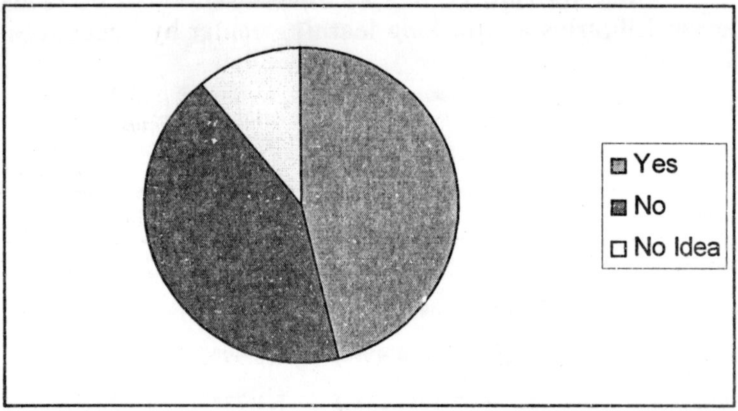

Graph 9(8): Library supports life long learning

1) Formal and Non-formal Education Center by Educational Qualification:

The next Table 9.24 represents data of respondents on State and District Libraries as a center of formal and non-formal education by occupation and has been analyzed below:

Table 9.24: Library as center of formal and non-formal education by educational qualifications

N=404

Educational Qualification	*Yes*	*No*	*No Idea*	*Total*
Under-matric	49(12.12%)	5(1.23%)	4(0.99%)	58(14.35%)
HSLC	114(28.21%)	11(2.72%)	9(2.22%)	134(33.17%)

Graduate	91(22.52%)	18(4.45%)	13(3.21%)	122(30.2%)
Post Graduate	84(20.79%)	4(0.99%)	2(0.49%)	90(22.27%)
Total	338(83.66%)	38(9.41%)	28(6.93%)	404(100%)

The above table affirms that 12.12% of the under-metric respondents agree State and District Library as the center of formal and non-formal education, whereas 1.23% does not agree. But the difference between 'Yes' and 'No' is quite high. Likewise, 28.21% of HSLC respondents affirm libraries as center of formal and non-formal education system. Again, 22.52% and 20.79% of both graduates and post-graduate respondents say 'Yes' respectively. On the other hand, 2.72% of HSLC, 4.45% of graduates and 0.99% of post-graduate respondents assured themselves that State and District Libraries are not a center of formal and non-formal education. In total, 83.66% of total respondents agree that State and District Libraries as center of formal and non-formal education, but 9.41% does not agree to that point, and still then, 6.93% have no idea about the statement.

2) Formal and Non-formal Education Center by Gender:

The following Table 9.25 signify data of respondents on State and District Libraries as formal and non-formal education center by gender and is analyzed to get the conclusion in this regards:

Table 9.25: Library as center of formal and non-formal education by gender

N=404

Gender	*Yes*	*No*	*No Idea*	*Total*
Male	252(62.37%)	3(0.74%)	5(1.23%)	260(64.36%)
Female	86(21.28%)	35(8.66%)	23(5.69%)	144(35.64%)
Total	338(83.66%)	38(9.41%)	28(6.93%)	404(100%)

The above table affirms that State and District Libraries is a center of formal and non-formal education for the society. Out of the total population, 62.37% of male and 21.28% of female respondents affirms this statement. On the other hand, 0.74% of male and 8.66% of female respondents do not agree to this statement; only 1.23% and 5.69% of male and female do not have idea respectively. This data is represented with Graph 9(9) below:

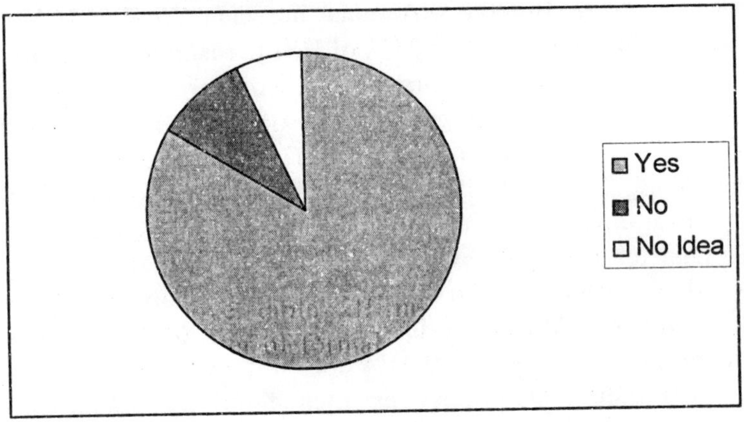

Graph 9(9): Library as formal and non-formal education center

10. State and District Libraries on Socio-cultural Development

State and District Libraries were established to meet not only educational programs of a country, but also to serve as recreation and information center of the society. An important role of State and District Libraries is to preserves the cultural heritage of the human race as represented by books and other documents. It functions as a cultural center of the society and promotes awareness of cultural heritage, appreciation of the arts and literature. It also provides cultural development of individual and social group. State and District Libraries may pay special attention to the children by providing special programmes or sections to foster creativity and reading habits. It should also extend special services or extension services to reach the disadvantaged sections of the society by providing specific materials in their respective way of life. Its services should cover all sections of the society irrespective of race, sex, religion, status or community.

1) Promoter of Social Life by Gender:

State and District Libraries of Mizoram have been served the state for more than twenty-eight years, its services were not much aware among the society as a whole. The social life of a nation is always influence by different factors. Library is one of such elements. The following Table 9.26 data is received and analyzed from respondents on State and District Libraries as promoter of social life by gender:

Table 9.26: Library as promoter of social life by gender

N=404

Gender group	*Yes*	*No*	*No Idea*	*Total*
Male	93(23.01%)	102(25.24%)	65(16.08%)	260(64.36%)
Female	24(5.94%)	76(18:81%)	44(10.89%)	144(35.64%)
Total	117(28.96%)	178(44.05%)	109(26.98%)	404(100%)

The above table depicts the declaration of the respondents on library contribution for the society as promoter of social life. Out of the total respondents, 25.24% of male affirms State and District Libraries do not promote social life, but 23.01% were against the later statement.

Likewise, 18.81% of female from the total respondents declared that it does not promote social life whereas 5.94% avow it promotes and 10.89% have no idea. By taking the whole picture, the researcher, therefore, conclude that the contributions of State and District Libraries, particularly state and district libraries of Mizoram, do not have much contribution for the promotion of social life of the community.

2) Promoter of Social Life by Educational Qualifications: Library as promoter of social education by educational qualifications has been tabulated under Table No.9.27 and is analyzed below:

Table 9.27: Library as promoter of social life by Educational Qualifications

N=404

Qualifications	*State Library*	*District Libraries*	*Both*	*None*	*Total*
Under Matric	-	23	3	32	58
		(5.69%)	(0.74%)	(7.92%)	(14.35%)
HSLC	11	46	11	66	134
	(2.72%)	(11.38%)	(2.97%)	(16.33%)	(33.18%)
Graduate	7	27	8	80	122
	(1.73%)	(6.68%)	(1.98%)	(19.8%)	(30.2%)
Post Graduate	10	27	10	43	90
	(2.47%)	(6.68%)	(2.47%)	(10.64%)	(22.27%)
Total	28	123	32	221	404
	(6.93%)	(30.44%)	(7.92%)	(54.7%)	(100%)

From the above table, it is clear that HSLC which has contributed 33.18% has highest as library as promoter of social life followed by Graduate, 30.2%, Post Graduate 22.27% and lowest in HSLC having 14.35% only. By analyzing the whole picture, 41.75% of the total respondents agreed State and District Libraries as promoter of social life, but 36.36% do not agree whereas 21.97% have no idea. Therefore, the researcher affirms that State and District Libraries is the promoter of social life to the Mizo community. The following diagram illustrates this total picture with Graph 9(10).

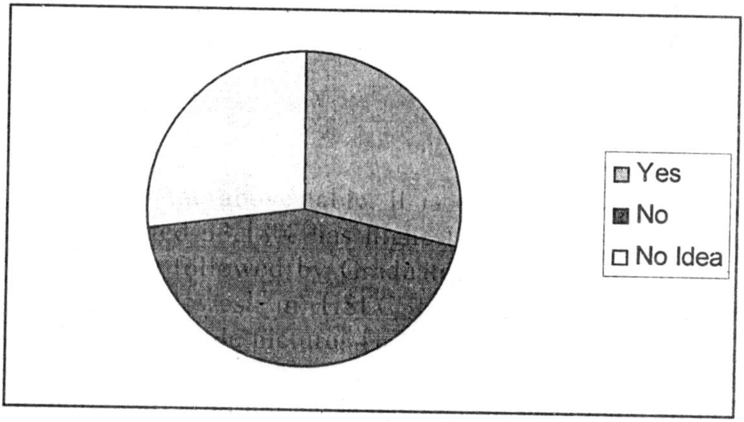

Graph 9(10): Library as promoter of social life

11. Preservation of Cultural Heritage

It is also stated earlier that State and District Libraries are center and preservation of cultural heritage. It does not preserve but also promotes through its activities or services render to the general community. In this regard, it can organize different programmes, like music concerts, dances, dramas, painting competition for children, exhibition of painting, etc.

1) Library as Preservation of Cultural Heritage by Age Group:

The following Table 9.28 is the representation of data receives from the respondents on library as preservation of cultural heritage by age and the same is analyzed as follows.

Table 9.28: Library as preservation of cultural heritage by age group

N=404

Age group	*Yes*	*No*	*No Idea*	*Total*
Below 18	30(7.42%)	31(7.67%)	25(6.18%)	106(26.23%)
19 – 30	71(17.57%)	42(10.39%)	35(8.66%)	148(36.63%)
31 – 40	44(10.89%)	13(3.21%)	23(5.69%)	80(19.8%)
Above 41	32(7.92%)	26(6.43%)	12(2.97%)	70(17.32%)
Total	177(43.81%)	132(32.67%)	95(23.51%)	404(100%)

The above table depicts State and District Libraries as promoter and preservation of cultural heritage. Out of the total population, 17.57% of 19-30 age group agreed and 10.39% does not agree to the statement, whereas 8.66% have no idea. Age group of 31-40 are also of the opinion that State and District Libraries as center of cultural heritage, 10.89% agree and only 3.21% does not agreed. According to below 18 years of age group, 7.42% of respondents declared State and District Libraries as center and promoter of cultural heritage, but 7.67% of them do not agree to that statement. The whole picture clearly affirms State and District Libraries as promoter and cultural heritage by constituting 43.81% as 'Yes' and only 32.67% against it.

2) Library as Preservation of Cultural Heritage by

Gender:

Table 9.29 represents data on State and District Libraries as preservation of cultural heritage is analized below:

Table 9.29: Library as preservation of cultural heritage by gender group

N=404

Gender	*Yes*	*No*	No Idea	*Total*
Male	120(29.7%)	78(19.3%)	62(15.34%)	260(64.35%)
Female	57(14.1%)	54(13.36%)	33(8.16%)	144(35.64%)
Total	177(43.81%)	132(32.67%)	95(23.51%)	404(100%)

The above illustrations clearly represent that out of the total respondents, 29.7% of male affirms State and District Libraries as preservation of cultural heritage, whereas 19.3% do not agree, and 15.34% have no idea. To female respondents, 14.1% agreed as male respondents, but 13.36% do not agree and 8.16% have no idea. In this regard, female has the same conclusion with male respondents. By taking the whole picture, State and District Libraries as preservation of cultural heritage, 43.81% of total respondents agreed, 32.67% do not agree and 23.51% have no idea to the statement, which is represented with Graph 9(11) below:

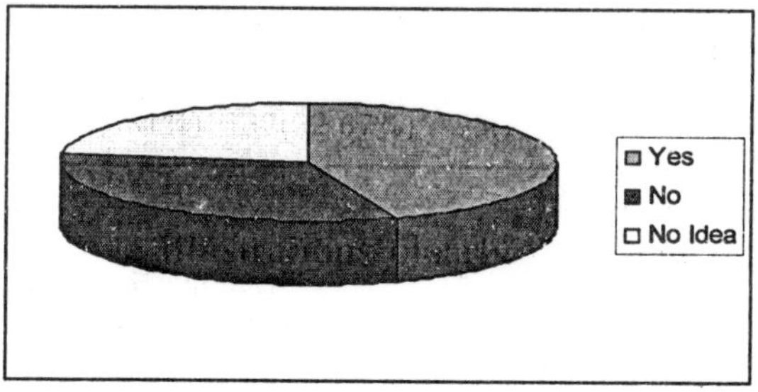

Graph 9(11):Library as preservation of cultural heritage

12. Development of Personal Creativity

It is also discussed earlier that State and District Libraries provide opportunity for personal creative development. It organizes service to stimulate the imagination and creativity of children young people. By developing love of books and reading habits among the community, the State and District Libraries creates well-informed educated citizens of the future. Some public libraries of the world use cassettes to distribute information on hygiene, health, animal husbandry and other topics relevant to people's daily life. Health campaigns, nutrition class are also organized for community. The State and District Libraries of Mizoram are also to provide some creativity programme or activities to educate the community, particularly children and youth groups to develop their creativity in their daily life.

1) Personal Creativity Development by Age Group:

The following Table 9.30 is data received from respondents on State and District Libraries as creativity development by age. The data is being analyzed below:

Table 9.30: Library as personal creativity by age group

N=404

Age group	*Yes*	*No*	*No Idea*	*Total*
Below 18	61(15.09%)	16(3.96%)	29(7.17%)	106(26.23%)
19 – 30	91(22.52%)	27(6.68%)	30(7.42%)	148(36.63%)
31 – 40	47(11.63%)	15(3.71%)	18(4.45%)	80(19.8%)
Above 41	50(12.37%)	16(3.96%)	4(0.99%)	70(17.32%)
Total	249(61.63%)	74(18.31%)	81(20.04%	404(100%)

The above table affirms that 15.09% of total respondents of below 18 years of age, declared State and District Libraries as personal creativity development; and 22.52% from 19-30 age group, 11.63% from 31-40 age group and 12.37% from above 41 age group. At the same time, 3.96% of below 18 years, 6.68% of between 19-30 age group, 3.71% of between 31-40 age grcup and 3.96% of above 41 age group says that State and District Libraries do not provides opportunity for personal creative development.

2) ***Personal Creativity Development by Gender***: Table 9.31 of the following illustrates data received from respondents on State and District Libraries as personal creativity development by gender and is being analyzed to get research result:

Table 9.31: Library as creative development by gender

N=404

Gender Group	*Yes*	*No*	*No Idea*	*Total*
Male	161(39.85%)	54(13.36%)	5(1.23%)	260(64.36%)
Female	88(21.78%)	20(4.95%)	36(8.91%)	144(35.64%)
Total	249(61.63%)	74(18.31%)	81(20.04%	404(100%)

The above table depicts that 39.85% of male and 21.78% of female affirms State and District Libraries as personal creative development of the local community, whereas 13.36% of male and 4.95% of female were against the statement. In total, 61.63% of respondents stated that State and District Libraries provides opportunity for personal creative development, but 18.31% of respondents are against the statement and 20.04% do not contribute their ideas. By analyzing the whole picture of the above data it can be represented with the help of Graph 9(12) as below for visual analysis.

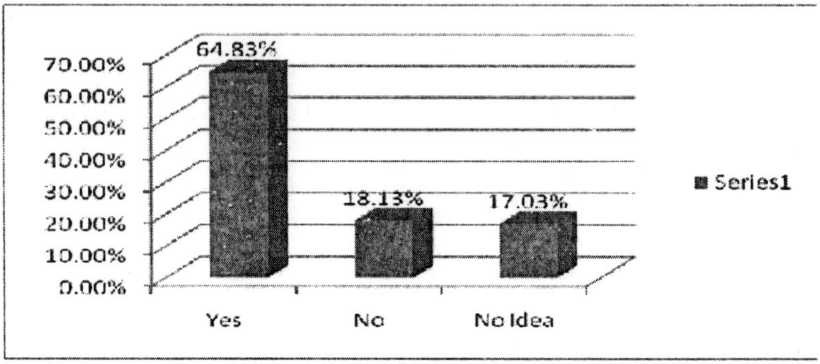

Graph 9(12): Library as creative development

13. State and District Libraries as a Place of Recreation and Leisure Interests

State and District Libraries is also regarded as a meeting place of local community at their leisure time to access information at various levels. It helps to develop understanding and strengthens democratic spirit and culture by appreciation of the differences in language, religion, customs and manners. It is a democratic institution, having the progress of the society as its prime mission. It also provides to one and all a harmless and elevating use of leisure.

1) State and District Libraries as a Place of Recreation and Leisure Interests by Age Group:

The following Table 9.32 representing data on State and District Libraries as a place of recreation and leisure interest by age group. It is analyzed below for the exhaustive research result.

Table 9.32: Library as a place of recreation and leisure interest by age group

N=404

Age group	*Yes*	*No*	*No Idea*	*Total*
Below 18	103(25.49%)	3(0.74%)	-	106(26.23%)
19 – 30	133(32.92%)	8(1.98%)	7(1.73%)	148(36.63%)
31 - 40	73(18.06%)	6(1.48%)	1(0.24%)	80(19.8%)
Above 41	60(14.85%)	10(2.47%)	-	70(17.32%)
Total	369(91.33%)	27(6.68%)	8(1.98%)	404(100%)

From the above table it is declared that 25.49% of below 18 years of age group respondents agree State and District Libraries as a place of recreation and leisure interests; on the other hand 0.74% of them do not agree. Among the age group of 19-30 years of age, 32.92% agree and 1.98% does not agree from the total respondents. By looking the age group of 31-40 years, 18.06% joins the idea of the later group and 1.48% does not. The senior group of above 41 year of age has also the same idea that 14.85% of them agree and 2.47% were against them. By looking the whole picture, it is affirm that 91.33% of the total respondents agree and 6.68% does not, and 1.98% has no idea on the State and District Libraries as a place of recreation and leisure interests.

2) State and District Libraries as a Place of Recreation and Leisure Interests by Occupation:

Table 9.33 below represents data received from respondents on State and District Libraries as a place of recreation and leisure interests by occupation fro the local community.

Table 9.33: Library as a place of recreation and leisure interest by occupation

N=404

Occupation	*Yes*	*No*	*No Idea*	*Total*
Student	159(39.35%)	18(4.45%)	3(0.74%)	180(44.55%)
Service	134(33.17%)	5(1.23%)	5(1.23%)	144(35.64%)
Self-employed	30(7.42%)	-	-	30(7.42%)
Others	46(11.38%)	4(0.99%)	-	50(12.37%)
Total	369(91.33%)	27(6.68%)	8(1.98%)	404(100%)

The above table clearly depicts that State and District Libraries as a place of recreation and leisure interest. Out of the total respondents, 39.35% of student group, 33.17% of service persons, 7.42% of self-employed persons and 11.38% others agreed State and District Libraries as a place of recreation and leisure interest. On the other hand, 4.45% of students, 1.23% of service, and 0.99% of others does not agreed. By looking the table, it is clear that all the respondents of self-employed group agree to the point. By analyzing the data, it is assured that State and District Libraries as a place of recreation and leisure interest

By analyzing the total data, it is clear that State and District Libraries act as a place of recreation and leisure interest for the local community by constituting 91.33% 'yes' and 6.68% 'no' and only 1.98% has no idea. This data can be illustrated with the help of the following Graph 9(13):

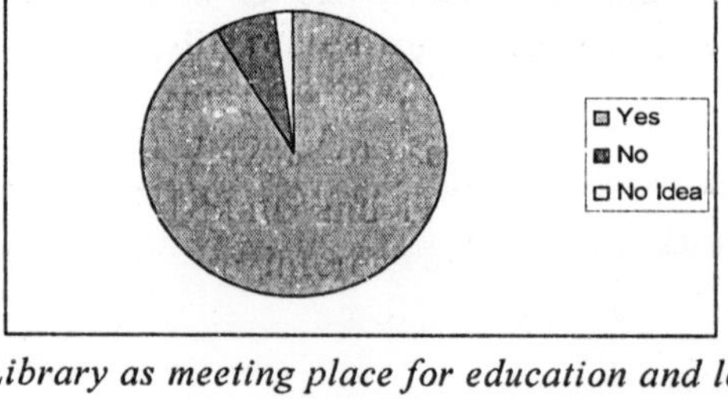

Graph 9(13): Library as meeting place for education and leisure interest

2. Findings:

The study reveals that State and District Libraries in Mizoram are engaged in the routine functions to meet the information needs of the community. Mizoram being the second highest literacy state in India and fast developing in the field of education, most of these libraries are having inadequate infrastructure and provide day-to-day services to meet the readers demand. There can be various reasons for which these libraries could not cope up with other developed libraries in providing different kinds of information to the community. As stated earlier, public library being a local gateway of information, they should abreast with latest developments to provide and bridge the gap between the information rich and information poor in education and socio-cultural development of the state.

From the preceding study on the problem stated, the researcher can draw the following specific findings on the basis of data collected, analyzed and interpreted:

1. There are two categories of Government established public libraries in Mizoram, viz., State Library and District Library. The State Library, located in the capital of the state and one each District Libraries at the district headquarters of Aizawl, Lunglei, Saiha, Kolasib and Champhai. Three districts, namely Mamit, Serchhip and Lawngtlai do not have district library.

2. At present, all the State and District Libraries, except Saiha District Library, do not have their own building and housed in a rented building; State Library and Kolasib District Library buildings are under construction.

3. None of these libraries have enough space to organize different sections of the library to

provide efficient services to the readers. These building were more over non-functional to serve the readers.

4. None of these libraries have adequate professional staff to take up technical works and to organize library services in scientific manner. There are two professional staff at State Library, one each at Lunglei, Kolasib and Champhai District Libraries, and no professional staff at Aizawl and Saiha District Libraries.

5. All of these libraries follow closed access system. Closed accessed system created certain problems for the library users unless there are no sufficient staffs to guide and help the readers to get their information needs quickly.

6. The daily average library users are ranging from 15 to 55 in these public libraries. Due to lack of space, reading room and stack area are not organized separately.

7. Technical work e.g., classification, cataloguing, subject heading, shelving, etc., is not properly maintained in these libraries; no added entries were provided in cataloguing that creates certain problems to the users to get their information needs.

8. Subscription of Periodicals/Journals is not adequate; and as such, there is no educational or research journals for students and research scholars. State Library subscribes two foreign journals, no other libraries subscribe foreign journal.

9. Budget allocation for these six public libraries is

Rs. 82.95 lakhs for 2007-08, which is 22.12% of the total budget allocation of the parent department, Art & Culture.

10. There are no proper rules for membership registration from the government. Membership fee is different ranging from Rs. 5.00 to Rs. 20.00 per head.

11. Mizoram being the ninth state of India with Library Legislation, there is no proper action from the concerned department to implement the Mizoram Public Libraries Act 1993 till date.

12. There is no proper system or policy for collection of documents to serve the community according to their information needs. Most of the collections are supplied and received from RRRLF under matching grant.

13. Library extension service is not properly provided to serve the rural people and disadvantaged persons as well as to give awareness of the State and District Libraries services to the community.

14. RRRLF provided grants for computerization of State Library, but the progress is very slow. None of these libraries are automated till today even without Internet facility.

15. There are 424 government-recognized village/ NGO libraries mostly run by NGO/CBO, viz., YMA, Students Union, etc., assisted by state government through RRRLF Matching Schemes. YMA contribution for the establishment of Village Library is very much appreciated.

16. Most of the State and District Libraries members are in the age group of 19-30 years and out of

which unmarried are more than married persons; and by gender, male are more than female.

17. In the frequency of library visits, unmarried-male between the age group of 19-30 visitors of State and District Libraries are having HSLC qualifications. The main purpose of readers to visit library is to borrow books. Books are the main source of information to all categories of readers.

18. Most of the readers' approaches are for educational and recreational information in nature. Approaches for social and cultural information are very low.

19. Services provided by these State and District Libraries are not satisfactory to the users to cater their information requirements. Only State Library has Photocopying machine, but is rarely utilized by the users.

20. Organization of library extension services, viz., book exhibition, seminar, lecture, quiz competition, workshop, etc., to aware public library services to the public is very limited. District Libraries do not organize such kind of programs at all, but the State Library organized Book Exhibition and Library Awareness Campaigns in five district capitals.

21. Although the State and District Libraries of Mizoram serve as local community information center they are facing the problems of inadequacy of reading materials to support formal and non-formal education as well as life long learning process. The findings clearly stated that

these libraries too contribute valuable services for the promotion of the social life of the local community but these services are neither properly organized nor made available at reader interests.

22. State and District Libraries preserve cultural heritage of the society through its collection of various documents. But no programs on cultural activities are organized to give awareness of library as center of cultural preservation.

23. State and District Libraries develop personal creativity of the community. Its various collections of documents on arts, music, health, house decoration, etc., are very helpful and informative to the creative persons for their personal creativity development. Further these libraries also serve as center of recreation and promote leisure interest of the community.

Public Library in India : 291-295
R. K. Ngurtinkhuma
Today and Tomorrow's Printers & Publishers, New Delhi-110 002 (India)

Chapter 9

SUGGESTION AND CONCLUSION

1. Suggestions

The study reveals that all the government established public libraries in Mizoram have been functioning as daily routine work to meet the information needs of the society. However, the functioning of these libraries are limited to collect, organize and serve the community due to various problems that are confronted by the government and the society. It is well known among the intellectuals that of all the four types of libraries, public library is the only library to serve the community as a whole without any distinction. Public libraries are basically established for the socio-cultural and educational development of the society, and its main purpose is to give, provide and serve the society in their various developmental activities, viz., education, economic, socio-cultural activities, health, employment, etc. This is an accepted fact that Public Libraries play a vital role for socio-cultural and educational development of the society in which the government has a lot to do.

This chapter, concerning about suggestions from the study has its foundation from the findings stated in the previous chapter. State and District Libraries in Mizoram has been serving the society for almost forty years, but its services are not much aware to the community for their educational or socio-cultural developments. Therefore, the researcher has suggested the following significant points for the development of public library system in general and State and District Libraries of Mizoram in particular, so that the community of the state could make use of educational resources through such libraries.

1. District Library may be established in all the district headquarters with modern Information Communication Technology to facilitate each access to the information needs of the local community.

2. State and District Libraries should have their own building with state-of-the-art at the central place of the locality for easy accessibility by the users.

3. Qualified professional staff should be recruited for smooth functioning of library services.

4. Library extension services, such as, Bookmobile, Book Exhibition, Workshop/Seminar, Library Lectures, Audio-visual Programs, Story Hours, etc. may be organized with emphasis on to promote library services and its importance to the local community.

5. Socio-cultural activities, like Cultural Exhibitions, Concerts, Field Trips, Film Shows, Craft Exhibitions, etc. may be organized at various places of the state to give awareness of public library services and its benefits to the society.

6. A section on Career Guidance may be established at the library to provide counseling to the users, particularly for the school children.

7. Mizoram Public Libraries Act 1993 should be

implemented for effective and efficient public library service in the state.

8. State and District Libraries should follow collection development policy of the government. Collection development policy may emphasize on information needs of the local community.

9. Internet facility should be provided to the library users, so that they may access their information needs easily. Libraries may be linked with or be a member of library resources in the country, e.g. DELNET.

10. Book Clubs or Readers' Club may be formed in each library locations to build up reading habits among the local community, particularly among the children.

11. Separate sections for children's literature, senior citizens, women and disable persons should be established in a library. Collections should also be organized systematically to meet their information needs.

12. Libraries need to be automated to meet the challenges of an information society with necessary hardware and software. Each library should create its own local database and provide effective and efficient computerized library and information services, such as Database Service, CAS, SDI, Reference Service, Document Delivery Service, etc.

13. The state government may continue contributions to RRRLF Matching Scheme and the amount may also be increased so that libraries in the state may receive more reading materials including Audio-

Visual through this scheme. Public libraries need a permanent source of finance both from the State and Central Government.

14. Library staff, both professional and semi-professional needs to be fully oriented towards application of ICT. The authority should organize such kind of regular training programs to acquire latest developments in the field. Special initiatives in orientation programs/computer literacy program may be organized for the library staff.

15. Due to inflation, library required more budgets from the state Government. More library budget will facilitate in developing a good collection of reading material for all category of users.

16. State and District Libraries are the center of local gateway to information particularly in providing reading materials. Most of the local community cannot afford to procure such reading material from their own resources. To meet their various information needs, libraries should subscribe more periodicals and journals in different subjects.

17. Public library may be transferred from State List to Concurrent List of the Indian Constitution to give more emphasis and recognized the importance of public library services by the Central and State Governments.

2. Conclusion

The present study concludes that the development of public libraries in India is making a steady progress in many of the states. It is evident that so far fourteen number of states have recognize the importance of public library service by enacting library legislation for socio-cultural and educational development. This has also been established that the public libraries play an important role for societal and national development. Although many of the states have not enacted public library act, they are still in the process and persuading the state government for early legislation.

Mizoram government has recognizes its importance and therefore enacted library legislation in 1993. This has resulted into wide coverage of public library form village level to state level. These libraries are also contributing a lot in promoting socio-cultural and educational activities in the state. This has also been established from the findings that these libraries are the vital source of information for the local community.

Public library in India, in general, and Mizoram in particular, are facing the constant problems of physical resources (building, furniture, equipment, including ICT infrastructure) acquiring and developing good collection of documentary and non-documentary resources, inadequacy of professional, semi-professional and non-professional staff as well as regular problems of financial resources.

The study further revealed that the impact of public libraries on socio-cultural and educational development could be further gear-up with active support from the state and central government. It is also concluded from the data analysis and findings that the government should encourage, establish and maintain public libraries in order to provide effective and efficient library services, which has a tremendous impact on socio-cultural and educational development of the local community. It is strongly suggested that the government of Mizoram should not only implement Public Libraries Act immediately but at the sane time it is equally important to strengthen physical documentary human and financial resources in the greater interest of the state.

Public Library in India : 297-302
R. K. Ngurtinkhuma
Today and Tomorrow's Printers & Publishers, New Delhi-110 002 (India)

BIBLIOGRAPHY

Books

Abraham, M. Francis (2006). Contemporary Sociology: An introduction to concepts and theories. New Delhi: Oxford University Press.

Barnett, Andy (2002). Libraries, Community and Technology. Jefferson: McFarland.

Bhatt, R.K. (1995). History and Development of Libraries in India. New Delhi: Mittal Publications.

Butler, Pierce (1933). An Introduction to Library Science. Chicago: Phoenix Books.

Ekbote, Gopala Rao (1987). Public Libraries System. Hyderabad: Ekbote Brothers.

Esparanza, M. (1995). Library and Information Science: Emerging Trends. New Delhi: Concept

Hage, Christine Lind (2004). The Public Library Start-Up Guide. Chicago: American Library Association.

Hluna, J.V. (1992). Education and Missionaries in Mizoram. Guwahati: Spectrum.

Hminga, C. L. (1987). The Life and Witness of the Churches in Mizoram. Lunglei: Literature Committee, Baptist Church of Mizoram.

IFLA (2001). The Public Library Service: IFLA/UNESCO Guidelines for Development. Munchen: K.G.Saur.

India. National Knowledge Commission (2007). Libraries- Gateways to Knowledge: A Roadmap for Revitalization.

India. Planning Commission. Tenth Five-Year Plan (2002-2007) Vol. II: Sectoral Policies and Programmes.

Jain, M.K. *ed.* (2000). 50 Years Library and Information Services in India (1947-98). Delhi: Shipra.

Kalia, D.R. (1990). Guidelines for Public Library Services and Systems. Calcutta: Raja Rammohun Roy Library Foundation.

Kalia, D.R. (1998). Public Libraries in 50 Years: Library and Information Services in India. New Delhi: Shipra.

Kaul, H. K. *ed.* (2002). National Round Table on Modernization and Networking of Libraries in India, January 5, 2002. New Delhi: DELNET.

Khanna, J.K. (1987). Library and Society. Kurukshetra: Research Publications.

Konnur, P.V., Asundi, A.Y. and Ragavan, S.Srinivasa. *eds.*; (2006). Seminar Paper on Best Practices in Library and Information Services (9-12 Aug. 2006). Bangalore: Bangalore University Library.

Kumar, S and Leena Shah (n.d). Public Library Acts in India. New Delhi: Ess Ess

Lahkar, Narendra *ed.*, (2007). Rural Libraries in the North East India: Problems and Prospects. Kolkata: Central Reference Library.

Lalrimawia (1995). Mizoram: History and Cultural Identity (1890-1947). Guwahati: Spectrum.

Liangkhaia (2002). Mizo Chanchin. Aizawl: LTL Publications.

Lianzawna, C. (1996). Mizoram Education Chanchin. Aizawl: H.Rokhumi

McCall, Major A.C. (2003). Lushai Chrysalis. Aizawl: Tribal Research Institute.

Mahajan, Baldev, Majumdar, Srilakha and Lallura, F. (1994). Educational Administration in Mizoram: Structure, Processes and Future Prospects. New Delhi: NIEPA.

Mahapatra, P.K. and Thomas, V. K. (1996). Public Libraries in Developing Countries- Status, Trends. New Delhi: Vikas.

Mangla, P.B. Kalia, D R and Jaganathan, Neela, *eds.* (2001). Library and

Information Services in India: States and Union Territories. Delhi: Shipra

Martin, Lowell A. (1998). Enrichment: A History of the Public Library in the United States in the Twentieth Century. Lanham: The Scarecrow Press.

Nagar, Murari Lal (1983). Foundation of Library Movement in India. Ludhiana: Indian Library Institute and Bibliographical Center.

Qureshi, Hasnain (2006). Principles and Practices of Library Science. New Delhi: Anmol.

Ranganathan, S.R. (1988). Five Laws of Library Science. Delhi: VBS

Ranganathan, S.R. (1973). New Education and School Library: experience of half a century. Delhi: Vikas.

Sahai, Shrinath (1973). Library and the Community. New Delhi: Today and Tomorrows.

Saiaithanga (1969). Mizo Kohhran Chanchin. Aizawl: The Regional Theological Literature Committee.

Sangkima (1992). Mizos: Society and Social Change (1890-1947). Guwahati: Spectrum.

Sharma, Pandey S.K. (1987). Libraries and Society. New Delhi: Ess Ess.

Singh, N.Giridhari and Singh, Ch.Ibohal, *eds.* (2007). Legislation Based Rural Library Service in India. Proceedings of III National Seminar of Ranganathan Society for Book Culture, Library and Informatics Studies. Imphal: RAS North East Chapter.

Totterdell, Barry *ed.* (1978). Public Library purpose: a reader. London: Clive Bingley.

Vashishth, C.P. *ed.*, (1992). Libraries as Rural Community Resource Centres. Delhi: B R Publishing Corporation.

Venkatappaiah, Velaga (1990). Indian Library Legislation. Vol. I: Union Library Bills and Acts. Vol. II: State Library Bills and Acts. Delhi: Daya

Viswanathan, C. G. (2005). Public Library Organization. 5th. ed. New Delhi: Ess Ess Publications.

Zatluanga (1997). Mizo Chanchin, vol. I. Aizawl: Zasanga

Periodicals/Journals

Augst, Thomas. American Libraries as Agencies of Culture. *American studies.* Vol.42 (3), Fall 2001

Barua, B.P. "Universal Accessibility to Information - Role of a Public Library in Indian Context". *Granthana.* 1(1), 1990; 19-24,

Bashiruddin, S. Role of Public Libraries. *Library Herald,* 3(4); Jan., 1961; 167-172.

Bhattacharjee, R. Role of Raja Rammohun Roy Library Foundation in the Promotion of Public Library Movement in India. *Herald of Library Science.* 38(1-2), Jan.-Apr., 1999; 14-19.

Buragohain, Alaka. Public Library scenario in India: Problems and Prospects. *Herald of Library Science,* 38(1-2), Jan.-Apr., 1999; 5-26.

Dasgupta, Kalpana. New Role of Libraries in a Developing Society with Particular Reference to India. *ILA Bulletin,* XVI (1-2), Jan.-June198; 37-46.

Esparanza, M. Role of Public Libraries in Socio-economic Development. *Herald of Library Science.* 25 (3-4), July-Oct. 1986; 189-193.

Kalia, D.R.; Biswas, S.C.; Kumar, Krishan & Barua, B.P. Guidelines for Public Library Systems and Services. *Granthana,* 2(1), Jan. 1991; 31-84.

Kaula, P.N. Adult Education and Public Libraries. *Herald of Library Science,* 38 (1-2), Jan.-Apr., 1999; 63-69.

Kumar, Krishan. Role of Public Libraries in the Promotion of Literacy. *Library Herald,* 30(2-4); July 1991-Jan.1992; 155-161.

Lianzama, C. Status Report of Public Library Development in Mizoram. *Granthana,* IV (1&2), Jan. & July 1993; 75-78.

Mangla, P.B. Role of the Public Library in Developing Countries with particular Reference to Literacy. *Journal of Library and Information Science.* 9(1), June, 1984; 1-15.

Rajan, T.N. The Role of Libraries in a Changing Society. *ILA Bulletin,* XVI (1-2), Jan-June 1980; 19-22.

Raj, Janak. National Policy on Education 1986 and Libraries. *ILA Bulletin,* XXIV (1), Apr.-Jun., 1988; 4-13.

Raju, K.A. Information Technology and Public Libraries in 21st. Century. *Herald of Library Science.* 38(1-2), Jan.-Apr., 1999; 52-61.

Ramanayya, I. V. Role of Public Library in Adult Literacy Work. *ILA Bulletin.* III (3&4), July-Dec.1967; 174-177.

Roush, Wade. The Infinite Library. *Span.* Jan/Feb, 2006; 8-14.

Venkatappaiah, V. State Policy for Public Library and Information Systems and Services. *Herald of Library Science.* 38(1-2), Jan.-Apr., 1999; 20-26.

Yancey, Kathleen Blake. "People's University: Our (New) Public Libraries as Sites of Lifelong Learning". *Change.* Mar/Apr. 2005; 13-19.

Websites

Blanes, Monica Medina. Grab that user: how can the public library service attract young people?

(http://www.ifla.org/IV/ifla71/papers/107-Blanes.pdf) accessed on 7.3.2007.

Davis, Donald G & Taher, Mohamed. Library History in India: Historiographical Assessment and Current Trends.

(http://www.worlib.org/vol03no2/davis_v03n2.shtml) accessed on 2.3.2007.

Hendrix, Frances. The Role of Public Libraries in the Information Society.

(http://www.hcu.ac.uk/events/beyondl/public.html) accessed on 2.4.2007

IFLA/UNESCO Public Library Manifesto 1994.

(http://www.ifla.org/vii/s8/unesco/eng.htm) accessed on 2.3.2007

Jambhekar, Neeta. National Policy on Public Libraries in India. (http://www.worlib.org/vol05no2/j_v05n2.shtml) accessed on 2.3.2007

National Library of India

(http://www.nlindia.org) accessed on 8.3.2007

Raja Rammohun Roy Library Foundation

(http://www.rrrlf.nic.in) accessed on 16.3.2007

The Role of Public Libraries in lifelong learning- a Project under the section of Public Libraries, IFLA

(http://www.ifla.org/VII/s8/project/rolepublib.htm) accessed on 2.4.2007

INDEX